Hixkaryana
and
Linguistic Typology

SUMMER INSTITUTE OF LINGUISTICS
PUBLICATIONS IN LINGUISTICS

Publication Number 76

EDITORS

Virgil L. Poulter　　　　　　　　　　Desmond C. Derbyshire
University of Texas　　　　　　　　　Summer Institute
at Arlington　　　　　　　　　　　　of Linguistics

ASSISTANT EDITORS

Alan C. Wares　　　　　　　　　　　Iris M. Wares

CONSULTING EDITORS

Doris A. Bartholomew　　　　　　　Phyllis Healey
Pamela M. Bendor-Samuel　　　　　Robert E. Longacre
Robert A. Dooley　　　　　　　　　Eugene E. Loos
Jerold A. Edmondson　　　　　　　William R. Merrifield
Austin Hale　　　　　　　　　　　　Kenneth L. Pike
　　　　　　　　　　　　　　　　　　Viola G. Waterhouse

Hixkaryana and Linguistic Typology

Desmond C. Derbyshire

A Publication of

The Summer Institute of Linguistics
and
The University of Texas at Arlington

1985

©1985 by Summer Institute of Linguistics, Inc.

Library of Congress Catalog Card No.: 85-050398

ISBN 0-88312-082-8

ALL RIGHTS RESERVED

No part of this publication may be reproduced, stored in a retrieval system, or transmitted in any form or by any means--electronic, mechanical, photocopy, recording, or otherwise--without the express permission of the Summer Institute of Linguistics, with the exception of brief excerpts in magazine articles and/or reviews.

Copies of this publication and other publications of the Summer Institute of Linguistics may be obtained from

Bookstore
Summer Institute of Linguistics
7500 W. Camp Wisdom Road
Dallas, TX 75236

CONTENTS

Preface   vii
Abbreviations   ix
Introduction   xiii

PART ONE: THE BASIC SYNTAX

1. The Word   3
2. The Phrase   25
3. The Main Clause   31
4. The Subordinate Clause   38
5. Embedded Clauses   50
6. The Sentence   56
7. Movement Processes   74
8. Reflexive and Reciprocal Constructions   80
9. Additional Constructions   86

PART TWO: SYNTACTIC TYPOLOGY: THE PLACE OF HIXKARYANA

10. The Basic Order of Constituents: OVS   95
11. Correlations between Hixkaryana and Existing Typologies   105
12. Major Differences between Hixkaryana and Existing Typologies   120
13. Discourse-related Phenomena   145
14. Conclusion   172

APPENDIXES

A. Phonology   177
B. Inflectional Morphology: Verb   187
C. Inflectional Morphology: Noun   199
D. Inflectional Morphology: Locative   205
E. Derivational Morphology: Verb Stem Formation   221
F. Derivational Morphology: Noun Formation   229
G. Derivational Morphology: Adverb Formation   237
H. Derivational Morphology: Relator Formation   243
I. Modifying Particles   245
J. Discourse Particles   247
K. Verification Particles   255

References   257

PREFACE

This work was initially written in 1979 as a doctoral thesis at the University of London, under the title **Hixkaryana Syntax**. It is published now as **Hixkaryana and Linguistic Typology**, a title which draws attention to what I believe to be the major contribution of the work, contained in Part Two. Part One is a general overview of the syntax of the language and is essentially a concise restatement (but arranged very differently) of Derbyshire (1979).

The only updating has been in the case of a few references to works which, at the time of the original thesis, were available only in manuscript form but have since been published. Apart from these, the only changes have been of a minor editing or reformatting nature.

In the six years since the thesis was written, there have been some notable advances, both in general research in linguistic typology and also in published (or soon to be published) studies in Amazonian languages. This published version of the thesis will enable interested scholars to make an even better evaluation today of the place of Hixkaryana in linguistic typology and Amazonian studies than was possible in 1979.

Desmond C. Derbyshire

ABBREVIATIONS

A, ADV	adverb
ACT	action
ADD	additive
ADVBLZR	adverbializer
ADVERS	adversative
ALT	alternative
AP	adverbial phrase
AUG	augmentative
CAUS	causative
CESS	cessative
COLL	collective
COMP	complement
COMPL	completive
CONT	continuative
CONTR	contrast
COP	copula
COUNTER-EXP	counter-expectancy
DEDUCT	deduction
DENOMLZR	denominalizer
DETRANS	detransitivizer
DEVLD	devalued
DIMIN	diminutive
DIST.PAST	distant past
EMPH	emphasis
EXCL	exclusive
FRUST	frustrative
GEN	general
HABIT	habitual
HSY	hearsay
I, IDEO	ideophone
IMM.PAST	immediate past
IMP	imperative

INCL	inclusive
INGR	ingressive
INTENSFR	intensifier
INTRANS	intransitive, intransitivizer
MISF	misfortune
MOT	motion
N	noun
NEG	negative, negation
NOMLZN	nominalization
NP	noun phrase
NONCOLL	noncollective
O, OBJ	object
OBLIG	obligatory
PERM	permanent
PERS	person
POSSD	possessed
POSSN	possession
PP	postpositional phrase
PREF	prefix
PRO	pronoun, pronominal
Prt	particle
PURP	purpose
QUANT	quantity
R	relator (postposition)
RECIP	reciprocal
REC.PAST	recent past
REF	referent
REFL	reflexive
RESP	response
REVERS	reversative
S	subject/sentence (in phrase-structure configurations)
SEQ	sequential
SIMULT	simultaneous
STEM FORM	stem formative
SUBJ	subject
SUPERL	superlative
TRANS	transitive
UNCERT	uncertainty
V	verb
VOC	vocative

Abbreviations

VP	verb phrase
I	first person
II	second person
III	third person
I+II	first person inclusive
I+III	first person exclusive

INTRODUCTION

The purpose of this study is to present the syntax of Hixkaryana, a language containing one basic feature that sets it apart from most other languages: the unmarked order of sentence constituents is Object--Verb--Subject. The effect of this feature on the rest of the syntax and its significance for typological studies are the major themes of the study.

Hixkaryana: genetic affiliation, location and number of speakers

Hixkaryana is a member of the Carib language family and is spoken by groups currently located on the rivers Nhamundá and Mapuera in northern Brazil, about halfway between Guyana's southern border and the Amazon (see map on p. 174). In 1979 there were about 350 speakers. The Nhamundá community is the larger one, and in April 1977 there were 237 inhabitants in the village of Kasawa on that river.

Linguistic classification

The classificatory work of Voegelin and Voegelin (1977) is misleading in its listing of Hixkaryana (p. 158) as "Hishkaryana ... Affiliation. Unknown." There are at least two references in earlier classifications, and both clearly identify it as Carib. Frikel (1958.132) has "Hichkaruyána" in his Parukotó-Charúma subdivision of "Karib"; and Loukotka (1968.207) includes "Hishcariana" in his Waiwai subdivision of "Karaib." So far as I am aware, Hixkaryana is not listed in other earlier classifications, but can probably be identified with Parukotó, or as part of that group, wherever it is referred to in the literature.

The most recent classification of the linguistic subdivisions of the Carib family is that of Durbin (1977), based on comparative phonological studies of a number of Carib languages. Hixkaryana ("Hishkaryana") is included in his "Southern Guiana Carib" grouping, one of the four divisions of Guiana Carib. The Guiana land mass includes Venezuela, Guyana, Surinam, French Guiana, and Brazil north of the Amazon. Most Carib languages are found in this area. The Southern Guiana group is part of the major division that he calls "Southern Carib," which also includes Carib languages in southeastern Colombia and in the Xingu basin of central Brazil. The other three Guiana groups are placed in "Northern Carib."

Historical notes

The Hixkaryana appear to be direct descendants of the Babui (Wabui), reported by Friar Francisco de São Marcos in 1725 to have moved from the river Trombetas westward to the Nhamundá (Frikel 1958.128). Frikel gives an interesting confirmation of the Wabui-Hixkaryana connection from his own experience on a trip to the Hixkaryana in the 1950s (p. 128, my translation):

> I once asked the Indians there (Nhamundá) if they had heard anything of the "Wabui." They laughed and answered: "That's who we are, here, on the Nhamundá. The Chawiyána, Hichkaru-yána, Kumiyána--they are all Wabui."

A short word list for "Uiaboy" ("Indios do Nhamundá") appears in Mansur Guêrios (1947.144-45), and it seems to be basically identical with Hixkaryana--(I attribute the differences to weaknesses in elicitation and transcription techniques.)

Frikel goes on to explain the designation "Parukotô-Charúma," which appears from time to time in the literature with reference to the various Carib-speaking groups between the Trombetas and the Nhamundá. In general, Charúma refers to groups in the eastern part of the region (Trombetas), and Parukotô to groups in the west (Mapuera and Nhamundá). In summarizing facts about the Charúma, he says (p. 151, my translation):

> Together with the Parukotô tribes of the Mapuera-Nhamundá, they constitute a uniform dialectal group.

Until very recently the name Hixkaryana pertained to just one of several clans (**-yana** 'kinship group'), who referred to themselves in general simply as **totokomo** 'people', and were scattered across a large area of Amazonian jungle between the river Jatapú to the west and the river Mapuera to the east. (Frikel, p. 153, gives the meaning of the root word **hichkaru** (Hixkaru-yana) as "veado vermelho," i.e., 'red deer'; this is inaccurate, however, since it means "veado branco," which is another species of smaller, whitish deer; the larger red deer is **koso**.) Fifty years ago their total population may well have run into thousands, but they were decimated by disease until, about thirty years ago, they were in danger of extinction. About that time they came together to form two main groups: the Hixkaryana, on and near the middle reaches of the river Nhamundá, and the Sherew, who have been living with another Carib tribe, the Waiwai, in southern Guyana.

Introduction

Frikel (1958.154) reports that, when he visited the Hixkaryana (in 1951 and 1955), there were four small villages with about eighty inhabitants, located on the Nhamundá between the rapids called "Fumaça" (downstream) and the mouth of the tributary "Wini" (upstream). He adds that they were reported by neighboring tribes to have been very belligerent in the past, but were now good and peaceful. Their war-like character fits in with what Guppy reports about the Waiwai being very much afraid of them (1958.98, where they are referred to as "Fishkaliena"). I should add here, however, that the Hixkaryana used to be equally afraid of the Waiwai, and it is to this group of "killer-people" that Kaywerye refers (although he does not actually identify them as Waiwai in the text) when narrating why his father left the river Mapuera to go to live on the Nhamundá (Derbyshire 1965.140-45).

In the last ten years most of the Waiwai and Sherew have moved to the river Mapuera in Brazil, and there has been much more frequent contact between them and the Hixkaryana, with a number of marriages taking place between individuals of the two groups. The Waiwai language is distinct from the Hixkaryana-Sherew language, but is more closely related to it than any other Carib language. In the last few years the Fundação Nacional do Indio, the Brazilian Government body responsible for Indian affairs, has established a post on the Nhamundá, but the Hixkaryana are still relatively isolated from the national Brazilian society, their only contacts being through the government official on the post and in connection with seasonal trade in Brazil nuts, which they gather and sell to traders who operate on the lower Nhamundá.

Cultural traits

Basso (1977.18-19) distinguishes three Carib "types," and in general the Hixkaryana still show most of the basic characteristics of her second type, which relates to "the majority of Guiana Caribs." She lists these following characteristics:

> Flexible social organization based on bilateral reckoning of kin; communal family households that constitute a political faction as well as a group of kin and affinally related persons; dependence upon bitter manioc (as opposed to maize, sweet manioc, or palm species); reliance upon shamanism for control and manipulation of nonhuman forces, but without the use of hallucinogenic drugs taken for that purpose; and the importance of girls' puberty rituals.

With reference to marriage and social rules, the Hixkaryana fit what Rivière (1977.41) calls the "pattern of culture that may be peculiarly Carib," e.g.:

... "wife givers" are superior to "wife takers" ... a tendency towards matrilocal residence, the lack of unilineal descent rules, and the absence of any corporate groups ....

Some of these traits have been modified in the last twenty-five years as a result of the influence of Christian teaching and practice that began through contacts with Christian Waiwai and developed during the course of the translation of the New Testament into their language ([Derbyshire] 1976).

The tropical forest environment and reliance on bitter manioc still dictate the basic life-style of the people. Men's work revolves around the annual cutting and burning of undergrowth and planting of manioc fields that goes on through the several months of the dry season and early rains (approximately August to February), and the daily hunting and fishing expeditions throughout the year. There is also gathering of wild fruits, plants, and nuts in the appropriate seasons. Women are daily occupied with harvesting manioc and preparing it and other items for food and drink. (Fock 1963 and Yde 1965 are excellent detailed studies of the culture of the Waiwai, whose patterns are very similar to those of the Hixkaryana.)

Field work

My wife and I lived with the Hixkaryana for various periods between 1959 and 1975, amounting to a total actual residence of about seven and a half years. My principal language teacher was Kaywerye, who was in his twenties when we began. We lived in his village, Kasawa, during the whole period. All the Hixkaryana on the Nhamundá, who formerly lived in several scattered villages, have moved into Kasawa during the course of the last few years. I cannot recall a single day that I lacked good language help when I needed it. In addition to Kaywerye, I worked closely at various times with Waraka, Mahxawa, Utxunu (who died in 1971), Tuhkoro, Wemko, Txekeryfu, Ahtxe, Yasɨhtxe, Ɨmrorunu, and Mawuhsa. Others also helped; indeed, everyone who lived at Kasawa contributed to some extent to our understanding of their language. I acknowledge my debt to all of them but must single out Kaywerye for my special thanks. He not only worked harder than all of them to teach me his language but also as village chief assumed the responsibility to see that our other needs were supplied.

In addition to published works (see References), various reports and papers on aspects of the language have been archived at the Brazil headquarters of the Summer Institute of Linguistics in Brasília. So far as I am aware, no one else has undertaken any linguistic or substantial anthropological field work among the Hixkaryana. (I have already noted Frikel's classificatory contribution and his two field trips to the Nhamundá; but if he has furnished any particular study on the Hixkaryana, I do not know of it.)

Introduction

Theoretical issues

Part One of this study presents a complete sketch of the syntax of the language, and Part Two attempts an assessment of the place of Hixkaryana in syntactic typology. There are eleven appendixes (A-K), which give detailed analysis and exemplification of other aspects of the language that are necessary for a full understanding of the syntax: phonology (A), inflectional morphology (B-D), derivational morphology (E-H), and clitic-particles (I-K). It is not written from any particular theoretical viewpoint, although the general orientation is slanted toward a (non-specific) transformational-generative approach, with some attention to developments in "relational grammar." It is, however, concerned with a number of theoretical issues. These are listed here, with references to the sections in which they are discussed:

Person distinctions in pronominal forms (1.2.2)

Universal status of "adjective" (1.3)

The category "postposition" (1.4)

The "Uniform Three-Level Hypothesis" of phrase structure (2.5)

Word order typology (Part 2, esp. chaps. 10 and 11; also 12.2.7)

Ergative features in Carib languages (10.3)

Word-order change (10.4)

The upward bounding constraint on rightward movements (11.2.8)

Functions of right-dislocated constituents in relation to "afterthought" hypotheses (12.2.4)

Identification of participants in discourse (12.2.4)

Proposed constraints on sentence-negative constructions (12.2.6)

Linear relationship between "traces" and moved constituents (12.2.6)

WH-Movement and the COMP node (12.2.6)

Universal status of "indirect object" (12.2.7)

Interaction of the discourse notions: focus, topic, theme-rheme, and given-new information (chap. 13)

Linear ordering of "theme" and "topic" constituents (13.2 and 13.3)

The functions of "mystery" particles (13.4.2)

Discourse factors involved in pronominal usage (13.5.2)

Conventions

In general, the conventions I have used follow the normal current practice. I use the local orthography throughout, except that á is replaced by ɨ to avoid confusion for the linguistically oriented reader. (The orthography was introduced only twenty years ago, but the Hixkaryana are now very familiar with it, and many of them can read and write with ease.) The literal translations for the forms cited consist in general of a separate gloss for each Hixkaryana word; there is a more precise morpheme glossing when this is relevant to the matter under discussion.

In a number of places citations are from Derbyshire (1965), and a page (sometimes also a sentence) reference is given. There are some discrepancies between the cited forms and the printed text, reflecting the better understanding I now have of what the transcription and/or gloss should have been.

Acknowledgements

I have already expressed my indebtedness to the Hixkaryana language teachers as well as others, without whose help this book could obviously not have been written.

I am particularly grateful to Geoffrey Pullum, my adviser in my doctoral program at University College London, for the many seed thoughts he planted in my mind. I take full responsibility for the content, but Pullum's contribution is much greater than the individual references I make to him would suggest. I also acknowledge the help and stimulating influence of Neil Smith, head of the Linguistics Section, and of all the staff members and postgraduate students who were in that Section of the Department of Phonetics and Linguistics at UCL from 1977 to 1979. Among the many linguists outside of UCL who have contributed to my thinking I would like especially to thank Bernard Comrie for his helpful suggestions, which were primarily in connection with the volume on Hixkaryana I prepared for the Lingua Descriptive Studies Series, but which sparked a number of ideas for this study.

I also thank my colleagues in the Summer Institute of Linguistics, especially those in the Brazil Branch, who have given linguistic advice and much practical help throughout the period my wife and I lived and worked among the Hixkaryana (thanks to permission granted by the Brazilian government, in recent years via the Fundação Nacional do Indio).

Finally, I acknowledge my debt to two persons whose contributions extend far beyond anything associated with Hixkaryana or linguistics, but who have ultimately had the greatest influence in the production of this study: my wife, Grace, closest human companion for over thirty years, and my God and Savior Jesus Christ, who has accompanied me and given direction to my life for even longer.

PART ONE

THE BASIC SYNTAX

PART ONE
THE BASIC SYNTAX

1 The Word

I shall distinguish six syntactic categories in Hixkaryana: verb (V), noun (N), adverb (A), relator (R), particle (Prt), and ideophone (I). They are distinguished primarily by syntactic properties and secondarily by morphological ones. In the sections that follow I shall discuss each of these in turn. My reasons for calling the heterogeneous class A <u>adverb</u> rather than <u>adjective</u> are explained in 1.3, and the reason for using the term <u>relator</u> for what are roughly postpositions is detailed in 1.4.

1.1 Verb (V). The V is the head of the verb phrase (VP), which is the obligatory predicate constituent of all finite clauses, that is, all main clauses except the equative. It is obligatorily inflected by means of a set of prefixes that mark the person and object (if any), and a set of suffixes containing the finite elements marking tense and aspect and, in some cases, mood and number. As a result of the presence of the subject-object agreement prefixes, the V can be, and often is, the only constituent of a clause and sentence.

There are three subclasses of V: transitive, intransitive, and the copula. These function in the corresponding types of clause (see 3.1), and they are also distinguished by the forms which the person-marking prefixes take (although there is a good deal of overlap); the suffixal forms are identical for transitive and intransitive, but there are some differences in the copula (see Appendix B.3.2).

The structure of the V is basically prefix-stem-suffix, but each of the three elements is affected by the possibilities for derivation: derivational prefixes occur immediately before, and derivational suffixes immediately after, the stem, leaving the inflectional affixes at the extreme boundaries of the word. There is also the possibility of stem compounds, although these are restricted to body part N stems followed by V stems. Full details of derivations and compounds are given in Appendix E.

The basic structure of the V is seen in the following examples:

wamano 'I felled it (tree)'
(w-ama-no
 1SIIIO-fell-IMM.PAST)--a simple transitive stem

komokno 'I have come'
(kɨ-omokɨ-no
 1S-come-IMM.PAST)--a simple intransitive stem

kosonyhoye 'I let myself be seen'
(kɨ-os-onye-ho-ye
 1S-DETRANSITIVIZER-see-CAUSATIVE-DIST.PAST COMPL)--
 an intransitive stem derived from a transitive stem after the latter has first undergone the causativizing process

V stems can also be the subject of a number of derivations that produce nonfinite forms (see Appendixes F.2 and G.2). Such forms function as N or A and are to be regarded as members of those word classes.

1.2 Noun and pronoun (N). Nouns and pronouns are regarded as members of the same class, since their syntactic function is basically the same. Pronouns, however, have some special properties which call for separate treatment at certain points. I shall assume they are identified by a feature [+PRO].

The syntactic properties that distinguish an N from words of other classes are as follows: (i) it may occur as the head of a simple NP; (ii) it may occur as the first element (possessor) in a possessed NP (see 2.2); (iii) it may occur with an R in a postpositional phrase (PP); (iv) it may have postposed to it the modifying particle **tho** 'DEVALUED STATE' (this is the only modifying particle [see Appendix I for complete list] that cannot also occur following a V, A, or R); and (v) it can be negativized by adding the suffix **-hɨnɨ** or, in a few cases, **-mnɨ**. (These suffixes can also be added to V stems to form derived N [see Appendix F.2, 4 for details and examples]).

1.2.1 Noun ([N, -PRO]). There are two parameters relevant to both the morphological structure and the syntactic function of [-PRO]N: possessibility and derivational status.

The parameter of possessibility distinguishes three (semantic) subclasses of [N, -PRO]: (1) obligatorily possessed--these can be depossessed by replacement of the possession-marking affixes with the suffix **-nano** 'DEPOSSESSION', but their normal form is the possessed form; (2) optionally possessed--here the unmarked form is the nonpossessed one, and the possessed form requires the addition of the possession-marking affixes (same set as for obligatorily possessed nouns); and (3) obligatorily nonpossessed—here the possession affixes never occur. Obligatorily possessed nouns include body parts and referential kinship terms; obligatorily nonpossessed forms include the names of plants, animals, persons, and natural phenomena. Possessed forms are marked in two ways: a prefix marking the person of the possessor; and a suffix indicating possession, tense, and number. Where the appropriate (third person) prefix occurs, the possessed noun may be preceded by another noun (possessor) to form the nucleus of a possessed NP (see 2.2). Details of prefixes and suffixes are given in Appendix C; the following illustrate the basic structure for each of the three subclasses:

obligatorily possessed:

ramorɨ 'my hand'
(ro-amo-rɨ
 I-hand-POSSN)

Haname yaworu 'Haname's uncle'
(y-awo-ru
 III-mother's brother-POSSN)

aworu 'his/her uncle'
(∅-awo-ru
 III-mother's brother-POSSN)

optionally possessed:

kanawa 'canoe'

akanawarɨ 'your canoe'
(a-kanawa-rɨ
 II-canoe-POSSN)

obligatorily nonpossessed:

xerye 'manioc'
Haname '(man's name)'

koso 'deer'
tuna 'water'

The parameter of derivational status divides [N, -PRO] into two groups: simple and derived. Derived N are complex morphologically, semantically, and syntactically. Morphologically, they have special affixes to mark the different derivations (see Appendix F). Semantically, there is a special relation among the meanings of the stem, derivational affix, and (if any) the inflectional affixes, for each derivation. Syntactically, N derived from verb stems are often marked for underlying subject and direct object, and they can function in constructions in which those and other clausal constituents, i.e., adjunct and complement (of the copula) can occur as free forms. The complexity can be seen in the following examples:

onhananthɨthɨyamo 'the ones taught by you'
(o-nɨ-hananthɨ-thɨ-yamo
 II-OBJECT NOMLZN-teach-PAST POSSN-COLL)

```
thenyehra tɨmryenon        komo yokarymanɨrɨ  Kaywerye wya
much       his(REFL)-people COLL telling-about Kaywerye by
'the telling of many things about his people by Kaywerye'

(y-okaryma-nɨ-rɨ
 III-tell about-ACTION NOMLZN-POSSN)
```

Although in general the range of syntactic function of derived N is the same as that of simple N, the complexity described above often results in "heavy" constructions, which are restricted in their normal usage in the following ways: they occur most frequently as either the predicate nominal in equative clauses (see 4.4 and 5.2) or the nuclear predication constituent in subordinate clauses (see 4). Where they occur in constructions that function as subject or direct object they often undergo a movement process involving left or right dislocation (see 7.3 and 7.4).

The language does not have a regular number-marking system in the sense of singular-plural, etc. It does, however, have a way of marking COLLECTIVE when the focus is on a group (I term the noncollective forms INDIVIDUAL when they need to be distinguished). There are collective forms for the categories V, A, and R, as well as for N. They are used only when the referent is human, defined for this purpose as including, in addition to human beings, animals and items regarded as an integral part of the culture or environment of the people. The use of the collective forms is optional in the sense that the speaker can decide whether he wishes to focus on the group or not. There are two forms of collective which occur with N: the more common one is the modifying particle **komo** (see Appendix I); the other, used mainly with some types of derived N, is the suffix **-yamo** (see Appendix C). Whichever form is used, it is usually in agreement with the collective marker in the V to which the N is related as either subject or direct object. (Occasionally, for reasons which I have not been able to determine, the agreement is lacking. See Appendix B.1.)

N are not formally divided into classes or genders, and none of the following categories are morphologically marked: definiteness, indefiniteness, and genericness.

1.2.2 Pronoun ([N, +PRO]). Pronouns are like obligatorily non-possessed nouns in that they do not take the sets of prefixes and suffixes that mark possession and do not, therefore, occur in a sequence of N as the possessed element. There are two properties which distinguish them from all other members of the category N: (i) there are distinct sets of [+PRO] forms for individual and collective number categories; and (ii) third person forms have parameters for animacy and deictic scaling. The complete [+PRO] paradigm is as follows:

	Animate		Inanimate
	Individual	Collective	
first person	uro		
first person inclusive	kɨwro	kɨwyamo	
first person exclusive	amna	amna	
second person	omoro	omnyamo	
third person nondeictic	noro	nyamoro	ɨro
third person near-deictic	mosonɨ	moxamo	onɨ
third person medial-deictic	mokro	mokyamo	moro
third person remote-deictic	mokɨ	mokyamo	monɨ

Pronouns are marked for the individual vs. collective distinction, like other N. The collective forms all involve the use of **-yamo** (see 1.2.1), but in idiosyncratic ways that do not follow the usual morphophonological rules, except in the case of **mokɨ**, **mokyamo** 'third person remote-deictic'. First person exclusive **amna** is idiosyncratic in a different manner, the same form being used for individual and collective. The individual form for first person inclusive, **kɨwro**, refers to two persons, i.e., the speaker and a single addressee, the collective form **kɨwyamo** when more than one addressee is included.

The deictic forms reflect different degrees of proximity to the speaker: the 'near-deictic' refer to entities near to the speaker, i.e., closer to the speaker than to the addressee; the 'medial-deictic' refer to entities nearer to the addressee, or at a distance from both speaker and addressee; and the 'remote-deictic' refer to entities in the far distance or not in view at all. The medial-deictic **mokro** is also sometimes used in referring to a person not in sight (the collective form is the same for both medial- and remote-deictic). The distinctions are obligatory except in the case of 'remote', where, in addition to the overlap of **mokro** and **mokɨ**, the nondeictic forms **noro** and **nyamoro** are also used. The deictic and nondeictic third person forms are used anaphorically in discourse (see 13.5.2).

There is a reduced form of **mokɨ** 'third person remote-deictic': **mo-** (alternating with **ma-** following the normal vowel harmony rule--see Appendix A). It occurs as a proclitic before verbs marked for third person subject with the **n(ɨ)-** prefix (see Appendix B.2), when the third person referred to is out of sight of the speaker and hearer. In the nonpast verb form it cooccurs with the suffix marking uncertainty: **monewehyano** 'he is taking a bath' (**mo-nɨ-ewehɨ-yano** OUT OF SIGHT-IIIS-take a bath-NONPAST UNCERT). The clitic is optional in the sense that the speaker can decide whether or not to draw attention to the fact that the person referred to is out of sight.

Free pronouns are, in general, optional, but there are two exceptions: **amna** 'first person exclusive' is always obligatory; and **uro** 'first person' is obligatory in the case of first person object in a predication of which the subject is second person, as in **uro menytxano** 'you heard me', which contrasts with **menytxano** 'you heard him' (the prefix **m(ɨ)-** with a transitive stem means 'second person subject' and, in the absence of a free form pronoun marking a different person, 'third person object' also--see Appendix B.2). This could conceivably also apply to second person subject acting on first person inclusive object, e.g., (?) **kɨwyamo mukurunhetxhe** 'you will protect us (inclusive, collective)', i.e., the free pronoun would have to be expressed. I do not, however, have any record of such a sequence, and presumably it is barred by the "inclusion constraint" (Postal 1966), which stipulates that overlap in reference between NPs that are clausemates universally reduces acceptability.

There are conditions under which free pronouns are obligatorily absent, and where the person is marked only by a prefix. This applies to first person, first person inclusive, and second person when these occur as possessors in N and derived A, or as the objects of R in PP: **rokanawarɨ** 'my canoe' (**ro-kanawa-rɨ** I-canoe-POSSN), never ***uro (ro)kanawarɨ**; **oyewehnɨtoko** 'when you take a bath' (**oy-eweht-nɨ-toko** II-take a bath-ACTION NOMLZN-SIMULTANEOUS ACTION), never ***omoro (o)yewehnɨtoko**; **kɨhyakanye** 'to us (inclusive and collective)' (**kɨ-hyaka-nye** I+II-to-COLL), never ***kɨwyamo hyaka**. This contrasts with third person forms, where the free pronoun is optional: **ɨkanawarɨ** or **noro kanawarɨ** or **mokro kanawarɨ**, all with the meaning 'his canoe'. The first and second person free pronouns can be used for emphasis in relation to 'my canoe', etc.; but a different kind of construction would result, involving parataxis and probably dislocation:

(1) uro ryhe ɨro ha,   rokanawarɨ
    I   EMPH that INTENSIFIER my-canoe
    'That is <u>my</u> canoe.'

This illustrates the use of the set of free pronouns with the possessive meaning (**uro** 'mine'), as well as for purpose of emphasis. There are no special pronoun forms expressing these functions, nor are there any relative pronouns. Where emphasis is involved, the pronoun is either fronted or has certain "emphasis" or "contrast" particles postposed, or both, in the same way as other sentence constituents (see 7.2 and 13.1).

There are five person distinctions in [+PRO]: I, I+II, I+III, II, and III. (I modify the formalism of Zwicky (1977) at this point, preferring I+III to his I-II, in order clearly to differentiate it from I, in a language that does not have clear-cut number distinctions). In the person-marking prefixes (both verbal and nominal) there are only four distinctions; I+III does not have a special prefixal form, but is expressed by the third person forms **n(ɨ)-** (with V) and **y-, ∅-** (with N, A, and R) cooccurring with the free pronoun **amna** 'I+III' (see Appendixes B and C). The fact that these third person prefix forms are used to express both III and I+III would appear to be unprecedented but theoretically predicted, in view of the statement by Zwicky (1977.728):

> The arrangement of features in (47) predicts one formal connection that has never to my knowledge been reported--between third person and exclusive first person (the +III and +I-II categories sharing the feature -Addressee and differing only in the feature +Speaker), as opposed to second person and inclusive first person ....

In Hixkaryana there are distinct free pronouns for the two categories: **amna** 'I+III' and **noro, nyamoro** 'III', but they cooccur with the same prefixal forms; **amna** obligatorily cooccurs, but **noro/nyamoro** are optional:

amna nomokno 'we (EXCL) have come'
(amna nɨ-omokɨ-no
 I+III III-come-IMM.PAST)

(noro) nomokno 'he has come'
((noro) nɨ-omokɨ-no
 (III)   III-come-IMM.PAST)

amna hokru 'our (EXCL) child'
(amna ∅-hoku-ru
 I+III III-child-POSSN)

noro hokru 'his child'
(noro ∅-hoku-ru
 III III-child-POSSN)

If **noro** is deleted before a possessed N, that N has a different form of the third person prefix: **ɨhokru** (**ɨ-hoku-ru** III-child-POSSN). In the case of V the same prefixal form occurs even when **noro** is deleted.

The free form **amna** 'I+III' has been seen already to be unique among the [+PRO] in two respects: it has the same form for both individual and collective; and it obligatorily cooccurs with the third person prefixes to express the category I+III. It is also unique in the rules which govern its position in the clause when it occurs as subject: (1) in the quotative clause it always occurs immediately after the verb -ka- 'say'; and (2) in all other finite clauses it occurs immediately before the V, even when there is also a free form direct object in the clause. This results in an order of constituents that virtually never occurs otherwise, namely OSV (see 10.2):

(2) a. **ɨtoko, omɨn   yaka, kekonɨ amna, owya**
go   your-house to   said-it I+III to-you
'We told you to go home.'

b. **kanawa amna nano**   (cf. **kanawa yano   toto**)
canoe I+III took-it   (canoe   he-took-it person)
'We took the canoe.'   ('The man took the canoe.')

Pronouns are used in special idioms, e.g., **uro uro ha** 'It is I' (in answer to a question) (**uro-uro-ha** I-I-INTENSIFIER); **noro rye** 'brothers, belonging to the same kinship group' (**noro-rye** III-SAMENESS); **norohnɨ tho** 'a nobody, someone of no importance' (**noro-hnɨ-tho** III-NEGATION-DEVALUED). First person inclusive forms are used in a generic way, substituting for nonspecific, indefinite pronouns such as 'one, anyone, whoever'. This is normally accomplished by means of the person-marking prefixes, but the free pronoun form is optionally added. The noncollective form is normally used, and the nonpast uncertainty suffix in the V:

(3) **ohxe kehtoko,   ɨtohra   tehxan**
good when-our(INCL)-being not-going we(INCL)-are

hamɨ,   (kɨwro), kohtxemanye   hyaka
DEDUCTION (I+II)   one-who-treats-us(INCL) to
'When one is well, one doesn't go to the doctor.'

1.3 Adverb (A). The category A is a heterogeneous class comprising what in other languages are often distinguished as adjectives and adverbs, and including also locative and time words, and numerals and quantifiers. The class includes both basic and derived forms. They are bound together into one class on the grounds of their common syntactic functions, either (i) as complement of the copula in copular clauses, or (ii) as adjunct in any type of clause. A, R, and V stems share the property of occurring in derived NEGATED and NOMINALIZED forms. The suffix **-hɨra** 'NEGATIVE' may be added to form a derived A. One subclass of A (including all basic, and some derived, forms) have related nominalizations with the suffix **-no** 'GENERAL NOMINALIZATION'. Another subclass (derived A having the **tɨ-** prefix) have nominalizations with the suffix **-mɨ** 'ADVERB (tɨ-) NOMINALIZATION' (see Appendixes F.3 and G for details).

The basic A forms include general modifiers such as **ohxe** 'good, well', **atxke** 'bad', **kawo** 'long, tall', **karye** 'high', the manner word **oske** 'thus', and the question word **ɨsoke** 'how?'. There are a few other forms which have components like prefixes or suffixes that suggest they are (historically) derived forms, but whose basic forms without those affixes no longer occur: **karyhe** 'strong, lively', **krawame** 'with difficulty', **fahfɨra** 'a little bit', **tɨmo** 'grouped', **tɨraho** 'lying down', **thatawo** 'standing, upright'. This is, so far as my records go, a complete listing of basic, nonderived forms of A (other than the locative, time, numeral, and quantifier words listed below).

There is a set of basic locative adverbs which match the deictic pronoun forms (see 1.2.2):

near-deictic: **tano** 'here', **xaro** 'to here', **oyoro** 'from here'

medial-deictic: **ɨto** 'there', **ɨsna** 'to there', **ɨsnyero** 'from there'

remote-deictic: **mono** 'over there', **meya** 'to over there', **monyero** 'from over there'

There are also a few nondeictic basic forms: **moxe** 'distant' (cf. the derived form **moxehra** 'near'), **monye** 'beyond, very far', and **moyoro** 'different place or direction'. Other locative forms either belong to R or are derived forms inflected for positional or directional possibilities, and are listed in Appendix D.

The only nonderived time words are **amnye** 'in the future', **mexe** 'a long time', and (possibly) **oroke** 'yesterday'. Other general time words are derived forms, or forms whose morphological structure suggests they are historically derived from some more basic form:

amnyerma 'now, today', **amnyehra** 'in the past, **awanaworo** 'tomorrow', **mexehra** 'a short time', **kokonye** 'in the afternoon', **awanaka** 'in the late afternoon', **kohsaya** 'at night', **enmahrɨ ro** 'early in the day', **emahona ro** 'all the time, every day', **amnye nyhe** 'later'.

There are only three basic numerals in everyday use: **towenyxa** 'one' (it is also used with the meaning 'alone, singly'); **asako** 'two, a couple or so'; and **osorwawo** 'three, a few'. As the glosses for the last two forms indicate, they are sometimes used without precision as to quantity. The form **harata me** 'three' is occasionally used instead of **osorwawo** (it is derived from the N, **harata** 'three-pronged fishing arrow', followed by the R **me** 'DE-NOMINALIZER', which makes it possible to use it as an adverbial). Even more rarely, three other derived forms are used as numerals: **towtɨnke rye** 'four' (derived adverb **towtɨnke** 'having a sibling', followed by the discourse particle **rye** 'SAMENESS'); **kamorɨ ɨrakayo me** 'five' (**kamorɨ** 'our (INCL.) hand(s)', **ɨrakayo** 'divided part, half', **me** 'DENOMINALIZER'); **kamothɨrɨ tkatxehkaxe ro** 'ten' (**kamothɨrɨ** 'our (INCL) hand(s), PAST POSSN', **tkatxehkaxe** 'completely', which is a derived A, and the Prt **ro** 'completely'). In recent years Portuguese numerals have come to be used freely and much more precisely than the traditional ones. They are incorporated as N, but they are normally used as A by adding the R **me**.

The only quantifiers that function as A are: **yake** 'many', **omeroro** 'all', and the derived forms **yakehra** 'few, not many', **thenyehra** 'much, many', **twahake** 'how much?', and **twararo** 'how many?'.

Derived A constitute by far the largest part of the class membership. There are three subgroups in terms of basic morphological features: (i) forms in which the prefix **tɨ-** 'ADVERBIALIZER' is obligatory; (ii) forms which take the set of nominal prefixes that mark person of the possessor and which are derived only from verb stems (the prefix refers to the person of either the subject of an intransitive stem, or the direct object of a transitive stem); and (iii) forms which are obligatorily nonpossessed and do not have the **tɨ-** prefix, but are marked by the general prefix (see Appendix B.2.3). Forms derived from verb stems frequently function as the nuclear constituent of subordinate clauses and are subject to certain constraints on the syntactic relations they enter into with other constituents (see chap. 4).

There are fifteen morphological processes by which A are derived. In terms of semantic types they can be classified as follows:

(1) State, derived from N stems, and action/state, from V stems (four processes): **tawasnye** 'light' (**tɨ-awas(ɨnɨ)-nye** ADVBLZR-daylight-STATE), **twoso** 'shootable, can be shot' (**tɨ-wo-so** ADVBLZR-shoot-ACTION ADV)

(2) Negative state, from N, A, and R stems, and negative action/state, from V stems (two processes): **ɨkamsukhura** 'bloodless, without blood' (**ɨ-kamsuku-hɨra** GEN.PREFIX-blood-NEGATIVE), **omomokhɨra** 'not waiting for you' (**o-momokɨ-hɨra** II-wait for-NEGATIVE)

(3) Time associated with action/state, from V stems (three processes): **romoknɨtoko** 'when my coming' (**ro-omokɨ-nɨ-toko** I-come-ACTION NOMLZN-SIMULTANEOUS TIME)

(4) Possession, and qualities associated with possessed items, from N stems (three processes): **tɨnyahke** 'having (nonmeat) food' (**tɨ-nyahɨ-ke** ADVBLZR-(nonmeat) food-having)

(5) Attempted action/state and unachieved action/state, from V stems (two processes): **twanotatxahke** 'trying to sing' (**tɨ-wanota-txahke** ADVBLZR-sing-desire/effort), **ɨwayehpaya** 'almost dying' (**ɨ-wayehɨ-haya** GEN.PREFIX-die-almost)

(6) Purpose of motion, from V stems (one process): **oyo-tahaxe** 'purposing to hit you' (**oy-otaha-xe** II-hit-MOT.PURP).

Details and examples of all processes are given in Appendix G.

There is a collective suffix **-nye** (see also 1.4) which occurs with derived A when they occur with one of the possessor person

son-marking prefixes that has a 'human' referent (see 1.2.1). When the possessor is a separate NP the collective category is marked in that phrase and the **-nye** suffix does not then occur with the A:

(4) **oyomokɨtxhenye   tasahxemtetxhe (oy-omokɨ-txhe-nye)**
    after-your-COLL-coming we-feast   (II-come- after-COLL)
    'After you all arrive we will have a feast.'

Compare (4) with the following example:

(5) **hawana komo yomokɨtxhe   tasahxemtetxhe** (not
    visitor COLL after-coming-of we-feast   ***yomokɨtxhenye**)
    'After the visitors arrive we will have a feast.'

Dixon (1977) has proposed a set of seven universal semantic types for the class of "adjective" and a further set of generalizations concerning the part-of-speech association of each type. Hixkaryana A items have some features that might warrant a reconsideration of some of his conclusions. They mostly relate to the fact that it is a language rich in derivational processes, and this is a typological dimension to which Dixon does not appear to attach any special significance (pp. 61-62). There are at least four features of this kind.

1. The lack of any distinction between adjective and adverb.

Dixon describes the class of adjectives (pp. 62-63) as:

   a set of lexical items, distinguished on morphological and
   syntactic grounds from the universal classes Noun and Verb.

In that definition he does not refer to an adverb class, and presumably considers it minor compared with the others, at least for some languages. In at least seven of the languages he discusses, however, there is a distinction drawn between adjectives and adverbs. In most cases the criteria for distinguishing the two classes are not given. There seem to be valid reasons for combining the two into one class in Hixkaryana: (i) there are very few basic (i.e., monomorphemic) forms that could possibly be called "adjective"; (ii) these basic forms function just like other forms that are clearly adverbials, and they have the same morphological properties, at least with regard to their derivational potential (see first paragraph of this section); and (iii) neither the basic nor the derived forms function in noun phrases, which is often one of the main criteria used for establishing an adjective class. The class could no doubt be termed either <u>adjective</u> or <u>adverb</u> or both, but since all but a few members of <u>this large class</u> pertain to semantic types usually associated with adverbs, and their syntactic properties correlate with (modifying or sentence) adverbials, it seems to me more appropriate to regard A as abbreviating adverb. The result is that most of the thirty-six "adjectival" concepts used by Dixon in his study belong to the A class, but they are forms derived from other classes of root.

2. Noun domination in derived adverbs.

In his typological dimensions Dixon allows only for verb or adjective domination (pp. 58-62). I assume this has reference to "the basic part of speech membership of the root" (p. 47), which he uses in his analysis of the selected concepts in seventeen languages. In fact, two of the languages seem to express many of the concepts as nouns (Hausa and Hua, p. 46), and it is not easy to see how he fits this fact into his statements about verb/adjective domination. In relation to Hausa, he refers to the "N/V syndrome" (p. 59), but appears to regard this as a minor subclass of the predominant A/V pattern (Hausa, in fact, has a small adjective class which accounts for concepts from four of the seven semantic types (p. 59), so there may be good grounds for treating N/V as relatively minor). In Hixkaryana the root forms for the concepts are 6 A, 6 V, 14 N, and 10 neutral. In the case of the neutral roots, which occur in words of all three major classes (N, V, A), it is the N form which is the least marked; so in these cases also the root can be considered more nounlike than verbal. It is clearly the noun root which is dominant in derived adverbs. (The neutral roots are described--in terms of verbal/nominal stems--in Appendix F.4.)

3. Antonymy expressed by negative suffix.

Except for English, Dixon does not discuss how the antonymy relation is expressed or to what extent, if any, there is a productive derivation process in the languages surveyed. He notes that in English the negative process un- applies to concepts in only three of the seven semantic types, and even then not for all the concepts included in those types (pp. 34-35). In Hixkaryana there is a highly productive negative process, and antonymy is almost exclusively restricted to pairs where one item is a negative form derived from the same root as the positive form: **kawo** 'long' and **kawohra** 'short' (the root is **kawo**, an A); **tɨyoke** 'sharp' and **tɨyohra** 'blunt' (the root is the N, -yo- 'tooth'); **atahurmakaxaho** 'one that is open' and **atahurmakahnɨ** 'one that is shut' (the root is a transitive V, -ahurmaka- 'open'). Dixon's discussion of the ways in which such oppositions are expressed in languages takes no account of this type of process (pp. 58-61).

4. The lack of any basic concept relating to speed.

One of the seven semantic types proposed by Dixon is speed (p. 31). The Hixkaryana language, reflecting cultural traits no doubt associated with the environment (closed-in jungle, placid river), does not have terms that refer primarily to speed. There are forms which can be used to express 'fast' and 'slow', but these are not the central meanings: **karyhe** 'strong, alive, lively'; **kɨrhɨraro** 'weak, flagging'; **amamehra** and **ɨramampɨra** 'not delaying'. There are, of course, many individual concepts that may be lacking in a particular language and culture. The notion of "universal semantic type", however, suggests something sufficiently basic that every language might be expected to have at least one or two concepts belonging to that type. The questions that need to be asked concerning "speed" are: (1) Does it include concepts that are really universal? (2) Do the forms used to express "speed" concepts across languages display a sufficient degree of distinctiveness in their morphological and syntactic properties to justify the setting up of a separate semantic type? Some of Dixon's own statements make the second question a valid one, as for example (p. 56):

> Turning now to the SPEED type, we can note a close dependence on the PHYSICAL PROPERTY type....

In his analysis of the seventeen languages, it is not self-evident that the relatively few differences there are in the morphosyntactic properties of "speed" and "physical properties" are of any greater magnitude than some of the differences he notes in the properties of concepts within a single semantic type.

1.4 Relator (R). The R occurs following an N or NP, and its semantic function is to relate that N(P) to the V or some other part of the sentence. All NPs except those which function as subject or direct object require an R (except a certain type of "topic"-- see 13.3):

(6) **koseryehyaha kamara hona**
    I-am-afraid jaguar to
    'I am afraid of jaguars.'

I use the term <u>relator</u> rather than the more conventional <u>postposition</u> for two reasons. First, the particle class described in 1.5 is also a class of postpositions, but with a quite distinct set of morphological properties and a different syntactic function; it seems to me inaccurate to call either class <u>postposition</u> to the (implied) exclusion of the other, and at times in the description it could be confusing. Second, the properties of the R include some which are not normally associated with postpositions: it can undergo the derivational processes of nominalization and negativization, and it can be inflected for person and collective number (these properties are described later in this section). In view of these factors (and I am sure they apply to other languages, in South America at least), the tendency by linguists to use the term <u>postposition</u> to characterize one particular class of word might merit some reconsideration. (I have continued to use the term <u>postpositional phrase</u> partly as a compromise, but also reflecting the fact that in function and general properties it is virtually identical with the term <u>(pre-/post-) positional phrase</u> as currently used).

The R can occur as a free form, but only when it has one of the set of person-marking N prefixes (or a reflexive/reciprocal prefix--see Appendix H), which substitutes for the N that would normally precede:

(7) **noseryehyaha bɨryekomo rohona (ro-hona)**
   he-is-afraid boy   to-me (I- to)
   'The boy is afraid of me.'

Relators mark the postpositional phrase (PP), which functions as a sentence adjunct or as the complement of the copula, in the same way as an A (or A-phrase). Members of the category Prt (see 1.5) are the only other elements that can occur in the phrase (see 2). In the two preceding examples the PP is a sentence adjunct; in the following it is the complement of the copula, and has a Prt sequence postposed:

(8) **koso xe   rmahaxa wehxaha**
   deer desirous-of very-much I-am
   'I like deer meat very much.'

An R cannot be stranded, in the sense of being separated from its object head, i.e., the noun (phrase) or prefix. (It is rare for postpositions to be stranded, but it has been reported for Dutch [see Koster 1978.577].) Where an NP is subject to a movement process, as in question-word fronting, any R associated with it will be moved also:

(9) **onok hona moseryehyano**
   who to   you-are-afraid
   'Who are you afraid of?'

In general R have the property of being subject to the same derivational processes as A: **-no** 'GENERAL NOMINALIZATION' (see Appendix F.4) and **-hira** 'NEGATIVE' (see Appendix H):

(10) a. **kuraha hokono   uro (hoko-   no)**
      bow   one-occupied-with I   (occ.with-GEN.NOMLZN)
      'I am one who is occupied with making a bow.'

    b. **omɨn   yawohra wahko (yawo-hira)**
      your-house not-in I-was (in- NEG)
      'I was not in your house.'

There are a few R forms that never seem to be negativized, notably **wya** 'to, by' and **ke** 'INSTRUMENT, CAUSE', and also the locatives where movement is involved, like **hona** 'to, towards'.

Relators express a variety of semantic functions. There is a relatively large group of forms to express locative functions (including a few which have reference also to location in time), and they are inflected for positional and directional possibilities--a full list of these is given in Appendix D. Of the rest, two forms occur more often than any others: **me** 'DENOMINALIZER', and **wya** 'to, by'. The form **me** has a primary syntactic function of enabling an N(P) to have the grammatical relation of adjunct or complement (of the copula) when no other R can be used, and in that sense it can be said to "denominalize" it so far as its grammatical function is concerned. In accomplishing that function it can also perform one of several different semantic functions: manner, purpose (see 4.2), function, essive, and translative:

(11) a. **yaskomo me   nehxakonɨ toto**
       shaman DENOMLZR he-was   person
       'The man was a shaman.'

   b. **toto   me   nomokye yaskomo mawaryenɨ**
       person DENOMLZR he-came shaman guardian-spirit-of
       'The shaman's guardian spirit came as a human being.'

   c. **Kaywerye wahanonkatxownɨ owto   yoh   me**
       Kaywerye they-chose-him village chief-of DENOMLZR
       'They chose Kaywerye to be chief.'

   d. **totxowɨ   totokomo Waraka yanoto   me**
       they-went people   Waraka servant-of DENOMLZR
       'The men have gone as Waraka's employees.'

The form **wya** functions as indirect object, but there do not appear to be any compelling syntactic reasons for having indirect object as a separate grammatical relation in Hixkaryana, since all adjuncts (oblique objects, including all R-marked constituents) behave in essentially the same way (see 12.2.7):

(12) **mukawa wɨmyako Waraka wya**
     shotgun I-gave-it Waraka to
     'I gave the shotgun to Waraka.'

It has a similar function in quotative sentences, where it marks the NP that refers to the addressee (see 3.4). It also occurs in causative constructions to mark the noun that refers to the causee (9.3), and in subordinate clauses to mark the underlying subject of a transitive verb (4.1). It is occasionally used to express a cause/source relation:

(13) **oyori   wya ayamotohye**
    your-tooth by you-became-weak
    'You have become ill through your (bad) tooth.'

It is quite often used with a cognitive function, in constructions like the following:

(14) **amnyerma nomokyano Waraka owya**
    today   he-comes   Waraka to-you
    'Do you think Waraka will come today?'

In a nominalized form it can express possession, but this is fairly rare:

(15) **owyano   oni, yawaka**
    to-you-NOMLZN this axe
    'This axe is yours' or 'This axe is for you.'

One possible explanation of this construction is that there is an underlying verb that has been deleted: -imi- 'give'; this would give **wya** an underlying recipient function. In at least some of its functions **wya** seems to have a case-marking role, and this fits a pattern found in some other languages in the Carib family (see 10.3). (See also 12.2.7 for the hypothesis that **wya** always signals an underlying subject.)

Other relators, with specific semantic functions, are as follows:

ke	'CAUSE, INSTRUMENT' (see 4.2)
yakoro	'with' (COMITATIVE)
hyaka	'for' (BENEFACTIVE; also LOCATIVE, meaning 'to (a person)'--see Appendix D)
hoye (ro)	'from' (SOURCE; also LOCATIVE)
hnawo	'in the absence of, without'
hoko	'concerning, occupied with' (also LOCATIVE)
kaxe	'because' (similar in function to **ke**, but it seems to relate to a reason or cause that is permanent or inherent)
wyaro	'like, in comparison to'
ywero	'knowing, acquainted with'
ywenyeke	'not knowing, unacquainted with' (the negative counterpart of **ywero**; these terms relate to knowledge that comes by tradition, personal acquaintance with somebody, or perhaps by intuition)

The Word

hahnoke   'near' (in time or place)

xe   'desirous of' (this R is the only way of expressing the concepts of desire, want, liking, love, there being no verb forms--see 4.2)

horɨ   'PURPOSE' (see 4.2)

yoho   'bigger than, more important than' (see 9.1.1, and compare the closely related LOCATIVE form **(y)ohoye** 'above' in Appendix D)

yosnaka   'smaller than, less important than' (see 9.1.1, and compare the LOCATIVE form **(y)osnawo** 'under' in Appendix D)

wararo   'to the ultimate point of, as close as possible to' (can be used as a LOCATIVE, but often the meaning is more general)

The foregoing items are illustrated in sequence in (16):

(16) a. **watma ke netahetxkonɨ toto heno homo**
    club with they-killed-them person dead COLL
    'The people used to kill them with clubs.'

   b. **rohetxe yakoro komokno**
    my-wife with I-came
    'I have come with my wife.'

   c. **nehekatno rohyaka**
    he-bought-it for-me
    'He bought it for me.'

   d. **yayhɨ hoye netmatxowɨ Waraka**
    tapir from he-gave-them-meat Waraka
    'Waraka provided them with meat from the tapir.'

   e. **romɨn yaka harha ɨteko, rohetxe hnawo**
    my-house to back I-went my-wife in-absence-of
    'I went back home when my wife wasn't there.'

   f. **kɨrwonako rotonɨr hoko**
    I-talked my-going concerning
    'I spoke about my going.'

   g. **rorwonɨ yonytxahra nehxatxkonɨ, anaro ro kaxe**
    my-talk not-hearing they-were other completely because
    'They didn't understand my words, because they were of a different (language group).'

   h. **tɨyɨmɨ wyaro naha Warya**
    his-father like he-is Warya
    'Warya is like his father.'

i. **Mawarye yexetxhɨrɨnhɨrɨ ywero natxhe totokomo**
   Mawarye his-being-long-ago knowing they-are people
   'The people know (what has been told of) Mawarye's
     doings long ago.'

j. **roywenyeke naha hawana**
   not-knowing-me he-is visitor
   'The visitor does not know me.'

k. **rototho hahnoke rmahaxa naha**
   my-going near   very   it-is
   'It is very near to the time of my going.'

l. **honyko xe   wehxaha**
   peccary desirous-of I-am
   'I want peccary.'

m. **tono   omsamtxemo, tuna horɨ**
   she-went young-girl   water PURPOSE
   'The girl has gone for water.'

n. **anaro kom yoho   rmahaxa   naha, Kaywerye, owto**
   other COLL greater very-much he-is Kaywerye   village

   yoh   kaxe
   chief-of because
   'Kaywerye is much greater than others, because
     he is the chief.'

o. **romuru yosnaka naha, omuru**
   my-son smaller he-is your-son
   'Your boy is smaller than mine.'

p. **tɨwyanye enahtoho   wararo   nasahxemtotxownɨ**
   by-them eat-'THING' NOMLZN ULTIMATE they-feasted
   'They feasted, eating as much as they possibly could.'

The collective suffix **-nye** (see chap. 3) occurs with R when their object has a human referent (see 1.2.1), but only when that object is marked by a prefix, without any preceding NP (where there is a preceding NP, the collective category is marked in that phrase):

(17) **ɨhokonye   kɨrwonɨmno (ɨ- hoko- nye)**
     occupied-with-them I-talked   (III-occ.with-COLL)
     'I was talking about them.'

This can be compared with the following:

(18) **Waraka hokru   kom hoko   kɨrwonɨmno**
     Waraka child-of COLL occupied-with I-talked
     'I was talking about Waraka's children.'
     (not *Waraka hokru kom hokonye ...)

Where semantically appropriate, R can be given a reflexive and/or reciprocal form by the addition of one of the set of detransitivizing prefixes (see 8.1 and Appendix H).

1.5 Particle (Prt). Particles (Prt) follow words of any class other than the ideophone, and never occur as free forms or in isolation. They are noninflected, nonderived words, and can be divided into three subclasses on the basis of function and position of occurrence in relation to other Prt in a sequence:

(1) Modifying Prt, which usually occur first in any Prt sequence and modify an N that is normally the head of the phrase in which they occur. (Where they occur in V or A phrases they refer to some N in the context and are considered to be modifying an ellipsed nominal head--see 13.5.1(5).) (See Appendix I for the set of modifying Prt.)

(2) Discourse Prt, which usually occur between the modifying and verification Prt in any sequence. The primary scope of the discourse Prt is the head word it governs, and it usually relates that word to some other part of the discourse--"usually," because, while the primary function of each Prt in the set is of a sentence connective or anaphoric type, there are some uses of a more general type of modification of the head word (see 13.4.2 and Appendix J).

(3) Verification Prt, which always occur last in any Prt sequence and are, therefore, always phrase final. Their function is to express the attitude or relationship of the speaker to what he is saying, including the degree of certainty and the authority for making the assertion (see 12.2.3 and Appendix K).

Particles are like clitics in that they are phonologically bound to their head word. This is reflected in some of their initial clusters, which do not occur in (phonological) word-initial position (e.g., **ymo** 'augmentative' (modifying), **rma** 'same referent' (discourse), **mpɨnɨ** 'certainty' (verification)). They are, however, considered a distinct (syntactic) word class on the grounds that (i) they are mobile compared with bound affixes, and (ii) at their boundaries they are not subject to the same morphophonological processes that apply at morpheme boundaries within words (see Appendix A.4). Furthermore, under normal definitions of clitic they could not be clitics, because they often bear stress. They might be termed associatives in the sense of Speiser (1941.166-67). Their mobility can be seen in the options available in such a sentence as the following:

(19) **namryekyatxkon   heno komo rma hatɨ,**
    IIIS-hunt-DIST.PAST CONT.COLL dead COLL same HSY

   kamarayana   komo
   jaguar-person COLL
   'Those jaguar people, now dead, used to still go hunting.'

The order of morphemes in the word **n-amryek(ɨ)-yatxkon(ɨ)** is fixed; the order of the sequence of Prt that follows can be changed to any of the following: **kom heno rma hatɨ, heno rma kom hatɨ, komo rma heno hatɨ** (sequences where **rma** occurs before both **heno** and **komo** are also possible, but less likely). Also, if the subject NP is fronted, the Prt **tɨ** can also be fronted with it: **kamarayana kom tɨ namryekyatxkon heno komo rma ha.**

Where either subject NPs or adjunct phrases (AP or PP) are fronted for emphasis (see 7.2), as in the last example, there is, in fact, a preference to place all or most of any Prt sequence in the fronted phrase rather than in the VP, where they would otherwise be placed (i.e., if either the VP itself, or the direct object NP, were sentence initial; see 7.7). In general, however, Prt can occur in any phrase in the sentence, including (left or right) dislocated phrases. In PPs, Prt normally occur after the R, but modifying Prt (frequently) and some discourse Prt (occasionally) can precede it:

(20) **[[$_{PP}$thetx   heno xaxa   [$_R$xe]]   nehxakonɨ]**
    his-wife dead SUPERLATIVE desirous-of he-was
    'He used really to love his late wife.'

In this example **heno** is a modifying, and **xaxa** a discourse, Prt.

There are a few other general conditions relating to Prt sequences. Verification Prt are mutually exclusive as a set, so only one can occur in any phrase. There is a subgroup of discourse Prt that usually occur before other discourse Prt and sometimes also before modifying Prt: **rha** 'in turn', **rma** 'same referent', **ro** 'habitual', **rye** 'sameness', and **xa** 'contrast'. There are a few special sequences of discourse Prt that have a meaning distinct from the sum of the individual meanings; these are listed separately in Appendix J. There do not seem to be any systematic restrictions on possible combinations of discourse Prt (or of modifying Prt, except that two of them, **txko** 'diminutive' and **ymo** 'augmentative', are mutually exclusive on semantic grounds). There are rarely more than five particles in any one phrase, and usually not more than three.

There is one other type of clitic-particle: a preverbal proclitic, of which there are two kinds: (1) a reduced pronoun form, **mo- (ma-)** 'third person, out of sight', that cooccurs with, and immediately precedes, the third person prefix in the V (see 1.2.

The Word

2); and (2) three forms that occur optionally preceding first person inclusive imperative V forms, **ɨpa** 'let's go', **omok** 'come (INDIVIDUAL)' and **omohtxok** 'come (COLLECTIVE)'. The last two are reduced forms of the second person imperative of the verb **-omokɨ-** 'come' (see 6.3).

Other members of the category Prt, with a highly restricted usage, are response (see 6.6) and vocative (see 6.7.2).

1.6 Ideophone. The ideophone is a noninflected, onomatopoeic word denoting an action that is normally expressed by a V. It is the only class of word that cannot be followed by a Prt. Ideophones occur very frequently in most types of discourse, with just one general constraint: they do not occur in embedded speech that functions as the direct object of the quotative verb **-ka-** 'say'. Ideophones function syntactically in one of three ways:

(i) As a sentence constituent, carrying the same meaning as the V of the sentence (i.e., the basic part of the V meaning, not including person, tense, etc.):

(21) **ɨpo,**   **nahatakaye**   **owto**   **hona**
    emerging-into-open he-came-out village to
    'Coming into the clearing, he arrived at the village.'

In this function the ideophone is usually sentence initial or sentence final, but it can occur between the V and some other constituent; it is often (left or right) dislocated, as in the example, but not necessarily so.

(ii) As the direct object of the verb **-ka-** 'say, do'. In this case the ideophone nearly always precedes the V, and exactly parallels the embedded speech constituent, which also functions as direct object of **-ka-** (see 3.1). Any other sentence constituent follows the **-ka-** phrase:

(22) **to**   **kay**   **hatɨ kamara**
    dropping he-did-it HSY jaguar
    'The jaguar dropped down (from a tree).'

(iii) In isolation, or with only an adjunct constituent following it, when it is not directly (grammatically) related to the sentences which precede and follow. In this usage it is regarded as a minor sentence type (see 6.7):

(23) **bo,**   **ɨrakataworo**
    falling-into-hammock in-the-middle-of-it
    'He (or any other person category) slept
     at night during the trip.'

Such a sentence is common in a travel narrative, when the person involved in the action is identifiable from the context.

The ideophone may be a single morpheme, as in the three preceding examples, or a sequence of reduplicated forms: **sɨh sɨh sɨh sɨh sɨh** 'stepping action in walking'. The number of repeats of the form may be from two to about ten, but is not usually more than six.

Ideophones show some variations from the normal phonology of the language: one or two additional phonological units occur, and in the phonotactics there are word-final consonants that do not occur elsewhere.

There are a few interjection forms, expressing feelings and attitudes, which have the same properties as ideophones, and are regarded as members of the same word class: **akay** (cry of pain), **poo** (expression of wonder).

2 The Phrase

The types of phrase and their respective functions are: verb phrase (VP), which functions as the obligatory predicate constituent of all finite clauses; adverbial phrase (AP) and postpositional phrase (PP), which function either as adjunct, in any type of clause/sentence, or as complement, in a copular clause; and noun phrase (NP), which functions as the subject or direct object of a clause, or as the object in a PP.

All phrases have two types of constituent: nuclear (obligatory) and peripheral (optional). The nuclear constituent consists of a single word (V, N, A, or (possessed) R). Except for the NP (see 2.2), the only peripheral constituent of phrases is the Prt, or Prt sequence (see 1.5).

2.1 Verb phrase (VP). The VP may consist of the V alone, or the V followed by one or more Prt. (I regard the preverbal proclitics described in 1.5 as part of the V; note also that I am not using VP to denote the constituent consisting of V and object NP; VP as used here might be thought of as analogous to Chomsky's "Verb" node in <u>Syntactic Structures</u>):

(24) a. **namryehtxowɨ totokomo**
 they-went-hunting people
 'The people have gone hunting.'

 b. **totokomo yonyetxkonɨ roro hatɨ,**
 people they-used-to-eat-them PERMANENT HSY

 kamarayana komo
 jaguar-person COLL
 'The jaguar-people used to eat people all the time.'

The Prt in (24b) are **roro** (discourse) and **hatɨ** (verification).

2.2 Noun phrase (NP). The nucleus of an NP is always an N. The peripheral elements are possessor NPs, preposed modifiers, and postposed Prt. Where an NP contains a possessor I will speak of it as a possessed NP.

Preposed modifiers are infrequent in NP, being restricted to numerals and the nominal form **anaro** 'another', both of which have other primary functions, either as adjuncts (numerals), or as head of an NP or object of a PP (**anaro**):

(25) a. **asak kanawa wenyo**
       two canoe I-saw-it
       'I saw two canoes.'

   b. **kanawa wenyo, asako**
      canoe I-saw-it two
      'I saw two canoes.'

   c. **anaro   owto   hona kahatakeko**
      another village to   I-came-out
      'I arrived at another village.'

   d. **owto   hona kahatakeko, anaro   hona**
      village to   I-came-out   another to
      'I arrived at another village.'

In (a) the numeral, and in (c) **anaro**, function as preposed modifiers; in (b) the numeral functions as adjunct; and in (d) **anaro** is the object of a PP, which is in a discontinuous paratactic relationship with the sentence-initial PP **owto hona**.

Postposed Prt occur frequently in NPs:

(26) a. **Utxun   heno**
       Utxunu now-dead
       'the late Utxunu'

   b. **Waraka haxa   ryhe**
      Waraka CONTRAST EMPHATIC
      'definitely Waraka, not anyone else'

   c. **kamara ymo hatɨ**
      jaguar AUG HSY
      'the big bad jaguar, it is reported'

In possessed NPs the possessor precedes the possessed, and it is the possessed which is the morphologically marked item (see 1.2.1 and Appendix C):

(27) a. **bɨryekomo yoknɨ**
       boy   pet-of
       'the boy's pet'

   b. **anaro   yowto   hona kahatakeko**
      another village-of   to   I-came-out
      'I arrived at another's village.'

   c. **karaywa   kanawarɨ komo rma hatɨ**
      non-Indian canoe-of COLL SAME HSY
      'The canoes of the non-Indians already referred to, it is reported'

The Prt in (c) are modifying (**komo**), discourse (**rma**), and verification (**hatɨ**).

The Phrase

In (27b) **anaro** is the possessor and **yowto** the possessed item, in contrast with (25c), where **anaro** is a preposed modifier and **owto** the (nonpossessed) N nucleus of the phrase. One way of describing this contrast (which is, as the glosses suggest, closely paralleled in English), would be to analyze **anaro** as capable of selecting a dummy or empty N, making possible contrasts like (28):

(28) a. (=25c).

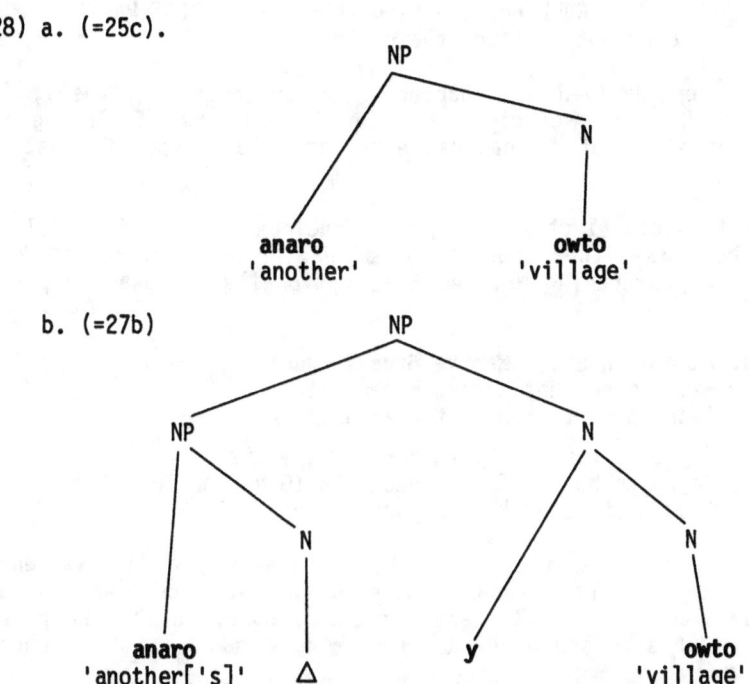

b. (=27b)

As in English, it is the NP--N structure that defines the possessed NP type and determines possession morphology (though in English it is the NP that is marked, while in Hixkaryana it is the N).

2.3 Adverbial phrase (AP). Most adverbial phrases are of the single-word (A) type, optionally followed by a Prt sequence, like VPs and NPs:

(29) a. **karyhe rmahaxa (ntoye)** b. **horyme nyhe txko (naha)**
    fast   very   (he-went)   big   more DIMIN (he-is)
    '(He went) very fast.'   '(He is) a little bigger.'

When the AP is the nuclear constituent of a subordinate clause, it can have a preposed NP <u>possessor</u>, which makes the construction very similar to a possessed NP (but the possessed item is a derived A, not an N):

(30) a. **Waraka yewehnɨtoko,...**
Waraka bathing-time-of
'When Waraka takes a bath,...'

b. **bɨryekomo komo hananɨhpɨra   (wehxakonɨ)**
child   COLL not-teaching-them (I-was-DIST.PAST)
'I used not to teach the children.'

See 1.3 on derived A, chapter 4 on subordinate clauses, and Appendix G for a complete list of derivations, including the possessed forms of A that can enter into this type of construction.

2.4 Postpositional phrase (PP). The nucleus of a PP is a Relator (R). The R is either preceded by an NP, or has a possessed form, without any preceding NP. The R is optionally followed by particle(s):

(31) a. **rakoro nteko   Waraka Manawsɨ hona**
with-me he-went Waraka Manaus to
'Waraka went with me to Manaus.'

b. **Kaywerye mɨn   yaka harha mpɨnɨ mɨtehe ha**
Kaywerye house-of to   back OBLIG you-go INTENSFR
'You must go back to Kaywerye's house.'

There are two PPs in (a), neither containing a Prt sequence: **rakoro** is the first person possessed form of the R **yakoro**, and **Manawsɨ hona** has an NP preceding the R **hona**. In (b) the phrase consists of a possessed NP **Kaywerye mɨn**, R **yaka**, and Prt sequence **harha mpɨnɨ**.

The NP that precedes the R may include a derived N functioning as the nuclear constituent of a subordinate clause (see 1.2.1 and chap. 4):

(32) **romararɨn ho owyanye   wewe yamanɨr   xe   wehxaha**
my-field in by-you-COLL tree felling-of desirous-of I-am
'I want you all to fell trees in my field.'

See 1.4 on R for further discussion and examples.

2.5 Implications for formalization of phrase structure rules. Certain facts in the foregoing sections suggest that there might be useful applications of the theory of Jackendoff (1977) to the facts of the Hixkaryana phrase types and Prt sequences. Jackendoff's monograph represents the most detailed and precise of recent studies of phrase structure. I will first sketch the kind of phrase structure rule system Jackendoff's analysis suggests, and then briefly discuss some of the problems in relating Jackendoff's theory to Hixkaryana.

The major lexical categories of Hixkaryana are V, N, A, and R (Jackendoff's P). Under Jackendoff's "Uniform Three-Level Hypothesis," the major phrasal categories must therefore be V''' (= S), N''' (= NP), A''' (= AP), and R''' (= PP). The hypothesis of three layers of structure seems at first to be particularly appropriate, in view of the fact that three distinct classes of Prt can be motivated internally to Hixkaryana on the grounds of syntactic and semantic properties. Suppose rules like the following were postulated:

(33) a. V''' → V'' (N''') (R''')* (A''')* (Prt''')
     V'' → V' (Prt''')*
     V'   → (X''') V (Prt''')*
   b. N''' → Art N'' (Prt''')
              N'''
      N'' → N' (Prt''')*
      N'   → N (Prt''')*

(Notice that the V' rule introduces X'''--that is, either NPs, PPs, APs, or direct quote Ss--to the left of V, in accordance with the standard view of what VP contains, rather than the view I have adopted in 2.1 for the purpose of this description generally.) One might then attempt to motivate the claim that the verification particles were those Prt that occurred under X''', the discourse particles those that occurred under X'', and the modifying particles those that occurred under X'.

In fact, the ordering restrictions between discourse and modifying particles are not quite as rigid as this would suggest (see 1.5). And there are two points at which the proposed rules might suggest a greater degree of parallelism between the structures than is actually present: (1) (Prt''') to the right of V''' implies that the verification particle is a sentence Prt, but syntax and semantics do not go hand in hand here; semantically, the scope relates to the whole sentence, but in the actual structures it always occurs as a phrase constituent (this means that when a verification Prt is dominated by N''' its semantic scope is not merely the domain of the constituent that immediately includes it, but the entire containing V''' (S); and (2) (Prt''')* to the right of V' relates to modifying particles, which do actually occur in VPs on the surface, but must, I feel, be regarded in the underlying configuration as part of an NP, whose nominal head is then deleted (see 1.5).

More generally, while I have not investigated the feasibility of applying Jackendoff's theory in detail to Hixkaryana, at first sight there appear to be some rather basic difficulties. These arise from the fact that, as Jackendoff points out (p. 38, fn.), "the X Convention says nothing about what to do with nonparallel structures." Thus, derived NP and derived AP which constitute the nuclei of subordinate clauses (see chap. 4) are sometimes parallel to S, with an NP preceding an NP or AP (derived from a V) corresponding to the NP that precedes the VP in S (cf. 34a and 34b). This parallelism does not, however, extend to intransitives (cf. 34c and 34d):

(34) a. **toto   heno komo yonothɨrɨ   (kamara wya)**
       person dead COLL eating-of-PAST (jaguar by)
       'the (past) eating of people (by the jaguar)'

   b. **toto   heno komo yonoye   (kamara)**
      person dead COLL he-ate-them (jaguar)
      '(The jaguar) ate people.'

   c. **toto   heno komo yamryekɨthɨrɨ**
      person dead COLL hunting-of-PAST
      'the people's hunting (in the past)'

   d. **namryekyatxkonɨ   toto   heno komo**
      they-went-hunting person dead COLL
      'The people used to go hunting.'

The ordering in (34c) is obligatory; in (34d) the NP could precede the VP, but this would be a marked order. A comparison between (34a) and (34c) reveals an even more crucial lack of parallelism: in (34a) the NP is the underlying object of the V (cf. 34b), but in (34c) the same NP, in the same position, is the underlying subject of the V. This difference, arising from the basic transitive-intransitive dichotomy, applies to all NP possessors that precede an N or A that is derived from a V, and marks the fundamental difference between subordinate clauses and main clauses (see 4.1). This makes for great difficulties in defining grammatical functions like subject and object, for while the N''' in V' is unambiguously an object, the N''' in A''' is variously a subject or an object. This, of course, reflects the fact that the category A does not properly correspond to English <u>adjective</u>. The same also applies to R (English P), for which there would also be problems in seeking to apply Jackendoff's theory as a whole to Hixkaryana.

3 The Main Clause

3.1 Taxonomy of clause types. One can classify Hixkaryana main clauses into five types by reference to their nuclear constituents: transitive (35a), intransitive (35b), copular (35c), equative (35d), and quotative (35e). The following examples contain only nuclear constituents:

(35) a. **kuraha yonyhoryeno biryekomo**
 bow he-made-it boy
 'The boy made a bow.'

    b. **newehyatxhe woriskomo komo**
 they-take-a-bath women COLL
 'The women are taking a bath.'

    c. **ohxe rmahaxa naha woto**   d. **romuru mosoni**
 good very it-is meat   my-son this-one
 'The meat is very good.'   'This is my son.'

    e. **kanawa yaryako rowti kano Waraka**
 canoe he-took-it my-brother he-said-it Waraka
 '"My brother took the canoe," said Waraka.'

The principal distinguishing features of each type can be summarized as follows. The transitive clause (a) has a direct object NP and a V with a transitive stem and one of the set of transitive person-marking prefixes. The intransitive clause (b) has no direct object NP, and its V has an intransitive stem and one of the set of intransitive person-marking prefixes. The copular clause (c) has an (AP) complement (it could also be a PP) and the V is the copula, which is the only V that can occur in this type of clause. The equative clause (d) does not have a surface V and its predicate constituent (**romuru**) is an NP, which distinguishes it from the copular complement. The quotative clause (e) has a direct object that is a finite clause (the embedded speech, which is usually a finite clause, but does not have to be) and the V **-ka-** 'say', which is the only V that can occur in this type of clause.

3.2 Order of constituents. The order of constituents in the examples is the preferred order, and this reveals a basic unity underlying all Hixkaryana main clause constructions that overrides the differences among the types outlined above. The basic order of constituents is OVS, whether the O is a direct object NP, a complement A, a predicate nominal, or an embedded speech finite clause. Variations in the order are permitted under stateable conditions (see chap. 7 and 13.1). The evidence for this order being the basic one is given in 10.2, and the whole of Part Two is concerned with its significance.

3.3 Subject and direct object agreement. Subject and direct object are obligatorily expressed in the verb by means of person-marking prefixes (see Appendix B for a complete listing); the transitive set consists of portmanteau forms that express both subject and object. The subject and object may be full NPs, as in the preceding examples, but they are often deleted under conditions of recoverability from the context (except in equative clauses). In transitive clauses there is often only one NP, the other having been deleted; and since a subject NP can be moved to a preverbal position (see 7.2 and 13.1), there is potential ambiguity as to whether the NP is subject or object. This ambiguity is usually avoided by the different prefixal forms in the verb: **n(ɨ)-** 'IIISIIIO' when there is no preceding object NP and **y-** 'IIISIIIO' when there is one:

(36) a. **toto yahosɨye   kamara**
     man it-grabbed-him jaguar
     'The jaguar grabbed the man.'

   b. **toto yahosɨye**
     man it-grabbed-him
     'It (jaguar) grabbed the man.'

   c. **kamara nahosɨye**   (or) **nahosɨye   kamara**
     jaguar it-grabbed-him   it-grabbed-him jaguar
     'The jaguar grabbed him.'   'The jaguar grabbed him.'

   d. **toto nahosɨye**   (or) **nahosɨye toto**
     man he-grabbed-it
     'The man grabbed it (jaguar).'

   e. **nahosɨye**
     'It grabbed him' or 'He grabbed it.'

Ambiguity only arises in (36e), where there is no NP at all, and this form is used only when the context makes the meaning clear. In the other cases the different prefixal forms avoid any ambiguity. The verb prefix does not always, however, disambiguate the function of a preceding NP. There are zero allomorphs of both **nɨ-** and **y-** which occur in the same environment, i.e., preceding a

The Main Clause

stem-initial consonant (see Appendix B); this is an absolute conditioning factor when the preceding NP functions as object:

(37) **Waraka hanan̯thyakon̯**   (Vb. stem: **-hanan̯h̯-** 'teach')
Waraka he-used-to-teach-him
'He used to teach Waraka.'

There are, however, two possibilities when the preceding NP functions as subject: (i) if the subject NP is phonologically dislocated (signalled here by comma), the zero allomorph of 'IIIS-IIIO' occurs; and (ii) if the NP is not dislocated, but phonologically bound to the verb, the **n-** allomorph of 'IIISIIIO' occurs.

(38) a. **Waraka, hanan̯thyakon̯**
Waraka, he-used-to-teach-him
'Waraka used to teach him.'

b. **Waraka nhanan̯thyakon̯**
Waraka he-used-to-teach-him
'Waraka used to teach him.'

Occasionally there is left dislocation of the object NP, and this results in genuine ambiguity, which is resolved only by the context.

3.4 Adjunct. I shall refer to just one type of peripheral clause constituent: adjunct (ideophones are regarded as constituents of the sentence rather than the clause--see 1.6 and 6.1). This term covers three types of construction: AP, subordinate clause in which the nuclear predicate constituent is a derived A, and PP (which may also have a subordinate clause embedded in it--see 2.4). It can occur in any type of clause, but in an equative clause it occurs only as a constituent of the predicate nominal. The preferred position for adjunct is following the subject, but it can, like the subject, be moved to clause-initial position. The adjunct is now shown (bracketed) occurring in each of the five clause types, and the various types of construction are illustrated:

(39) a. **wewe yametxow   hat̯ hawana komo, [towto**
tree they-fell-it HSY visitor COLL their-village

kom hona harha t̯tohra   ronye   rma haka]
COLL to back their-not-going time-COLL CONT yet
'The visitors say they will fell the trees before
they go back to their village.'

b. **[ohxehra] d̯kno, [thenyehra tuna ymo yomokn̯r ke]**
not-good I-slept much   water AUG coming-of because
'I didn't sleep well, because it was raining heavily.'

c. ekeh   me   wehxaha, [atunano wya]
    sick-one DENOMLZR I-am   fever   by
    'I am sick with fever.'

d. [ɨsna]   ɨtosaho   mokro
    to-there one-that-went   that-one
    'That is the one who went there.'

e. [awanaworo] nomokyatxhe harha, kekonɨ   Waraka,
    tomorrow   they-come   back   he-said-it Waraka

    [amryehxemo   kom   hoko]
    ones-who-hunted COLL concerning
    '"They will return tomorrow," said Waraka, about
    the hunting party.'

In (39b) there are two adjuncts in the intransitive clause: the first is an A and precedes the V; the other is a PP with an embedded subordinate clause, and it is clause final. It is also possible, and quite common, to have a single complex adjunct, consisting of two or more phrases in paratactic construction, each phrase having the same grammatical relation and the same basic semantic content (see 12.2.4):

(40) neryeye   ɨsna,   warata hona
      he-put-it-down   to-there   shelf onto
      'He put it down there, on the shelf.'

There are also two adjuncts in the quotative clause (39e), but in this case one of them is part of the embedded speech finite clause (the time adverb **awanaworo**) and the other occurs in final position in the main clause (the postpositional phrase **amryehxemo kom hoko**). In (39a) the adjunct is a relatively long subordinate clause with a derived A as the nuclear constituent.

Copular clauses can have both complement and adjunct, as seen in (39c), where **ekeh me** is the complement and **atunano wya** the adjunct. The semantically more prominent constituent functions as complement, and this normally precedes the (copula) V, with the adjunct following. Since, however, the complement can occasionally occur after the V, and the adjunct is often fronted, it is not always clear which is complement and which is adjunct, although the criterion of semantic prominence usually is sufficient to distinguish the two. Some constructions occur almost exclusively as complement: the negation subordinate clause, which has the negative derived A as its nuclear constituent; and the desiderative PP governed by the R **xe** 'desirous of'. Other constructions rarely occur as complement, mainly as adjunct: the subordinate clauses time, purpose, and cause (see 4.2 and 4.3).

The Main Clause

The indirect object seems to be best interpreted as a subtype of adjunct; it is expressed by a PP governed by the R **wya** 'to, by':

(41) a. **yawaka yɨmyako   bɨryekomo rowya**
       axe   he-gave-it boy   to-me
       'The boy gave the axe to me.'

   b. **ɨtohra   exko kano   wosɨ thokru   wya**
      not-going be   she-said-it woman her-child to
      '"Don't go," said the woman to her child.'

The preferred position is clause final, as with other adjuncts. The **wya**-phrase is not restricted to the usual semantic functions associated with indirect object, e.g., recipient, addressee (as in the preceding examples). It also occurs with the copula (39c), in a quite different semantic role. It also occurs in subordinate clauses to express the underlying subject of the predicative element (see 4.1), and in causative constructions to express the role of causee (see 9.3). It has the same possibilities as other adjuncts (and subject) of movement to clause-initial position. There does not seem to be any good syntactic reason for setting up indirect object as a separate clause constituent (see 12.2.7 for fuller discussion).

3.5 Copular and equative clauses. The copular complement differs from the direct object NP of a transitive clause in that the copula only rarely occurs without it; when it does, the result is a subject-copula construction (the subject is then normally fronted):

(42) a. **kamɨmɨ nehxakonɨ**
       sun   it-was
       'There was sun (all the time).'

   b. **roharɨ   mpe   nay ha**
      my-grandson DOUBT he-is INTENSFR
      '"Do I have a grandson?"'

This construction is more frequent when the subject is an embedded equative clause (see 5.2), but such a clause includes a predicate nominal, which is the equivalent of a complement/direct object.

In equative clauses, where there is no overt copula, the normal verbal category of tense-aspect is not expressed; the more restricted tense distinctions that apply to N, and especially derived N, are available (see 1.2.1, 4.7, and Appendixes C and F). This is seen in (39d), where the derived noun **ɨtosaho** is marked for 'PAST', distinguishing it from **tɨtosomɨ** 'the one who is going/will go'.

Apart from this difference in marking of tense-aspect, copular and equative clauses are very similar in many of their main functions and can often be substituted for each other. This applies to defining, identity, and role functions.

(43) a. **toto   me   naha**   (or)   **toto   noro**
       person DENOMLZR he-is   person he
       'He is a man.'   'He is a man.'

   b. **romuru me   naha mosoni** (or)
       my-son DENOMLZR he-is this-one
       'This is my son.'

      romuru mosoni
       my-son this-one
       'This is my son.'

   c. **owto   yoh   me   naha**   (or)
       village chief-of DENOMLZR he-is
       'He is chief.'

      owto   yohi   noro
       village chief-of he
       'He is chief.'

The foregoing examples highlight the structural differences in the two clause types. The equative nucleus has only nominals, in contrast with the copular complement, which must be a PP or AP; the copula is present or absent; and the subject is an obligatory constituent of the equative, but not of the copular, clause.

3.6 Use of the quotative verb without embedded speech direct object. In quotative clauses the (embedded speech) object always occurs immediately preceding the main verb **-ka-** 'say'; that verb can, however, occur with an adjunct preceding instead of embedded speech, in which case it functions like any other transitive V without an object NP:

(44) **oni wyaro nkekoni   biryekomo, tiyoni   wya**
      this like he-said-it boy   his-mother to
      'This is what the boy said to his mother.'

See 1.6 for occurrence of ideophone with **-ka-** 'say, do'.

3.7 Number of constituents in main clauses. The verb is frequently the only constituent in a clause. At the other extreme it is possible to have all the nuclear constituents and one or more adjuncts occurring in a single clause. The preferred pattern is to delete subject and object NPs whenever possible, and to spread adjuncts across two or more clauses, so that the average number of constituents per clause is probably about two, or a little over.

The Main Clause

This does not necessarily mean short clauses; in addition to the fact that adjuncts (and sometimes subject and object) can be subordinate clause, there is also frequent use of the complex paratactic construction (see 12.2.4). This results in a sequence of phrases, whose purpose is to modify, coordinate, or clarify one central argument, functioning as a single constituent at the clause level.

3.8 Collective number agreement. The collective number agreement between verb and subject and object noun phrases is discussed in 1.2.1 (see also Appendix B.1).

4 The Subordinate Clause

4.1 Nonfinite constructions. All subordinate clauses have nonfinite verbal forms, either derived N or derived A, as their main predication element. Tense-aspect is not marked in the subordinate clause, only in the superordinate clause. Apart from the nonfinite form of the verb, the subordinate clause differs syntactically from the main clause in the ways in which the underlying subject and direct object are expressed: (i) the subject of the intransitive and copula, and the object of the transitive, normally function as possessor of the derived form in a possessed noun phrase relationship (see 2.2 and 2.3); and (ii) the subject of the transitive is usually expressed by means of a separate PP governed by the R **wya** 'to, by'. The possessor relationship, as elsewhere in the language, is expressed obligatorily by one of the set of nominal person-marking prefixes and optionally by a preceding NP (see 1.2.1). Adjuncts and copular complements occur in subordinate clauses in the same form as they do in main clauses.

4.2 Postpositional phrase as nuclear predication constituent. Derived N occur in PPs with R, acting as nuclear elements of a variety of subordinate clause types: cause/result, with the R **ke** 'because' (45a); manner, with the R **me** 'DENOMINALIZER' and **wya** 'to, by' (45b, c); purpose, with the R **horɨ** 'PURPOSE' (45d) and **me** following the nominalizing suffix **-toho** 'THING ASSOCIATED WITH AN ACTION' (45e); negative purpose, with the R **hona** 'to' following the nominalizing suffix **-nɨrɨ** 'ACTION NOMINALIZATION' (45f); and desire, with the R **xe** 'desirous of' (45g):

(45) a. **ɨtohra   wahko, thenyehra tuna   yomoknɨr ke**
     not-going I-was   much   water coming-of because
     'I didn't go because it was raining heavily.'

   b. **teryewryero rowanotanɨr me   kewehyaha**
      loudly   my-singing DENOMLZR I-take-a-bath
      'I take a bath singing loudly.'

The Subordinate Clause

c. **wayehtxownɨ, watma ke totahatxho komo wya**
they-died club with the-hitting-of-them COLL by
'They died through being hit with a club.'

d. **kuraha wanɨmno, ɨhoko ryesnɨrɨ horɨ**
bow-wood I-picked-it-up occ.-with-it my-being PURP
'I picked up the bow-wood with a view to working on it.'

e. **kosohtxemehe, rahohsɨra atunano yehtxoho me**
I-treat-myself not-catching-me fever its-being DENOMLZR
'I treat myself with medicine so that the fever won't get me.'

f. **temenye kɨrwonɨmno, anar komo wya enytxanɨr hona**
whispering I-spoke other COLL by hearing-it towards
'I spoke in a whisper, so that other people could not hear it.'

g. **honyko wonɨr xe wehxaha, Waraka wya**
peccary shooting-of desirous-of I-am Waraka by
'I want Waraka to shoot peccary.'

The negative purpose type (45f) can also be expressed by the purpose relator **horɨ** following the nominalizing suffix **-hɨtorɨ** 'NEGATIVE ACTION NOMINALIZATION, POSSD':

(46) **temenye kɨrwonɨmno, anar komo wya enytxahtor horɨ**
whispering I-spoke other COLL by not-hearing-it PURP
'I spoke in a whisper, so that other people could not hear it.'

4.3 Derived adverb as nuclear predication constituent. Derived A express a different set of subordinate clause types, functioning either as adjunct or copular complement: time, for which there are three forms, marked by the adverbializing suffixes **-toko** 'SIMULTANEOUS ACTION' (47a), **-txhe** 'after' (47b), and **-wawo** 'during the time of' (47c); negative, marked by the suffix **-hɨra** 'NEGATIVE' (47d); and motion purpose, marked by the suffix **-so/-xe** (47e):

(47) a. **tɨwya tɨyɨm yonyetoko, nekahtɨmyako bɨryekomo**
by-him his-father him-seeing-when he-fled boy
'When he saw his father the boy ran away.'

b. **bɨn yaye tahatakatxhe, nosompotɨye**
his-house from his-coming-out-after he-looked-up

horykomo
adult-man
'When he came out of his house the man looked up.'

c. **waha me ryexwawo, toto heno**
fighting-man DENOMLZR my-being-during person dead

komo wetahekon╪
COLL I-killed-them
'When I was a fighting man I used to kill people.'

d. b╪ryekomo komo hanan╪hp╪ra naha   wos╪, tano
   child   COLL not-teaching she-is woman here
   'The woman does not teach the children here.'

e. romarar╪n ho wewe yamaxe   nomohtxow╪
   my-field in tree PURP-to-cut they-came
   'They have come to fell trees in my field.'

4.4 Syntactic functions of subordinate clauses. The types of subordinate clause discussed and illustrated so far all function as either adjunct or copular complement. Any derived N in a postpositional phrase will constitute the nucleus of a subordinate clause with a similar function, i.e., adjunct or complement. This applies, for example, to phrases governed by locative (48a), comparative (48b), and comitative (48c) R:

(48) a. kowommo   tuna kwaka, tahtunye tehxem╪   kwaka
        I-went-in water into   deep   being-NOMLZN into
        'I dived into the river, into (the part that) is deep.'

   b. karyhe oton╪r   yoho,   karyhe ╪tehe
      fast   your-going   more-than fast   I-go
      'I will run faster than you.'

   c. Xatapu hona t╪tosom   kom yakoro nteko   Mahxawa
      Jatapú to   one-going COLL with he-went Mahxawa
      'Mahxawa has gone with the people who are going to
       the (river) Jatapú.'

Derived N can also constitute the nucleus of subordinate clauses that function as subject (49a), direct object (49b), and the predicate nominal in an equative clause (49c):

(49) a. Manaws╪ hoye omohxemo   komo, Kaywerye yakoro
        Manaus from ones-who-came   COLL Kaywerye with

        n╪rwonatxhe
        they-talk
        'The people who came from Manaus are talking
         with Kaywerye.'

   b. txetxa wawo wewe yomokoton╪r╪ wenyo
      forest in   tree falling-of   I-saw it
      'I saw a tree falling in the forest.'

   c. ohxe ╪hanan╪hn╪r╪   komo on╪   wos╪ wya
      good teaching-of-them   COLL this-thing woman by
      'The woman is teaching them well.'

The Subordinate Clause

In (49c) the subject constituent of the predicate nominal, **wosɨ wya**, is dislocated from the rest to follow the other equative clause constituent, the subject **onɨ**; it illustrates the nonpreferred ordering in transitive subordinate clauses, and is frequent where there is both an adjunct (**ohxe**) and a subject in the clause (see 7.6).

4.5 Number and ordering of constituents in subordinate clauses.
The number of constituents in subordinate clauses is even more restricted than in main clauses, and the complex paratactic construction which is so common in main clauses does not occur within the subordinate clause. Transitive subordinate clauses often have two constituents (the **wya**-phrase subject, and the possessor NP object) in addition to the nonfinite verbal form, but otherwise there is not usually more than one such additional constituent. Where the message requires additional elements, a paratactic sequence of subordinate clauses, with repetition of the nonfinite verbal form, is used.

(50) **nomokyako ehtxemanye   Manawsɨ hoye, ekeh**
     he-came   one-who-heals-him Manaus   from   sick-one

   me   Waraka yexetxhe,   atunano wya
   DENOMLZR Waraka his-being-after   fever   by

   exetxhe,   mexe   rmahaxa exetxhe
   his-being-after   long-time very   his-being
   'The doctor came from Manaus after Waraka became sick, after he was sick with fever, when he had been sick a long time.'

The preferred order of constituents in subordinate clauses is different from that in main clauses: Adjunct-Subject-Object-Nonfinite verb (transitive, e.g., 47a and 47e); Adjunct-Subject-Nonfinite verb (intransitive, e.g., 45a); and Complement-Subject-Nonfinite copula (copular, e.g., 45e). In the case of transitive subordinate clauses there is frequent postposing of the subject after the verb, which results in an order for the nuclear elements that is the same as the basic order in main clauses, i.e., OVS (see 7.6). This transitive subject is sometimes dislocated altogether from the subordinate clause and placed to the right of the verb in the superordinate clause (see 7.6). This can also happen when the superordinate clause is a nonverbal equative clause, in which case the subordinate clause subject is placed to the right of the main clause subject, as in (49c).

There is one proviso to the foregoing statement on preferred order: where a transitive subordinate clause is the complement of the copula, the subject (**wya**-phrase) and adjunct constituents are more often than not dislocated from the subordinate clause and placed to the right of the main clause. This is a similar process to that described in the preceding paragraph for the subject only (of a transitive subordinate clause) when it is postposed to the right of any main clause verb. Where the main clause is a copular, however, it is much more frequent, to the point of being the preferred pattern, and it applies to adjunct as well as subject. The desire and the negative subordinate clauses usually occur as complements of the copular, and for these two clauses the pattern described here is illustrated in (45g), where it is the subject of the subordinate clause that is moved to the right of the copula, and (47d), where it is the adjunct (**tano**) that is moved to the right of both the copula and its subject (**wosɨ**). It is possible to place both these constituents in the subordinate clauses to which they logically belong, and they would then occur in the clause-initial position, but this is the less dominant pattern. This right-dislocated postposing applies to indirect object (adjunct), which has the same form (**wya**-phrase) as the subject of a subordinate clause:

(51) **yawaka yɨmrɨ   xe   nay   hatɨ Waraka, owya**
     axe   giving-of desirous-of he-is HSY Waraka to/by-you
     'Waraka says he wants to give you the axe' or
     'Waraka says he wants you to give the axe (to someone).'

The context would normally resolve the ambiguity, which is present whether or not the **wya**-phrase is dislocated from the subordinate clause (cf. 9.3).

4.6 Position in main clause. In general, subordinate clauses have the position in the main clause normally associated with the constituent they express, i.e., adjunct (clause final), copular complement (preceding the copula), etc. Since they are relatively "heavy" constructions, however, they are often the subject of movement and dislocation processes (see chap. 7). In particular, subordinate clauses functioning as subject are often clause-initial, and those functioning as direct object postverbal.

4.7 Restricted tense-marking of derived nouns. As stated earlier, the normal tense-aspect marking is expressed in the superordinate clause, and not in the subordinate clause. Some derived N forms, however, occur with the restricted form of tense-marking expressed in the possession-marking suffix paradigm with possessed N. The suffixes that express 'PAST' are **-thɨrɨ** and **-nhɨrɨ**, and their COLLECTIVE counterparts **-thɨyamo** and **-nhɨyamo** (see Appendix C).[1] These forms do not occur in the cause, manner, purpose, negative

---
[1] The restriction of tense-marking to possessed nouns is reported for Potawatomi by Hockett (1948:73). Hixkaryana also has tense distinctions signalled by different derivational affixes in some nonpossessed nouns: cf. **tɨtosomɨ** 'one who

The Subordinate Clause

purpose, and desire clauses, but they are available in some of the other syntactic functions of derived nouns, and then express a time in the past prior to the time of the action expressed in the main verb:

(52) a. **watma ke toto heno yotahanyenhɨyamo,**
club with person now-dead ones-who-had-killed

   nekahtɨmtxownɨ hatɨ
   they-fled   HSY
   'The people who had killed the man with clubs fled.'

   (y- otaha- nye- nhɨ- yamo)
   (III-kill/hit-'DOER' NOMLZN-PAST-COLL)

b. **amna nomokyako, amna wya ɨsna ɨpatxowɨ**
I+III came   I+III by to-there let-us-go

   katxhɨr   hona
   say-PAST NOMLZN to
   'We (EXCL) came to where we said we were going.'

   (∅- ka- txhɨrɨ)
   (III-say-ACTION NOMLZN,PAST)

4.8 Negation in subordinate clauses. The negation of a V in a subordinate clause can never be expressed by the negation of the V in a superordinate clause--that is, there is no analogue of "Negative Raising." When a V is negativized in a subordinate clause, it functions syntactically as the complement of a derived form of the copula, and results in an embedded subordinate clause inside another subordinate clause:

(53) **neryehotetxkonɨ totokomo, Manawsɨ hona ɨtohra**
they-were-happy people   Manaus to not-going

   Waraka yesnɨr   ke
   Waraka his-being because
   'The people were happy, because Waraka didn't go to Manaus.'

Another example is (45e), where the negative is embedded in a purpose clause whose nucleus is the derived copula form **yehtxoho** 'thing associated with its being'. (See also chap. 5 on embedded constructions.) There is an alternative construction in which the

---

is going/will go' (**tɨ-to-so-mɨ** ADV-go-ACT.ADV-NOMLZN) and **ɨtosaho** 'one who has gone' (**ɨ-to-saho** GEN.PERF-go-SUBJ.OF PAST ACTION) (see Appendixes F.2, F.3, and G.2).

The modifying particles **heno** 'dead' and **tho** 'DEVALUED' (see Appendix I) also play a part in signalling tense distinctions, mainly of the kind Anderson (1972) describes as relating to the existence of an entity: **romuru heno** 'my late son'; **romini tho** 'my old house (that for all practical purposes does not exist any more)'.

The Subordinate Clause

copula is not used, but the scope of the negation seems to be exactly as in the foregoing example; this is to apply the derivational process **-hɨto-** 'NEGATIVE ACTION NOMINALIZATION' to the verbal element which is the nuclear predication constituent of the subordinate clause:

(54) **neryehotetxkonɨ totokomo, Manawsɨ hona Waraka**
they-were-happy people   Manaus to   Waraka

    tohtor   ke
    his-not-going because
    'The people were happy, because Waraka didn't go to Manaus.'

    (∅- to-hɨto-   rɨ)
    (III-go-NEG.ACT.NOMLZN-POSSN)

See also (46) for the use of **-hɨto-** in a purpose clause. This suffix also cooccurs with the derived A suffix **-toko** 'SIMULTANEOUS ACTION':

(55) **hawana komo yomokɨhtotok   haka, nyah**
visitor COLL when-their-not-coming yet   food

    yonyhoryetxkonɨ   worɨskomo komo
    they-were-preparing-it women   COLL
    'Before the visitors arrived (lit., when they still had not come), the women were preparing the food.'

    (y- omokɨ- hɨto-   toko)
    (III-come- NEG.ACT.NOMLZN-SIMULT)

The scope of the negation can be extended to include the whole of the subordinate clause by the addition of the negative suffix **-hɨra** to the R governing the PP, or to the suffix of the derived A:

(56) a. **mokro   yakoro ramryeknɨr xehra   wehxaha**
    that-one with   my-hunting desirous-of-NEG I-am
    'I do not want to go hunting with that fellow.'

  b. **nat   yehetawawohra   tehxatxow hamɨ**
    plant fruit-bearing-during-NEG we-are   DEDUCT
    'It is evident we are not yet in the season of fruit-bearing of those plants.'

  c. **kyakwe ɨwono,   tonotho   mehra   mak**
    toucan I-shot-it eating-of-it DENOMLZR.NEG ADVERS

    ha,   ahothɨr   xe   xa
    INTENSFR its-wing-feathers desirous-of CONTR

    ryesnɨr ke   mak   ha
    my-being because ADVERS INTENSFR
    'I shot the toucan, not for the purpose of eating it, but only because I wanted its wing feathers.'

The Subordinate Clause

```
          (t-          ono- toho         me-        hɨra)
          (III(GEN.PREF)-eat-'THING' NOMLZN DENOMLZR-NEG)
```

There are some R (**ke** 'because', **wya** 'to, by') and derivational suffixes (**-toko** 'SIMULT.ACTION', **-txhe** 'after') which never seem to occur with the negative suffix **-hɨra**, and there is no simple way to express the kind of negation scope just described for the subordinate clauses which they govern. The effect can, however, usually be obtained by either a separate negative sentence, or by a subordinate clause in an emphatic positive form that implies a related negative:

(57) a. **takoronomahoryehra   nahko. wakoronomano mak**
     not-fit-to-be-helped he-was I-helped-him COUNTER-EXP

   ha,   rowtɨ   me   esnɨr   ke
   INTENSFR my-brother DENOMLZR his-being because
   'He didn't deserve to be helped, but I helped
    him because he is my brother.'

b. **rowtɨ   me   esnɨr   ke   ryhe wakoronomano**
   my-brother DENOMLZR his-being because EMPH I-helped-him
   'It was because he is my brother I helped him.'

Both of the above utterances could be glossed as 'I helped him, not because he deserved to be helped, but because he is my brother.' But it is not possible to say: **wakoronomano, takoronomahorye esnɨr *kehra, ...** (I-helped-him, fit-to-be-helped his-being because-NEG) 'I helped him, not because he deserved to be helped, ...'

4.9 Subordinate clause functioning as main clause. There is one construction, the contrary-to-fact conditional, which consists of two subordinate clauses, and the second one functions as a main clause. The first clause is a time subordinate clause, marked by the derived A suffix **-toko** 'SIMULTANEOUS ACTION' (general conditional (i.e., 'if') clauses are expressed by two of the forms used to express time: **-toko**, and **-txhe** 'after'). The second clause in the sequence has a derived N nuclear constituent, marked by **-nɨrɨ** 'ACTION NOMLZN.POSSD' or **-hɨtorɨ** 'NEGATIVE ACTION NOMLZN.POSSD', followed by the modifying Prt **tho** 'DEVALUED', followed by the discourse Prt **haryhe** 'FRUSTRATIVE':

(58) a. **ekeh   mehra   ryehtoko,   Waraka**
       sick-one DENOMLZR-NEG my-being-when/if Waraka

       yakoro rotonɨrɨ tho   haryhe
       with   my-going DEVLD FRUST
       'If I hadn't been sick, I would have gone with Waraka.'

b. **rakoro ayamryeknɨtoko, koso wohtorɨ**
with-me your-hunting-when/if deer not-shooting-of

tho haryhe rowya
DEVLD FRUST by-me
'If you had gone hunting with me, I would not
have shot the deer.'

4.10 Constraints on cooccurrence of possessor and wya-phrases with derived N and A. Some derivational affixes forming N and A are incompatible with possession morphology, and the forms they derive never have the person-marking prefixes, nor do they cooccur with **wya**-phrases that express an underlying subject (see Appendixes F and G, in which obligatorily possessed and nonpossessed derived forms are distinguished). These nonpossessed forms can be used to express the nuclear constituent of a subordinate clause, but the underlying subject and object are not distinct constituents in the clause:

(59) a. **Kasawa ho enusaho mokro**
Kasawa at one-who-was-born that-one
'He was born at Kasawa.'

b. **amamehra tonosom me naha**
without-delaying thing-to-be-eaten DENOMLZR it-is
'It is to be eaten without delay.'

In some derived A forms the possessor prefixes are used only to express the underlying direct object. Intransitive stems do not have any possession markers, and the subject of transitive stems is not expressed by a **wya**-phrase. In both cases the subject is null, and understood as anaphoric to the subject of the superordinate clause. The forms subject to this constraint are **-txahke** 'DESIRE INVOLVING EFFORT' (and its corresponding negative **-txakomra**), **-hɨra** 'NEGATIVE', **-so/-xe** 'PURPOSE OF MOTION', and **-haya** 'almost':

(60) a. **wewe ke rotahatxahke nahko (r-otaha-txahke)**
wood with trying-to-hit-me he-was (I-hit- trying)
'He was trying to hit me with a stick.'

(not **tɨwya rotahatxahke nahko*
by-him trying-to-hit-me he-was)

b. **oroke Waraka yonyhera wehxako (y- onye-hɨra)**
yesterday Waraka not-seeing I-was (III-see- NEG)
'I didn't see Waraka yesterday.'

(not **rowya Waraka yonyhera wehxako*
by-me Waraka not-seeing I-was)

The Subordinate Clause 47

    c. **Kasawa hona ɨteko, ɨto   rma   Kaywerye yonyxe**
       Kasawa to   I-went there same Kaywerye PURP-to-see

      (y- onye-xe)
      (III-see- MOT.PURP)
      'I went to Kasawa to see Kaywerye there.'

      (not *rowya Kaywerye yonyxe)

    d. **koso wohaya   mahko   wayɨ ke**
       deer almost-shooting you-were arrow with

      (Ø- wo- haya)
      (III-shoot-almost)
      'You almost shot the deer with the arrow.'

      (not *owya   koso wohaya   mahko
          by-you deer almost-shooting you-were)

With intransitive stems the above derivations are marked by the adverbializing **tɨ-** prefix, or by the 'GENERAL PREFIX' (see Appendix B.2.3) instead of the person-marking prefix:

(61) a. **twanotatxahke nahko (t-   wanota-txahke)**
       trying-to-sing he-was (ADVBLZR-sing- trying)
       'He was trying to sing.'

    b. **oroke   ɨtohra   wehxako (ɨ-   to-hɨra)**
       yesterday not-going I-was (GEN.PREF-go-NEG)
       'I didn't go yesterday.'

    c. **owto   yoh   yakoro ɨrwonɨmso   nomokno**
       village chief-of with   PURP-to-talk he-came
       'He has come to talk with the chief.'

      (ɨ-   rwonɨm-so)
      (GEN.PREF-talk- MOT.PURP)

    d. **enurhaya   nay   hatɨ Masarɨ hokru**
       almost-be-born she-is HSY Masarɨ child-of
       'They say Masarɨ's child is about to be born.'

      (Ø-   onu(ru)-haya)
      (GEN.PREF-be born-almost)

There is one context in which a possessed form of the negative is used with intransitive stems (see Appendix G.2 (iv)), but it then functions, not as complement of the copula to express normal sentence negation, but as an adjunct in a special kind of time expression:

(62) **wɨmyaha   harha akatxho, yawaka, rotohra   ro**
     I-give-it back your-thing axe   my-not-going TIME

```
    rma   haka (ro-to-hɨra)
    CONT yet  (I- go-NEG)
    'I will give you back your axe before I go (lit.,
     while I (am) still not yet going).'
```

The derived N forms which normally cooccur with both possessor prefixes (to express subject of intransitive and object of transitive) and the **wya**-phrase (to express subject of transitive) are the following: **-nɨrɨ** 'ACTION NOMLZN.POSSD' and its past tense counterpart **-thɨrɨ**; **-hɨtorɨ** 'NEGATIVE ACTION NOMLZN.POSSD'; and **-toho** 'THING, TIME, or PLACE ASSOCIATED WITH THE ACTION'. The **wya**-phrase does not occur, however, where the subject of the subordinate clause is zero, anaphorically related to the subject of the superordinate clause (i.e., in "Equi" cases):

```
(63) a. Waraka wya honyko  wonɨr      xe           wehxaha
        Waraka by  peccary shooting-of desirous-of I-am
        'I want Waraka to shoot peccary.'

     b. honyko  wonɨr      xe          wehxaha
        peccary shooting-of desirous-of I-am
        'I want to shoot peccary.'

        (not *rowya honyko wonɨr xe wehxaha
              by-me ...)

     c. temenye      kɨrwonɨmno, anar  komo wya enytxahtor
        whispering I-spoke     other COLL by  not-hearing-it

        horɨ
        PURP
        'I spoke in a whisper, so that other people would
         not hear it.'

     d. meya ɨtono,  enytxahtor     horɨ
        away I-went not-hearing-it PURP
        'I walked away so I wouldn't hear it.'

        (not *rowya enytxahtor horɨ)
```

In the purpose clause marked by **-toho me**, the **wya**-phrase seems to be optional, when the subject referents in main and subordinate clauses are the same:

```
(64) wayamakasɨ ɨkahyaha  (rowya) oyowakryetxho        me
     comb        I-make-it (by-me) benefitting-of-you DENOMLZR
     'I am making combs so that I can benefit you
      (i.e., give them to you).'
```

The possession marking and **wya**-phrase are obligatory with the three types of "time" adverb: **-toko** 'SIMULTANEOUS', **-txhe** 'after', and **-wawo** 'during'.

The Subordinate Clause

There are two forms of derived N which always have the possession markers but never cooccur with the **wya**-phrase: **-nye** 'doer of the action', in which the possessor prefix marks the object of the action, but the subject is part of the derivation itself; and **-nɨ- ... -nɨ-** 'object resulting from action', where it is the direct object that is the central part of the derivation, and the possessor prefixes in this (unique transitive) case mark the subject of the action:

(65) a. **Manawsɨ hona Waraka nyaknye   uhutwehe**
      Manaus to   Waraka one-who-send-him I-know-him

   (**∅- nyake-nye**)
   (III-send-DOER)
   'I know the one who is sending Waraka to Manaus.'

b. **Manawsɨ hona Waraka nɨnyaknyɨrɨ   uhutwehe**
   Manaus to   Waraka one-whom-he-sends I-know-him

   (**∅- nɨ-   nyake-nɨ-   rɨ**)
   (III-OBJ.NOMLZN-send- ACTION NOMLZN-POSSN)
   'I know the one whom Waraka is sending to Manaus.'

There are two other derived N forms where the possessor prefixes occur with the normal function for intransitive and transitive stems, but the **wya**-phrase never occurs since the subject of an underlying transitive is completely out of focus:

(i) **-hɨyemɨ** 'PERSON ASSOCIATED WITH THE ACTION AS COMPANION': **ownɨkhɨyemɨ** 'your sleeping companion' (**ow-nɨkɨ-hɨyemɨ** II-sleep-COMPANION); **ronyakhɨyemɨ** 'the one who is sent with me' (**ro-nyake-hɨyemɨ** I-send-COMPANION)

(ii) **-txhetɨ** 'PAYMENT FOR THE ACTION': **ototxhetɨ** 'payment for your trip' (**o-to-txhetɨ** II-go-PAYMENT); **kana yanɨmɨtxhetɨ** 'payment for catching fish' (**kana-y-anɨmɨ-txhetɨ** fish-III-lift-PAYMENT)

5 Embedded Clauses

A common type of embedding is where one subordinate clause functions as a constituent of another (higher) subordinate clause (5.1). There are only two types of embedded main clause, but these are also very common: equative clauses can be embedded as a constituent of some higher clause (5.2); and any clause, including finite clauses, can be embedded as the direct object of the quotative verb **-ka-** 'say' (5.3).

5.1 Embedding of subordinate clauses. All nonfinite clauses are embedded, with the exception of the contrary-to-fact conditional clauses mentioned in 4.9. We are concerned here with subordinate clauses embedded in other subordinate clauses. One example of such embedding, already discussed in 4.8, is where a negative subordinate clause is embedded in other types of subordinate clause, which have a nominalized or adverbialized form of the copula. This kind of embedding is particularly common with negative clauses, but it also occurs frequently with other subordinate clauses that function as the complement of the copula: desire embedded in a cause clause (66a); desire involving effort, embedded in a motion purpose clause (66b); and manner (**me**) embedded in a nonmotion purpose clause (66c):

(66) a. **Kasawa hona nteko, Kaywerye yakoro tɨrwonɨmrɨ**
Kasawa to   he-went Kaywerye with   his-talking

    xe   tesnɨr   ke
    desirous-of his-being because
    'He went to Kasawa, because he was wanting to talk with Kaywerye.'

  b. **komokno, wewe horye tokayɨmtxahke   ehxe**
    I-came   tree along trying-to-climb PURP-to-be
    'I have come so that I can try to climb the tree.'

  c. **karyhe wewe yamanye   me   ryehtxoho**
    strong tree one-who-fells DENOMLZR my-being(PURP)

         me,   kotkukmekonɨ
         DENOMLZR I-was-testing-myself
         'I used to train myself, so that I could be
         a strong tree-feller.'

In each of the preceding sentences (66a-c) the "higher" of the
two subordinate clauses has a derived form of the copula as its
nuclear constituent, and the "lower" embedded clause is the complement of that copula. The derived form of the copula can also
occur in the "lower" of the two subordinate clauses (67a), and
other combinations of subordinate clauses, in which the copula is
not involved at all, occur. Motion purpose embedded in a nonmotion
purpose clause (67b) and a clause governed by the comitative
relator embedded in a time clause (67c) are two examples:

(67) a. ɨhok   ihxe   romoknɨr xe   nehxakonɨ
        occ.-with-it PURP-to-be my-coming desirous-of he-was
        'He was wanting me to come to work on it.'

     b. enmahrɨro tasanɨmyatxhe, wewe yamaxe
        early   we-get-up   tree PURP-to-fell

        totho   menye
        our(INCL)-going(PURP)   DENOMLZR-COLL
        'We will get up early so that we can go to fell trees.'

     c. Kanaxen hoye omohxemo   kom yakoro
        Kanashen from ones-who-came   COLL with

        rorwonɨmnɨtoko, uro manyekyako
        when-my-talking me you-called
        'You called me when I was talking with the
        people who came from Kanashen.'

The examples cited thus far do not exhaust the possible subordinate clause types that can be involved in this type of embedding. There are, however, one or two general constraints that
tend to make certain combinations unlikely. In the discussion on
subordinate clauses (4.5) it is noted that there are severe restrictions on the number of constituents; this is even more no-
ticeable when one subordinate clause is embedded in another. In
particular, embedding is usually avoided if it would necessitate
both possessor NPs and **wya**-phrases to mark subject and object, and
if such do occur there will almost certainly not be any peripheral
constituent in the same clause. Subordinate clauses in which such
subject and object constituents are normal are not, therefore,
likely to occur together with one embedded in the other. Such
clauses include time, cause, and nonmotion purpose. Peripheral
clause constituents are also relatively rare, and when they occur
are restricted to simplex forms. There is rarely more than one
degree of recursion in the embedding; when there is, it is un-

likely that there will be any constituents other than the nuclear predication elements:

(68) **rohyaka nmenheko, romohtoho hutwanɨr**
to-me he-wrote-it time-of-my-coming knowing-of

xe tesnɨr ke
desirous-of his-being because
'He wrote to me, because he was wanting to know the time of my coming.'

Here there are two degrees of recursion and only the nuclear constituent in each of the three subordinate clauses.

5.2 Embedding of equative clauses. Equative clauses frequently occur as the embedded subject of the copula. They are placed immediately before the copula (which is the less preferred position of subject in other copular clauses—see 3.5). This is the usual position of the copular complement, but when an equative clause occurs there it is not marked by the relator **me** 'DENOMINALIZER', which is required to enable a noun phrase to function as the complement. A complement constituent may also occur in the same clause, either after the copula or between the equative clause and copula.

(69) a. **nomokye hawana. horykomo tho mokro nehxakonɨ**
he-came visitor adult-man DEVLD that-one he-was
'A visitor came who was an old man.'

b. **foru heno utxuramsaho nehxakonɨ**
plantain QUANT one-that-ripened it-was

xamata mkawo
rocky-island on-top-of
'Plantain plants that had ripened were on the rocky island.'

c. **ɨton mokɨ nahko kana heno**
there-NOMLZN that-one it-was fish QUANT
'That lot of fish was over there.'

In (69a) the equative clause **horykomo tho mokro** is the subject of the copula that follows it; its main (semantic) function is to give further identification of the subject NP of the preceding sentence, and this is a common usage of the equative. In (69b) there is a complement constituent that follows the copula, and in (69c) there is another part of the subject constituent, which follows the copula and is in (discontinuous) paratactic sequence with the equative clause.

The predicate nominal constituent of the equative clause (usually the first NP) can be a derived N, and the nucleus of a sub-

Embedded Clauses

ordinate clause. This results in another type of embedded subordinate clause:

(70) a. ɨto   rma   oknomxemo   mokyamo   nehxatxkon hatɨ
    there same ones-who-were-left those-people they-were HSY
    'They were the people who were left there.'

   b. oske kanye   mokɨ   nexeye ahakheno
      thus one-who-says-it that-one he-was my-dead-father
      'My late father was the one who said that.'

In (70b) the predicate nominal is a nominalized form of the quotative verb **-ka-** 'say' cooccurring with an adjunct constituent. Nominalized forms of **-ka-** also occur with a direct speech finite clause preceding, in its usual syntactic function of direct object (see 5.3), and this leads to another form of embedding: a finite clause embedded in a (**-ka-**) subordinate clause that is the (predicate nominal) constituent of an equative clause, which is the embedded subject of the copula:

(71) oske nehxatxkonɨ amnyehra, kanye   mokɨ
    thus they-were   long-ago one-who-says-it that-one

    nexeye ahakheno
    he-was my-dead-father
    'My late father was the one who said, "That's
     how they were long ago."'

An equative clause can also be embedded as the subject (72a) or direct object (72b) of a (noncopular) verbal clause:

(72) a. nuxe   rma   mokro   raheno
       my-younger-brother SAME REF that-one he-seduced-me
       'My younger brother is the one who seduced me.'

   b. owotɨ   mosonɨ   arko   ha
      your-meat this-one take-it INTENSFR
      'Take this meat for yourself.'

5.3 Direct speech embedding in quotative clauses. The direct speech that is embedded as the direct object of the quotative verb **-ka-** 'say' can be any type of main clause, a subordinate clause (usually in answer to a question), or any minor sentence type, including responses to utterances of any kind (see 6.6 and 6.7). This is the only way in which finite clauses can be embedded (see (35e) in 3.1 for an example of a quotative clause).

A quotative clause can be embedded in another quotative clause. There is not usually more than one degree of recursion:

(73) **ɨhokohra   exko ɨkan   haxa owya,**
     not-occ.-with-it be I-said-it CONTR to-you

   kekonɨ   ɨyɨmɨ   buru   wya
   he-said-it his-father his-son to
   '"But I said to you, 'Don't do it,'" said the
   father to his son.'

The quotative V often occurs in the form of a derived N or derived A, and it then functions as the nuclear constituent of a subordinate clause. This results in finite clause embedding in subordinate clauses, which are themselves the embedded constituents of some higher clause (see chap. 4). There are two irregular derived forms of **-ka-: tawro** 'saying', which is the action nominalization derivation (not ***kanɨrɨ**, but the past tense counterpart **katxhɨrɨ** is regular--see Appendix F.2); and **tatoko** 'when saying', which is the simultaneous action derivation (not ***kantoko**--see Appendix G.2). Subordinate clauses containing a derived form of **-ka-** can be any of the types described in 4.2-4 and can function as copular complement (74a), adjunct (74b), subject (74c), or direct object (74d):

(74) a. **awanaworo tamryekyatxhe   kahra**
        tomorrow we-INCL-COLL-hunt not-saying-it

   nehxako Kaywerye amna wya
   he-was Kaywerye I+III to
   'Kaywerye did not say to us, "We'll all go
   hunting tomorrow."'

   b. **teko, omokhɨra   harha mpɨnɨ   wehxaha**
      he-went not-coming back CERTAINTY I-am

   ha   tawro   me
   INTENSFR saying-it DENOMLZR
   'He went away saying, "I will never come back."'

   c. **ohxe wehxaha, karaywa   yanoto   kaxe**
      good I-am   non-Indian employee-of because

   kanye   komo, nosonkuhtetxhe
   one-who-says-it COLL they-deceive-themselves
   'People who say, "I'm O.K., because I work for a
   non-Indian," deceive themselves.'

   d. **nomokyaha karyeno   ymo katxho   menytxano,**
      it-comes high-thing AUG thing-said you-heard-it

   karaywa   wya
   non-Indian by
   'Did you hear what was said by the non-Indian,
   "The airplane is coming"?'

Embedded Clauses

Where a **wya**-phrase is used to express the underlying subject of the derived form of **-ka-**, it often occurs dislocated from the subordinate clause and following other constituents of the higher clause (74d). It can also initially, before the direct speech constituent of the subordinate clause, but it only rarely occurs immediately after **-ka-**, i.e., between **-ka-** and the nuclear constituents of the higher clause (see 4.5 and 7.6).

The derived form **katxho**, which is the nominalization 'THING, TIME, OR PLACE ASSOCIATED WITH THE ACTION', is frequently used in a special way to refer to humans, when it has the meaning: 'person about whom the thing is said' or 'person associated with the thing said':

(75) **waha   komo mokyamo, anhɨ   komo**
     killer COLL those   bad-one COLL

   katxho   kom hona   amna   noseryehyaha
   one-assoc.-with-thing-said COLL towards I+III are-afraid
   'We are afraid of the people about whom it is said,
    "Those people are killers, evil men."'

The direct speech object of **-ka-** can be more deeply embedded by the embedding of its subordinate clause in another, "higher," subordinate clause (see 5.1):

(76) a. **amnyerma wehemehe owyanye   tawro   yonytxahra**
        today   I-pay-it to-you-COLL saying-it not-hearing

   mahko   hamɨ   rowya
   you-were DEDUCT by-me
   'You evidently did not hear me say, "I am going
    to pay you today."'

   b. **amryekhɨra wahko, amararɨn   hoko   kakoronomehe**
      not-hunting I-was your-field occ.-with I-help-you

   tawro   xe   ryesnɨr ke
   saying-it desirous-of my-being because
   'I didn't go hunting, because I was wanting to say,
    "I will help you work on your field."'

In (76a) the **-ka-** subordinate clause functions as the possessor (i.e., direct object) in a negative subordinate clause. In (76b) the **-ka-** clause is embedded as the head of the R in a desire clause, and this in turn is embedded as the complement of the copula derived form in a cause clause.

6 The Sentence

6.1 Declarative sentences. Declarative sentences normally take the form of a single main clause. A sequence of clauses can be intonationally bound to form one sentence (see 6.4), and sequences of embedded speech clauses occur to form one quotative sentence (see 6.5). All subordinate clauses function as constituents of a main clause or as the main clause itself (in contrary-to-fact statements), so they do not occur as a separate sentence-level constituent (see chap. 4). There are, however, two constituents that are regarded as associated with sentences rather than clauses: the ideophone (when it does not occur as the object of **-ka-** or as a separate sentence--see 1.6); and a special topic constituent, which is not grammatically related to the clause with which it is associated in the sentence (see 13.3). In generative grammatical terms, these items would be regarded as what Green (1976) has called Main Clause Phenomena (MCP), but unlike most, if not all, of the phenomena which she describes, they never seem to occur in (finite or nonfinite) embedded clauses, so they could be defined, far more strictly than her MCPs, as categories that occur only in a root sentence. A root S in Hixkaryana is purely and simply an S which is never itself dominated by any node.

6.2 Interrogative sentences. There are two basic types of interrogative sentence: yes-no questions (see 6.2.1); and question-word (or "wh") questions (6.2.2). Both types are marked by intonation, and also (optionally) by certain particles with restricted functions. Word order changes apply only to question-word questions. Rhetorical questions, which are indirect speech acts with the same form as interrogative sentences, are discussed in 12.2.2.

6.2.1 Yes-no questions. There are two intonation patterns that apply to interrogative sentences: (i) normal interrogative and (ii) peremptory (see Appendix A). The latter applies also to other types of speech acts, such as imperative, vocative, and exclamative. The normal interrogative pattern is a rising pitch through the sentence, reaching high on the penultimate syllable, which is stressed, and then falling sharply on the final syllable. It occurs with all nonperemptory interrogatives:

(77) **yutu   mɨkahno   (yutu mɨkähno)**
    manioc-squeezer you-made-it
    'Have you made the manioc-squeezer?'

In the peremptory pattern the pitch continues to rise through to the final syllable, which is also heavily stressed:

(78) **ɨhme menahno   hampe   (ɨhme menahno hampe)**
    egg you-ate-it DOUBT
    'Did you really eat the egg?'

Peremptory intonation most often occurs with certain particles: **ha** 'INTENSIFIER', **mpɨnɨ** 'CERTAINTY', **we** 'COUNTER-AFFIRMATION', **mpe** 'DOUBT', but it can also occur without any of these.

Interrogative sentences are also marked by the verb suffix **-yano/-yatxowɨ** 'NONPAST, UNCERTAIN', but this relates only to nonpast forms, where it contrasts with **-yaha/-yatxhe** 'NONPAST', which normally occurs with declarative sentences (see Appendix B):

(79) a. **nomokyaha**   b. **nomokyano**
       IIIS-come-NONPAST   IIIS-come-NONPAST UNCERT
       'He is coming.'   'Is he coming?'

The nonpast forms also occur with a noninterrogative meaning, only some kind of uncertainty being expressed.

Interrogative sentences are normally neutral, not being marked for expecting an affirmative or negative answer. A leading question may, however, be signalled by the context, or by the occurrence of certain particles, particularly those of the verification set, e.g., (78), where the particle **hampe** expresses the speaker's scepticism and suggests that the answer should be in the negative.

Alternative in interrogative questions is expressed by the particle **katɨ** 'ALTERNATIVE', which is normally postposed to the first constituent of the sentence, although its scope is usually the whole sentence. It can occur in a simple yes-no question, expressed either as a single sentence or as a sequence of two sentences in which both possibilities are spelled out:

(80) a. **owto   hona katɨ mɨteko**
       village to   ALT you-went
       'Did you (or did you not) go to the village?'

   b. **owto   hona mɨteko. ɨtohra   katɨ mehxako**
       village to   you-went not-going ALT you-were
       'Did you go to the village? Or did you not go?'

The same question could be put without using **katɨ** at all, either as **owto hona mɨteko** 'did you go to the village?' or as **owto hona ɨtohra mehxako** 'did you not go to the village?' Multiple alternatives are also expressed by using this particle, but question words are then normally involved (see 6.2.2).

In yes-no echo questions the verb phrase is obligatory. Other elements of the first speaker's sentence may or may not be repeated in the echo:

(81) A. **tuna yohokoso   ɨtehe**
water to-edge-of I-go
'I'm going to the river bank.'

B. **(tuna yohokoso)   mɨteno**
(water to-edge-of) you-go
'You're going (to the river bank)?'

A. **ɨtɨ, ɨtehe (ɨsna)**
yes, I-go (to-there)
'Yes, I'm going (there).'

Speaker B would not use only the phrase *****tuna yohokoso**, without the verb, as an echo question.

Question echo questions do not appear to be used at all, so that an exchange like the following would be deviant:

(*82a) A. **tuna yohokoso mɨteno** 'Are you going to the river bank?'
B. **tuna yohokoso ɨteno** 'Am I going to the river bank?'

B's utterance could, however, be an echo response to a command in the form:

(82b) A. **tuna yohokoso ɨtoko** 'Go to the river bank.'
B. **tuna yohokoso ɨteno** 'Shall I go to the river bank?'
A. **ɨhɨ, ɨtoko ɨsna**   'Yes, go there.'

6.2.2 Question-word questions. The basic question words are: **onokɨ** 'who', **etenɨ** 'what', **ɨsoke** 'how', **henta** 'where', **twahake** 'how much', 'how many', **twararo** 'how many', 'to what extent', and the derived forms: **ɨsokentoko** 'when' (**ɨsoke-no-toko** how-NOMLZN-SIMULT. ACTION) and **ɨsok tawro** 'why' (**ɨsoke-tawro** how-say/do NOMLZN)

There is an obligatory fronting rule which moves a question word to the sentence-initial position. If the question word is in a PP, the Relator is also moved along with the question word, so that the whole phrase occurs sentence initial.

Question-word questions are similar to yes-no questions in the intonational patterns that can be used, and also in the use of the 'NONPAST, UNCERTAINTY' verb forms. The particle **katɨ** 'ALTERNATIVE' is also used with question words, and a multiple choice is then either implied or made explicit:

(83) a. **Waraka omoro. onok katɨ omoro**
  Waraka you who ALT you
  'Are you Waraka? Or who are you?' or
  'Are you Waraka or are you someone else?'

 b. **ɨsok katɨ weryano owotɨ. ɨyen   katɨ. uhuryan**
  how ALT I-fix-it your-meat I-boil-it ALT I-smoke-it

  katɨ. ɨkanyhoryan   katɨ
  ALT I-slow-roast-it ALT
  'How shall I fix your meat? Shall I boil it? Or shall I smoke it? Or shall I slow roast it?'

In (83b) **katɨ** could optionally be omitted in the first and second sentences, but it would almost certainly occur in the third and fourth sentences, where it could also be optionally reinforced by another particle, **haxa** 'CONTRAST' (**uhuryan haxa katɨ. ɨkanyhoryan haxa katɨ**), without any change of meaning.

Certain suffixes can be added to question words. The nonnominals can be nominalized by the addition of **-n(o)** 'GENERAL NOMINALIZATION' and **-h(ɨ)nɨ** 'NEGATIVE NOMINALIZATION' (see Appendix F):

(84) a. **ɨsoken   komo mokyamo**
  how-NOMLZN COLL those
  'What kind of people are they?'

 b. **ɨto ehxera natxhe. hentanohnɨ   komo.**
  there not-being they-are where-NOMLZN-NEG COLL

  Fumasa honohnɨ   komo
  Fumaça at-NOMLZN-NEG COLL
  '"They are not there." "The ones who are not where?" "The ones who are not at Fumaça."'

The suffix **-yana** 'people, tribe', and modifying particles, such as **tho** 'DEVALUED' (see Appendix I), also occur with question-word nominals:

(85) a. **onokyana   omoro. hexkaryana uro**
  who-people you   Hixkaryana I
  '"What tribe are you?" "I am Hixkaryana."'

 b. **onokɨ tho   mokro   mekyano**
  who DEVLD that-one you-bring-him
  'Who is that poor fellow you are bringing?'

Any constituent of the main clause, other than the verb, can be replaced by a question word. In (86a) there are four constituents other than the verb; these are in turn replaced by question words in (86b-e):

(86) a. bɨryekomo komo yonyetxkonɨ kamara
child COLL he-was-eating-them jaguar

txetxa wawo amnyehra
forest in long-ago
'The jaguar used to eat children in the forest long ago.'

b. onokɨ tho yonyetxkonɨ kamara
who DEVLD he-was-eating-them jaguar
'Whom did the jaguar used to eat?'

c. onokɨ bɨryekomo komo yonyetxkonɨ
who child COLL he-was-eating-them
'Who used to eat children?'

d. henta bɨryekomo komo yonyetxkonɨ
where child COLL he-was-eating-them
'Where did he used to eat children?'

e. ɨsokentoko bɨryekomo komo yonyetxkonɨ
when child COLL he-was-eating-them
'When did he used to eat children?'

In quotative clauses the constituent that is questioned precedes the embedded speech if that speech is fairly short. Otherwise the question word is placed in a separate formulaic sentence that precedes or follows the sentence with the embedded speech:

(87) a. onokɨ ɨtoko omɨn yaka kano rowya
who go your-house to he-said-it to-me
'Who said to me, "Go home"?'

b. onokɨ wya ɨtoko omɨn yaka mɨkano
who to go your-house to you-said-it
'To whom did you say, "Go home"?'

c. onokɨ, onɨ wyaro nkano. koso wono
who, this like he-said-it deer he-shot-it

Ewka, yake, kano
Ewka many he-said-it
'Who said, "Ewka has shot a lot of deer"?'

In equative clauses only one of the constituents can be questioned, the predicate nominal:

(88) **eten onɨ.   wayamakasɨ moro**
what this-thing comb   that-thing
'"What is this?" "That is a comb."'

In copular clauses any constituent other than the copula can be replaced by a question word. The complement may be an A or a PP, and this is reflected in the form of the question word (or phrase):

(89) a. **ɨsok manaye. ohxe wehxaha**
how you-are good I-am
'"How are you?" "I am well."'

b. **eten xe   manaye. kanawa xe   wehxaha**
what desirous-of-you-are canoe desirous-of I-am
'"What do you want?" "I want a canoe."'

In the above examples the question word occurs in a complete sentence. This is the normal pattern, but occasionally question words are used in incomplete sentences, either alone, or with an element other than the V, usually the subject of the copula (90b):

(90) a. **kanawa yano   bɨryekomo. henta**
canoe he-took-it boy   where
'"The boy has taken away the canoe." "Where?"'

b. **henta ohetxe**
where your-wife
'Where is your wife?'

There is a preference not to use question words in subordinate clauses, but they can be used, especially in echo questions, and any constituent other than the V can be questioned. The subordinate clause then occurs in sentence-initial position, or the rest of the main clause may be omitted altogether:

(91) a. **wayamo wanɨmyako.   henta oyehtoko**
turtle I-picked-it-up where when-your-being

(manɨmyako)
(you-picked-it-up)
'"I picked up a turtle." "Where were you when (you picked it up)?"'

b. **ɨkowontano, kamara wya ronyetoko.   onokɨ**
I-yelled   jaguar by when-seeing-me who

wya oyonyetoko,   (okowontano)
by when-seeing-you (you-yelled)
'"I yelled when the jaguar saw me." "When what saw you (you yelled)?"'

In NPs, only the N head of a simple phrase, and only the possessor N in a possessed NP, can be replaced by question words:

(92) a. **onokɨ ryhe menyo.   anaro horoto   wenyo**
    who EMPH you-saw-it other spider-monkey I-saw-it
    '"What did you see?" "I saw another spider-monkey."'

   b. **onok yowtɨ   komo mokyamo. Waraka yowtɨ**
    who brother-of COLL those   Waraka brother-of

    komo moxamo
    COLL these
    '"Whose brothers are those people?" "These are
      Waraka's brothers."'

There is no way of replacing the possessed item with a question word, so there is no exact equivalent for 'Waraka's what?'. None of the peripheral elements (modifiers, particles) can be replaced with a question word.

In a PP, there are two possibilities for assigning question words. First, the NP can be a question word, and this is subject to the constraints described above in the case of single NPs and possessed NPs:

(93) a. **eten ke   wewe mamano.   yawaka ke   wamano**
    what with tree you-felled-it axe   with I-felled-it
    '"What did you fell the tree with?" "I felled
      it with an axe."'

   b. **onok mɨn   yaye momokno. rowtɨ   mɨn**
    who house-of from you-came my-brother house-of

    yaye komokno
    from I-came
    '"Whose house have you come from?" "I've come from
      my brother's house."'

Second, the whole postpositional phrase may be replaced by a general question word that does not require the use of a relator:

(94) **henta mɨnomno.   tuna yohoye ɨnomno**
   where you-left-it water above I-left-it
   '"Where did you leave it?" "I left it at the river bank."'

Only one sentence constituent can be questioned, so that it is not possible to say **onokɨ, eten xe naye* (who, what desirous-of he-is) 'Who wants what?' or **etenɨ, onok yonkukmeno* (what, who it-baffles-him) 'What baffles who?'.

The Sentence   63

In echo questions the question word may occur as the only element in the echo, or it may occur with one or more other elements, one of which must be the verb:

(95) a. A. **tuna yohokoso ɨtehe**
water to-edge-of I-go
'I'm going to the river bank.'

   B. **henta ya (mɨteno)**
where to (you-go)
'Where (are you going) to?'

b. A. **omuru wenyako domenku ho**
your-son I-saw-him Sunday on
'I saw your son on Sunday.'

   B. **onokɨ (menyako)**   (or)   **ɨsokentoko (menyako)**
who (you-saw-him)   when (you-saw-him)
'Whom (did you see)?'   'When (did you see him)?'

Subordinate clause echo questions are discussed and illustrated earlier in this section.

6.3 Imperative sentences. Imperative sentences are marked in the verb morphology (see Appendix B) and by the potential (and frequent) usage of the peremptory intonation pattern (see Appendix A). The subject NP is normally deleted with the person categories I, I+II, and II, but it can occur with any of these; it is obligatory with I+III (**amna**), and the usual discourse considerations will determine if it is present with III (see 13.5.2). The morphological elements affected are as follows: (i) the verb suffix is one of the set which constitutes the imperative mood paradigm; (ii) the usual person-marking prefixes are replaced by the general prefix in second person (II) imperative forms, except for a subclass of intransitive stems (see Appendix B); and (iii) the discourse particle **hak(a)** 'IMPERATIVE, right now' is obligatory with III imperative forms and optional with other forms. There are two parameters in the imperative suffix paradigm: individual vs. collective number; and nonmotion vs. motion, specifically as to whether motion is, or is not, involved in the performance of the intended action (see Appendix B).

The order of constituents is, in general, the same for imperative as for other sentences. As elsewhere, variations from the basic order frequently occur when the person of the subject is I, I+II, or II: the subject pronoun, if it occurs at all, often precedes the verb; and the direct object NP is optionally moved to follow the V (see 7.4):

(96) a. bɨryekomo komo ɨhananɨhtxoko   (or)   omoro ɨhananɨhtxoko
        child   COLL teach-them   you   teach-them

        bɨryekomo komo   (or)   omoro bɨryekomo komo
        child   COLL   you   child   COLL

        ɨhananɨhtxoko
        teach-them
        'Teach the children.'

    b. (uro) wamaxe   wewe (or) wewe wamaxe   (uro)
        (I) I-fell-it-IMP   tree   tree I-fell-it-IMP   (I)
       'Let me fell the tree.'

    c. karaywa   tewakryetxe   (kɨwyamo)
       non-Indian let-us(INCL)-be-kind-to (I+II-COLL)

       (or) kɨwyamo   karaywa   tewakryetxe
             I+II-COLL   non-Indian let-us(INCL)-be-kind-to
       'Let us be kind to the non-Indian.'

The fronting of the pronoun emphasizes the person.

   Third person imperative is expressed by the same verb suffix forms that have the meaning 'IMMEDIATE PAST': **-no** and (COLLECTIVE) **-txowɨ**, plus the particle **hak(a)**. This particle can follow the verb, but there is a strong preference to move it to occur immediately after the first constituent of the sentence, and the subject of III forms is normally fronted so that **haka** can occur with it:

(97) a. nomokno haka   b. toto   kom hak nomohtxowɨ
        he-came IMP   person COLL IMP they-came
        'Let him come.'   'Let the people come.'

    c. xar   hak nomohtxowɨ toto   komo
       to-here IMP they-came   person COLL
       'Let the people come here.'

With other person categories **haka** is optional, but where it occurs it is again normally a part of the sentence-initial constituent:

(98) a. kamryehsɨ (haka)   b. uro hak kamryehsɨ
        I-hunt   (IMP)   I   IMP I-hunt
        'Let me go hunting.'   'I must go hunting right now.'

With the second person imperative **haka** adds a high degree of peremptoriness. In the following three ways of expressing a simple command there is an increasing degree of peremptoriness:

(99) ɨtoko;   ɨtok; ha   ɨtok haka
     go   go   INTENSFR   go   IMP/right-now
     'Go!'   'Go!'   'Go right away!'

The Sentence

The pronoun **amna** 'I+III' is unique again in the imperative form it takes (see 1.2.2 for other ways in which **amna** is unique). It continues to cooccur with the III form prefix, but the suffix imperative form is not that which occurs with III (**-no/-txowɨ**), but that which occurs with I: **-si/-sɨnye** (**-xe/-xenye**) (the COLLECTIVE form occurs only when the direct object is collective):

(100) **wato   hak amna nexe,   omɨnɨ   (n- e-   xe)**
      shelter IMP I+III make-it your-house (III-make-IMP (I))
      'Let us (EXCL) build a shelter, (to be) your house.'

The motion imperative forms do not include any special form for III. For I+II motion imperatives there is an option to add a proclitic before the regular verb imperative form, either **ɨpa** 'let's go' or **omok/omohtxok** 'come' (see 1.5):

(101) a. **(ɨpa)   tewehtxe**
         (let's-go) let-us-COLL-take-a-bath
         'Let's all go take a bath.'

      b. **(omok) tamanye   onɨ   wewe**
         (come) let-us-two-fell this-one tree
         'Come, let's fell this tree.'

When used as a clitic in this way the form **ɨpa** does not change for collective number (101a), but there are two forms involving **ɨpa** that are frequently used as substitutes for **tɨtonye** 'let us (two) go' and **tɨtotxe** 'let us (COLL) go', and here the collective distinction is made: **ɨpaha** 'let us (two) go' and **ɨpatxowɨ** 'let us (COLL) go'.

With I and II imperatives, the motion category is obligatorily expressed with a distinct set of suffixes (see Appendix B). In these cases the motion is directed to a location away from the speaker and addressee for the performance of the intended action:

(102) a. **wewe hak wamatxano**
         tree IMP I-go-fell-it
         'Let me go fell the tree' or 'I will go fell
         the tree right now.'

      b. **kana anɨmtatxko**
         fish go-lift-it-COLL
         'All of you go catch fish.'

Negative imperative sentences follow the general pattern for sentence negation. The copula is marked with the imperative suffix and with the person-marking prefixes (II is the general prefix, which in the case of the copula is zero-marking). The negated element is the A derived from a V stem by adding the suffix **-hɨra**

'NEGATIVE', and it functions as the complement of the copula. There is no motion category for the copula:

(103) a. **ronyhera   ehtxoko**
not-seeing-me be-COLL
'Don't all look at me!'

b. **ekehɨ   tho   yahehra   (hak) wehxe**
dead-one DEVLD not-touching (IMP) I-am-IMP
'Don't let me touch the dead body' or 'I must not touch the dead body.'

c. **amryekhɨra   tehtxe**
not-hunting let-us-COLL-be
'Let's not go hunting.'

d. **katxhonano yarhɨra   hak nahko**
goods   not-taking IMP he-was
'Don't let him take away the goods.'

There is one other way to express the imperative: without using any form that specifically marks imperative. This is where there is a command to do something at a future time. It is expressed by the nonpast verb form followed by the particle **ha** 'INTENSIFIER':

(104) **awanaworo mɨtehe ha**
tomorrow you-go INTENSFR
'Go tomorrow' or 'You must go tomorrow.'

6.4 Sentence coordination. There are no formal means in the language for expressing coordination at either the sentence or phrase level, i.e., no simple equivalents of 'and', 'but', and 'or' (certain discourse particles [see Appendix J] can sometimes be used to express these notions, but this is not their primary function, nor can they be used in all contexts where coordination is required to be expressed). The primary means of expressing coordination of clauses or sentences is juxtaposition, with or without the addition of a discourse particle. This is basically another example of the paratactic construction that occurs most often as a sequence of phrases in a clause, and where coordination is one of several possible functions (see 3.7 and 12.2.4).

A sequence of main clauses can be coordinated to constitute one sentence. This is signalled by the intonation patterns: the final clause has the terminal pattern; the preceding clauses in the sequence, the nonterminal pattern (see Appendix A). The following example is from Derbyshire (1965.110):

(105) **oskeno   tho   yoskekonɨ   xarha;**
       thus-NOMLZN DEVLD he-used-to-kill-him also

   dom, dom, dom,   nonyekonɨ   ha;
   eating (IDEOPHONE) he-used-to-eat-him INTENSFR

   nomokyakonɨ   harha tɨ, horykomo
   he-used-to-come back HSY   chief-man
   'The (jaguar-man) chief used to kill anyone like that
   (visitor), eat him, and then return (home) again.'

The intonation patterns of the (tape-recorded) text are not shown
in Derbyshire (1965), but they are as indicated above: **xarha** and
ha, the final elements in the first two clauses, have nonfalling
pitch; the final clause has a succession of falling pitches on
harha tɨ and **horykomo**, which is a typical example of the terminal
pattern.

A coordinating function also seems to be involved when there is
a sequence of short sentences in which the subject and object
referents do not change and are marked only in the verb prefixes,
and where other constituents are minimal (in this case each main
clause in the sequence has falling pitch (the terminal pattern),
and is, therefore, a distinct sentence). The following is from
Derbyshire (1965.44):

(106) **hohtyakonɨ   hatɨ, txetay.   nenahyakonɨ**
      she-was-picking-it HSY, picking (IDEO) she-was-eating-it

   hatɨ. narɨrɨkekonɨ   hatɨ, tɨnyo   hyaka
   HSY   she-was-tossing-it-down HSY   her-husband to
   'She was picking (the fruit), eating it, and tossing
   it down to her husband.'

Such sequences may also have an adversative ('but') linkage as in
the following from Derbyshire (1965.113):

(107) **amotohpɨra nehxakonɨ toto. meya   tɨ nexeye**
      not-tiring he-was   man   far-apart HSY he-was

   ha;   kamara hama   tho   namotohye
   INTENSFR jaguar change DEVLD he-tired
   'The man was not tiring, but the jaguar was far
   different, in an abnormal state of exhaustion.'

There are sequences of sentences in which a discourse particle
is the primary marker of coordination. The particles most commonly
used with this function are **xarha** 'ADDITIVE' and **mak(e)/mah**
'ADVERSATIVE, CONTRARY TO EXPECTATION'. The following is from
Derbyshire (1965.14, 31):

(108) a. **oskeno   tho   yosahtotxownɨ**
      thus-NOMLZN DEVLD they-provided-a-place-for-it

   hatɨ saraho tho. wewe yamatxownɨ   xarha,
   HSY manioc DEVLD tree they-felled-it ADD

   esarɨ,   saraho yosarɨ
   its-place manioc place-of
   'They provided a place for that thing, the manioc, and
   they felled trees, a place for (planting) the manioc.'

   b. **weryeko   yarymetxkonɨ,**
      fire-stick they-were-throwing (rubbing)-it

   xɨk xɨk xɨk xɨk xɨk xɨk atahohsɨra   mak nehxakonɨ
   rubbing-stick (IDEO)   not-being-caught ADV it-was
   'They were rubbing the fire-stick, trying many times,
    but it was not catching alight.'

There are several ways of expressing 'or' coordination. The particle **katɨ** 'ALTERNATIVE' is used in interrogative sentences (see 6.2). Since 'or' often implies some kind of uncertainty, the verification particle **hana** 'UNCERTAINTY' is frequently used. Where contrast is in focus the discourse particle **haxa** 'CONTRAST' may be used, either alone or with **hana**. Some of the (noninterrogative) possibilities are as follows:

(109) a. **nɨmyan   hana. tɨmpɨra   (haxa) hana**
      he-give-it UNCERT not-giving-it (CONTR) UNCERT

   nay   ha
   he-is INTENSFR
   'Maybe he will give it, maybe he won't' or 'Either
    he will give it or he won't.'

   b. **Kasawa hona hana   ɨten ha.   Mutuma hona**
      Kasawa to   UNCERT I-go INTENSFR Mutuma to

   (haxa) hana   ɨten ha
   (CONTR) UNCERT I-go INTENSFR
   'I may go to Kasawa or to Mutuma.'

   c. **Kasawa hona hana   ɨten ha.   ɨsna   ɨtohra**
      Kasawa to   UNCERT I-go INTENSFR to-there not-going

   ryehtoko,   Mutuma hona haxa   ɨtehe
   if-my-being Mutuma to   CONTR I-go
   'I may go to Kasawa. If I don't go there,
    I'll go to Mutuma.'

The English sentence 'I'm going to Kasawa or to Mutuma' carries an inference that the speaker is definitely going somewhere. This inference is not present in (109b), but it is in (109c).

6.5 Direct speech multiple clause units. The embedded speech which functions as the direct object of the quotative verb **-ka-** sometimes consists of more than one main clause. Where a discourse contains a long stretch of monologue direct speech, there is frequent repetition of the **-ka-** verb, with or without other constituents of the quotative margin, such as subject NP or adjunct (addressee **wya**-phrase or other type of adjunct). This frequently occurs after each main clause of direct speech, in which case there is simply a succession of quotative sentences of the usual form: O (speech) - V (**-ka-**) - (S) - (A). Where, however, there are two or more main clauses of direct speech preceding **-ka-**, a more complex unit occurs. The two (or more) clauses which form the direct object would normally be considered separate sentences, but in this case I regard them as a special type of complex quotative sentence (an alternative interpretation would be to regard them as separate sentences and the whole unit another type of 'sentence cluster'--see 13.6):

(110) **amna namryekyako, Waraka yakoro. ɨpa tamryeknye;**
I+III hunted   Waraka with   let's-go let-us-two-hunt

honyko woso   hak tɨtonye, keknano
peccary PURP-to-shoot IMP let-us-go he-said-it

noro rowya
III to-me
'I went hunting with Waraka. "Let's go hunting. Let us go to shoot peccary," he said to me.'

There is another type of complex quotative sentence which occurs frequently in discourse: the main clause direct speech which precedes **-ka-** is repeated (often with identical words) after **-ka-** and any other constituents of the quotative margin, without being followed again by the **-ka-** verb. This construction occurs usually when the direct speech is an imperative or interrogative sentence, but it can also occur with other types. The following examples are from Derbyshire (1965.46,114):

(111) a. **omokhɨra   nahtxoko, kekonɨ   hatɨ, notxwakomo**
not-coming they-were she-said-it HSY   old-woman

ha.   omokhɨra   nahtxoko
INTENSFR not-coming they-were
'"Nobody has come," said the old woman.
"Nobody has come."'

b. **ehtxemahra   exko ha,   kekonɨ   hatɨ.**
not-treating-him be   INTENSFR he-said-it HSY

ehtxemahra   exko ha
not-treating-him be   INTENSFR
'"Don't treat him with medicine," he said.
"Don't treat him with medicine."'

6.6 Response sentences. Response sentences are of three types: answers to questions (6.6.1), responses to commands (6.6.2), and echo responses (6.6.3). They all have in common the potential for including a response particle.

6.6.1 Answers to questions. Answers to yes-no questions can be unmarked, in which case they are an ordinary declarative sentence, but there are two ways in which they can be marked as a distinct speech act: (i) use of the response intonation pattern, consisting of a relatively low pitch through the sentence until the last syllable, when there is a sharp rise to high (see Appendix A); and (ii) the occurrence of one of the set of interrogative response particles.

The response intonation pattern is mostly restricted to short answers, often a single word, and it occurs especially in negative answers:

(112) A. **huhyaye mɨtono**   B. **ɨtohra**   (**ɨtohrá**)
    downriver you-went   not-going
    'Did you go downriver?'   'No, (I did) not go.'

The interrogative response particles are: **ɨhɨ**, **ɨ?ɨ**, and **m?m** (there are similar, but distinct, particles which occur as responses to commands--see 6.6.2). They may occur alone or with a complete sentence of a normal declarative type:

(113) A. **huhyaye mɨtono**   B. **ɨhɨ** (**ɨtono**)
    downriver you-went   RESP (I-went)
    'Did you go downriver?'   'Yes, (I went).'

The three forms seem to be optional variants functioning to show affirmation or agreement. Affirmative answers to questions in a positive form usually contain a particle (114a); negative answers to questions in a positive form do not (112); and negative answers to questions in a negative form may or may not (114b):

(114) a. A. **Fumasa hona mɨteko**   B. **ɨhɨ, ɨsna   ɨteko**
       Fumaça to you-went   RESP to-there I-went
       'Did you go to Fumaça?'   'Yes, I went there.'

   b. A. **osonyhera   wehxano**
       not-being-seen I-am
       'Can I not be seen?'

     B. **(ɨhɨ), osonyhera   manaha**
       (RESP) not-being-seen you-are
       '(That's right), you can't be seen.'

When the person does not know the answer, the form used is **ɨna hana** 'I don't know'; **ɨna** is a particle that is used frequently as

The Sentence

a response to a command or other noninterrogative utterance; the verification particle **hana** has the meaning 'UNCERTAINTY':

(115) A. **Waraka nomokno** B. **ɨna hana, nomokno hana**
    Waraka he-came   RESP UNCERT he-came UNCERT
    'Has Waraka come?'   'I don't know, he may have
                           come.'

B's response could be the form **ɨna hana** alone, without any verb phrase or other constituent.

There is a preference for answers to be in the form of complete sentences, both to yes-no questions and to question-word questions, but incomplete sentences sometimes occur. In the case of yes-no questions, such incomplete sentence answers take the form: (i) response particles occurring alone (113), or (ii) deletion of the copula in negative answers (112). There is greater freedom to use incomplete sentences as answers to question-word questions:

(116) a. A. **hentano   tho   ɨtxemyano**
          where-NOMLZN DEVLD I-poison-it
          'What place (on the river) shall I do
           the fish-poisoning?'

      B. **ehnɨ tho   ymo mak   hatɨ**
         river DEVLD AUG COUNTER-EXP HSY
         'The mainstream, contrary to what you might expect.'

   b. A. **ɨsok mahko**   B. **atxke ha**
         how you-were   bad INTENSFR
         'What happened to you?'   'Something awful.'

In both answers the verb is omitted.

6.6.2 Responses to commands. Verbal responses, marked by the use of a special response particle, are common in the case of second person imperatives. The particle is one of a set that is distinct from those used in answer to questions, and consists of: **hɨɨ**, **ɨɨ**, and **mm**, all of which are noncommittal or mildly positive, and **ɨna hamɨ**, which is strongly positive (for the form **ɨna** see 6.6.1; **hamɨ** 'deduction' is a verification particle):

(117) a. A. **ahatakako**   B. **hɨɨ**
            come-out   RESP.
            'Come out.'   'All right.'

      b. A. **orwonɨmko akoro**
            talk   with-him
            'Talk with him.'

B. **ɨna hamɨ, kɨrwonan hamɨ, akoro**
   RESP DEDUCT I-talk   DEDUCT with-him
   'Sure, I'll surely talk with him.'

6.6.3 Echo responses. Echo responses occur when the person who is primarily the hearer (of a monologue, or in a section of a dialogue where the other party is doing the main part of the speaking) makes responses which echo something the speaker has just said or which acknowledge the speaker's statements. They take the form of either response particles, or the repetition of one or more elements in the speaker's previous sentence, or both particle and repeated element. The verb form is changed where appropriate, and the particle **hamɨ** 'DEDUCTION' is often added. It is a feature of Hixkaryana discourses where one person is doing all the talking and another is listening, and the echo responses can occur after almost every sentence.

6.7 Minor sentence types. The minor sentence types discussed here are rhetorical (6.7.1) and exclamatory (6.7.2). Other minor sentence types described elsewhere are contrary-to-fact (4.9), ideophonic (1.6 (iii)), and incomplete sentences of the kind that occur in questions (6.2) and responses (6.6).

6.7.1 Rhetorical minor sentence type. Rhetorical sentences often take the form of a major type: the interrogative sentence, functioning as an indirect speech act (see 6.2). They can also occur as incomplete sentences, and this is what constitutes the minor sentence type. The minimal form is the rhetorical question phrase occurring alone (118a, b). The expanded form adds to that question phrase an incomplete-sentence answer in the form of a subordinate clause (118c):

(118) a. **ɨsok tawro harha**
        how doing back-again
        'What's going on here?' or 'This is something strange.'

   b. **henta haryhe**
      where FRUST
      'Where on earth is it?' or 'It should be
      here, but it isn't.'

   c. **ɨtohra   nahko. ɨsok tawro hana   ohxehra**
      not-going he-was how   doing UNCERT not-well

      tesnɨr   ke   hamɨ
      his-being because DEDUCT
      'He didn't go. Why? Because he wasn't
      feeling well, evidently.'

The Sentence   73

In (118c) the complete sentences would be: **ɨsok tawro hana ɨtohra nahko ha. ɨtohra nahko, ohxehra tesnɨr ke hamɨ.** 'Why did he not go? He didn't go because he evidently wasn't feeling well'. The deleted element, **ɨtohra nahko** 'he didn't go', is needed to account for the prefixal form used in the derived noun in the subordinate clause: **t(ɨ)-** 'III REFLEXIVE' in **tesnɨr** 'his being' identifies the person as the same referent as the subject of the superordinate clause, which is part of the deleted element.

6.7.2 Exclamatory minor sentence type. Exclamatory sentences are brief nonverbal utterances, usually with peremptory intonation (see Appendix A), and may consist of almost any type of word or words, other than a verb. They include vocatives, which are optionally marked by the particle **y** 'VOCATIVE' postposed to the word (usually a proper name or kinship term) that is the focus of the vocative:

(119) a. **nor ha**
     III INTENSFR
     'He (is the one).'

b. **Waraka y**
   Waraka VOC
   'Waraka!'

c. **hay**
   call-of-greeting
   'Hi!'

d. **poo**
   (expression of surprise)
   (interjection)
   'How big!'

e. **eme   y**
   mother VOC
   'Mother!'

f. **owya   ymo xako**
   to-you AUG MISFORTUNE
   'You've had it' or
   'You are in trouble.'

7 Movement Processes

7.1 Question-word fronting. There is an obligatory rule that moves question words and phrases to the sentence-initial position (see 6.2.2).

7.2 Fronting for emphasis. The basic order of constituents is OVS, with adjuncts normally following the subject. There is an optional rule which moves the subject or an adjunct to the clause-initial position for purposes of emphasis. It is optional in the sense that there are no conditions of the sentence grammar that bring the rule into operation, but there are stateable discourse conditions under which it applies. These are discussed in 2.4.1. The rule does not apply to constituents of a subordinate clause, but it applies to the subordinate clause as a whole in its function as subject or adjunct. It applies to all types of main clauses, but in quotative clauses it is largely restricted to those that have short clauses of direct speech embedded in them as direct object; where the embedded speech is longer, a separate formulaic-type sentence will be added for fronting the constituent that is emphasized, as is the case also with question words (see 6.2.2). The following examples show fronting of the subject of a transitive clause (120a), subject of an intransitive (120b), subject of a copular (120c), simple adverb adjunct (120d), indirect object adjunct (120e), and subordinate clause adjunct (120f):

(120) a. **okomkurusu bɨryekomo heno yoskeko**
   bushmaster child   dead it-bit-him
   'It was a bushmaster (snake) that bit the child.'

   b. **Waraka haxa nehurkano asama yawo**
   Waraka CONTR he-fell   trail on
   'It was Waraka (not someone else) who fell on the trail.'

   c. **rowtɨ   hokyamo   ekeh   me   natxhe**
   my-brother children-of sick-one DENOMLZR they-are

   atunano wya
   fever   by
   'My brother's children are sick with fever.'

d. **towahke   rma   totokom hok   nehxakonɨ karaywa**
   friendly CONT people occ.-with he-was   non-Indian
   'Yet the non-Indian was friendly towards the people.'

e. **ohetxe   wya woto wɨmno   enmahrɨro**
   your-wife to meat I-gave-it early-in-the-day
   'I gave the meat to your wife early in the day.'

f. **ohxehra tesnɨr   ke   amryekhɨra nahko**
   not-good his-being because not-hunting he-was
   'It was because he was not well he didn't go hunting.'

Certain discourse particles frequently occur with constituents fronted for emphasis, especially those associated with contrast, emphasis, and continuity of referent, as in (120b, d). Only one constituent can be fronted in any clause; in (120b, c, d, e) there are other post-verbal constituents, which must remain in that position once the other constituent in each case has been selected for emphasis, although in another context they could also be fronted. When a subordinate clause is fronted, it usually also involves left dislocation (see 7.3); but this is not necessarily so, especially if it is relatively short and not, therefore, a "heavy" construction, as in (120f).

In a paratactic sequence of phrases which normally follows the verb, i.e., subject or adjunct, one phrase only of the sequence can be selected for fronting, leaving the rest of the sequence in the post-verbal position, and thus forming a discontinuous constituent. The following is from Derbyshire (1965.113):

(121) **noro htxero nomokye ha,   kamara yohɨ   ymo**
      III first he-came INTENSFR jaguar chief-of AUG

   htxero kamarayana   ymo htxero
   first jaguar-people AUG first
   'It was he who arrived first, the jaguar chief,
   the jaguar-man.'

7.3 Left dislocation. Left dislocation of a constituent sets it off from the rest of the clause, in initial position, by means of a pause break and a separate intonation pattern, usually of the nonterminal kind (see Appendix A). The constituent may be a subject or adjunct that is fronted for emphasis, or the direct object or copular complement. It is usually a "heavy" construction, i.e., one that is syntactically, morphologically, or semantically complex (often with all three types of complexity), such as derived nouns (122a), subordinate clauses (122b), and paratactic sequences (122c). Noncomplex constructions are also sometimes dislocated (122d), when the only purpose seems to be to give added emphasis:

(122) a. **onekarymatxhɨrɨ   yaworohra naha**
   the-thing-told-by-you not-true it-is
   'What you reported is not true.'

   b. **tɨwya kana heno yanɨmɨtxhe, towto**
   by-him fish QUANT after-lifting his-village

   hona harha nteko
   to   back he-went
   'After catching a lot of fish, he went back
   to his village.'

   c. **ɨwahathɨyamo, aknyohnyenhɨyamo   tho,**
   his-killers   ones-who-had-burned-him DEVLD

   oske nketxkonɨ
   thus they-said-it
   'His killers, the ones who had burned him, said thus.'

   d. **noro wya ryhe, mukawa wɨmno**
   III to EMPH shotgun I-gave-it
   'It was to him I gave the gun.'

The constraint against the fronting of more than one constituent (see 7.2) does not operate to the extent that one of the fronted constituents is also left dislocated (122b).

Left dislocation of direct object or copular complement is rare. When it occurs, it appears to be for the purpose of special emphasis (I regard the normal, clause-initial position of direct object as the case of unmarked emphasis, since an object NP only occurs when there is some kind of highlighting or focusing of the constituent):

(123) **amna kanawarɨ, anhɨntahra   harha txeryko**
   I+III canoe-of not-going-wrong again fix-it
   'Our (EXCL) canoe, don't let it go wrong again.'

7.4 Direct object to postverbal position. There are two conditions under which the direct object is optionally moved to the right of the verb: (i) where it cooccurs with a I, I+II, or II subject; and (ii) where it is a "heavy" construction, and where the rightward movement also involves dislocation and is the reverse process of the left dislocation of subject and adjunct phrases (see 7.3):

(124) a. **wenyhoryetxehkan   ha,   ɨro   ha**
   I-finished-making-it INTENSFR that-thing INTENSFR
   'I have finished making that thing.'

   b. **ɨsna   taryatxow   hamɨ katxhonano**
   to-there we(INCL)-take-it DEDUCT goods
   'We must take the goods there, evidently.'

Movement Processes 77

    c. **ɨtxemko tɨ kana, epepe   yotɨ**
       poison-it HSY fish my-older-brother meat-of
       'Poison fish, food for my brother.'

    d. **nahohsatxkon   hatɨ, amryehxaho**
       he-grabbed-them HSY   one-that-had-gone-hunting

       tho   hatɨ
       DEVLD HSY
       'He used to grab them, anyone that had gone hunting.'

    e. **ɨto   nenamtxownɨ   ha   marar ho harha,**
       there they-planted-them INTENSFR field in become

       for   heno komo, mahe   heno komo, menkar
       plantain patch COLL bell-potato patch COLL banana

       heno komo
       patch COLL
       'They planted them there in the field, the plantain patch, the bell-potato patch, and the banana patch.'

Where the direct object cooccurs with first or second person subject, it may or may not be dislocated when it is moved to the right (cf. (124a) and (124b)). When the object is moved to the right, any constituent that normally occurs to the right of the verb may either stay in its normal position and (usually) precede the object, as one part of the adjunct constituent does in (124e), or it may be fronted for emphasis, as in (124b), and as the other part of the adjunct constituent does in (124e).

Where the direct object is expressed by a paratactic sequence, the whole sequence may be moved to the right, as in (124e). Quite often, however, the first phrase in the sequence is left in the normal position preceding the verb and the rest of the sequence moved to the right:

(125) a. **hakrya wotxownɨ   ha,   koso heno komo**
       peccary they-shot-it INTENSFR deer GROUP COLL
       'They shot peccary and some deer.'

    b. **rotɨ   yɨmyako,   kana**
       my-meat he-gave-it fish
       'He gave me meat, that is, fish.'

In (125a) there is coordination of the two elements in the sequence, and in (125b) a greater degree of specification (see 12.2.4 for these and other functions of paratactic constructions). The other possibility is that the whole paratactic sequence precedes the verb, but this is rare, and left dislocation is probably always involved.

Copular complements are not normally moved to the right of the copula, unless some other constituent is fronted, as in (126), where the subject has been fronted and the PP **arkaxah wawo** is postposed:

(126) **toto yamotho   nehxakon⁺, arkaxah   wawo**
      man hand-of-past it-was thing-vomited in
      'A man's hand was in the vomit.'

7.5 Right dislocation of subject and adjunct. The normal position of a subject or adjunct phrase is to the right of the verb. There is an option for the speaker to make them a part of the main intonation pattern of the clause or to dislocate them by means of a pause break and a separate intonation pattern. There are no clearly discernible conditions which determine how the option will be exercised. There is always dislocation between phrases in a paratactic sequence.

7.6 Subject of subordinate clause moved to right. The subject in subordinate clauses is expressed by either a possessor NP (usually with intransitive stems) or a **wya**-phrase (with transitive stems), and the preferred ordering is for that subject to precede the derived N or A, which normally occurs clause-final (see 4.5). There is an option to move that subject constituent, whether a possessor NP or **wya**-phrase, to a position following the derived form that is the nucleus of the clause, and even to move it to the right of all main clause constituents (127c). This position to the right seems to be preferred when there is also an adjunct in the subordinate clause, or when that clause is in some other way a "heavy" type of construction, as in (127c):

(127) a. **amamehra   t⁺nyakny⁺r   ke   rowya,**
         not-delaying sending-of-him because by-me

   totwet⁺   nomyako
   his-hammock he-left-it
   'Because I sent him in a hurry, he left
    behind his hammock.'

   b. **notkukmetxkon⁺,   omokh⁺ra   haka ehtokony**
      they-were-practicing not-coming yet when-their-being

   haka, kurumyana   komo
   yet   buzzard-people COLL
   'They were practicing, when the buzzard-people
    still had not yet come.'

   c. **tan⁺hnohtoho   komo ywenyeke   rma**
      fact-of-their-destruction COLL not-knowing SAME-REF

   hak nehxatxkon ham⁺, tuna ymo wya
   yet they-were DEDUCT water AUG by
   'They did not yet know about their (coming)
    destruction by the flood.'

Movement Processes

In (127a) **rowya** would normally occur immediately before **tɨnyaknyɨr**. The normal order in (127b) would be **omokhɨra haka kurumyana kom yehtoko** (the collective suffix **-ny(e)** being deleted when a possesor NP with **kom(o)** 'COLLECTIVE' precedes.

7.7 Verification particle movement. The scope of verification Prt relates to the whole clause (when they occur in a dislocated phrase, the scope relates to that phrase). When a clause has normal word order, with (O)V in initial position, the verification Prt occurs in the VP and is usually preceded by the Prt **ha** (in sequences such as **hatɨ** 'HEARSAY' **hana** 'UNCERTAINTY'). Where a subject or adjunct is fronted for emphasis, the verification Prt is often moved to occur as part of that fronted constituent. The **ha** part of the sequence is never moved to the left; it usually remains following the V, but can be deleted:

(128) a. **nomokye hatɨ, owto   hona**
         he-came HSY   village to
         'He came to the village.'

   b. **owto   hona tɨ nomokye ha**
         village to   HSY he-came INTENSFR
         'He came to the village.'

There is one verification Prt to which this process does not seem to apply: **mɨ** 'DEDUCTION'. It always occurs in the VP, usually preceded by **ha**, or in the subject NP of an equative clause.

8 Reflexive and Reciprocal Constructions

8.1 The set of detransitivizing prefixes. The set of detransitivizing prefixes occurs primarily with V stems and has the effect of changing a transitive into an intransitive stem. It is the most general way of expressing reflexive and reciprocal meanings, but it can also have a pseudopassive meaning (see 9.4), or a simple intransitive meaning (see Appendix E). (In Relational Grammar terms, the detransitivizing prefixes indicate that the final 1 is also a 2 at some level). The set consists of **e-**, **os-**, **ot-**, **as-**, **at-**, and they occur between the (intransitive) person-marking prefix and the verb root:

(129) a. **bɨryekomo komo yompamnohyako Nonato, karaywa**
       child   COLL he-taught-them Nonato non-Indian

   rwon   hoko
   talk-of concerning
   'Nonato was teaching the children Portuguese.'

   b. **nosompamnohyatxoko   bɨryekomo**
      IIIS-DETRANS-teach-REC.PAST COMPL.COLL child

   komo, karaywa   rwon   hoko
   COLL non-Indian talk-of concerning
   'The children taught themselves Portuguese' or
   'The children taught each other Portuguese.'
     (It could also mean 'The children were taught
        Portuguese' or 'The children learnt Portuguese.')

The two examples show the typical changes associated with the use of the detransitivizer prefix: the direct object **bɨryekomo komo** (129a) becomes the subject (129b); there is a change in the person-marking prefix from the transitive **y-** 'IIISIIIO' (a) to intransitive **n-** 'IIIS' (b); and the intransitive form is marked for 'COLLECTIVE' in the suffix (**-yatxoko**) to agree with the subject NP (b), whereas the transitive form follows the normal pattern of not having 'COLLECTIVE' marked in the verb when there is an object NP (**-yako** in (a)). In both sentences the phrase **karaywa rwon hoko** is an adjunct, not a direct object.

Reflexive and Reciprocal Constructions

Verb stems that have had the detransitive prefix applied to them can be the subject of processes that result in derived N and A, so that subordinate clauses can also have this form of reflexive or reciprocal relation:

(130) **bɨryekomo komo weynyo,   tuna kwaka**
child   COLL I-rebuked-them water into

ataymomrɨ   komo ke
ducking-themselves/each other COLL because

(∅- at-   aymomɨ-rɨ)
(III-DETRANS-duck- ACT.NOMLZN.POSSN)
'I rebuked the children, because they were ducking themselves/each other in the water.'

The detransitivizing prefixes also occur with some R stems (see Appendix H). With one subset of stems the resulting form can have either the reflexive or reciprocal meaning:

(131) a. **ɨx(e)   wehxaha**   b. **osox(e)   wehxaha**
III-desirous-of I-am   REFL-desirous-of I-am
'I love her.'   'I love myself.'

c. **osox(e)   natxhe**
REFL/RECIP-desirous-of they-are
'They love themselves' or 'They love each other.'

With another subset of R stems the detransitivizing prefix carries only the reciprocal meaning. These include: **othoko** 'occupied with each other' (**ot-hoko** RECIP-occ. with) and **otɨwyaronye** 'like each other, alike' (**otɨ-wyaro-nye** RECIP-comparable to-COLL). The reflexive with these stems is formed by adding the third person reflexive prefix **tɨ-** and the particle **rma** (see 8.3). Whenever the detransitivizing prefix occurs with an R stem, it replaces the person-marking prefix which normally occurs with those stems when there is no preceding NP.

8.2 The third person reflexive prefix tɨ-. The set of person-marking prefixes that occurs with N, derived A, and R forms includes the prefix **tɨ-** 'III REFLEXIVE'. It identifies the third person possessor as having the same referent as the subject of the same clause or of a superordinate clause:

(132) a. **thetxe   yaryako   Waraka Manawsɨ hona**
III REFL-wife-POSSN he-took-her Waraka Manaus   to
'Waraka took his wife to Manaus.'

b. **xaro   tomokɨtxhe,   Wayway kom**
to-here III REFL-come-after Waiwai COLL

> yokaytɨ yokarymehe Ewka
> news-of he-tell-it Ewka
> 'When he comes here, Ewka will tell us the news
> of the Waiwai people.'

The prefix **tɨ-** can relate to the subject of the same subordinate clause in which it occurs:

(133) a. ..., **thokru   kom hananthrɨ**
     III REFL-child-POSSN COLL teaching-of

    ke   wosɨ wya
    because woman by
    '..., because the woman (was) teaching her own children.'

  b. **Waraka wenyako, towto   hona**
    Waraka I-saw-him III REFL-village-POSSN to

    harha ɨtontoko
    back when-his-going
    'I saw Waraka when he was going back to his village.'

The subject of the subordinate clause in (133a) is the **wya**-phrase because the nominalized verb form (**hananthrɨ**) is transitive. In (133b) it is marked by the possessor prefix **ɨ-** 'III' in **ɨtontoko**, which is an adverb form derived from an intransitive stem. Both the **ɨ-** prefix and the **t-** 'III REFL' in **towto** are anaphors of **Waraka** in the superordinate clause, but that antecedent is not the subject of its clause and does not, therefore, govern the reflexive prefix in the subordinate clause, as can be seen by comparing (133b) with the following:

(134) **Waraka wenyako, ewto   hona rotontoko**
   Waraka I-saw-him III-village-POSSN to   when-my-going
   'I saw Waraka when I was going to his village.'

The embedding of subordinate clauses can result in a succession of forms marked by the reflexive prefix:

(135) **wewe mahyaka nteko   bɨryekomo, rowya tonyɨr**
    tree behind he-went boy   by-me III REFL-see-NOMLZN

    xehra   tesnɨr   ke
    desirous-of-NEG III REFL-be-NOMLZN because
    'The boy went behind the tree, because he didn't
    want me to see him.'

The reflexive prefix may occur in any constituent other than the verb or subject of the main clause, i.e., in (underlying)

Reflexive and Reciprocal Constructions 83

subject of a subordinate clause (132b and 135), direct object of main (132a) or subordinate (133a) clauses, copular complement (135), adverbial adjunct (132b), or postpositional phrase adjunct (133b).

8.3 Reflexive function of the discourse particle rma. The discourse Prt **rma** 'SAME REFERENT' (see Appendix J) is used to express reflexivity in a restricted context: it occurs with the R **wya** 'to, by' when this R occurs with a possessor prefix that has the same referent as the subject of the same clause; if this is the third person, the prefix is **tɨ-** 'III REFL' (see 8.2), but it may also be any other person marker:

(136) a. ...   kekonɨ,   Waraka, tɨwya   rma
      (direct speech) he-said-it Waraka   III REFL-to   SAME-REF
      '..., said Waraka to himself.'

   b. **oskarymako**   **owya rma**
      tell-about-yourself   II-to   SAME-REF
      'Confess just to yourself.'

The Prt **rma** also occurs with other R with a reflexive meaning, but in these cases it is optional:

(137) a. **rohoko**   **(rma)**   **kɨrwonɨmno**
      I-concerning   (SAME-REF)   I-talked
      'I was talking about myself' or 'I was talking to myself.'

   b. **thoko**   **(rma)**   **newatxarkano bɨryekomo**
      III REFL-concerning   (SAME-REF)   he-played   boy
      'The boy was playing by himself.'

It is also optionally used to reinforce the reflexive element in other places where **tɨ-** is used:

(138) **towtɨ**   **(rma)**   **yaryako   Waraka**
      III REFL-brother-POSSN   (SAME-REF)   he-took-him   Waraka
      'Waraka took his own brother.'

8.4 Reciprocal forms. The primary means of expressing the reciprocal relation is the set of detransitivizing prefixes (see 8.1).

There is an idiom that has a specifically reciprocal meaning: **meya rha** 'each other', composed of the locative A **meya** 'to over there' and the discourse Prt **rha** 'in turn':

(139) **meya   rha   tɨmnye**
      to-there   in-turn   let-us(two)-give-it
      'Let us give to each other.'

The reciprocal meaning is sometimes carried by the discourse Prt **rye** 'SAMENESS, TOGETHERNESS, MUTUALLY RELATED.' It cooccurs with the pronoun **noro** 'III' to form **noro rye** 'belonging to the same kinship group, mutually related people'. With the locative A **ɨto** 'there (near)' it forms **ɨto rye** 'involved in the same action as each other'. With the time A **ɨtoko** 'at that time' it forms **ɨtoko rye** 'at the same time as each other'. The resulting meanings may or may not be reciprocal in the full sense, depending on the context:

(140) a. **ɨtoko   rye   tehemehe**
at-that-time TOGETHER we(two)-pay for-it
'We will pay each other at the same time' or
'We will both pay (someone else) at the same time.'

b. **nɨrwonɨmtxownɨ nyamoro rye**
they-talked   they   TOGETHER
'They talked with each other' or 'They all
talked at the same time.'

The Prt **rye** is also involved in sequences with two other Prt, **ro** 'EXCLUSIVE' and **rma** 'SAME REFERENT', with a reciprocal meaning:

(141) a. **ɨrwomra   ehtxoko rohoko   omnyamo**
not-talking be-COLL concerning-me II-COLL

ro   rye   rma
EXCL TOGETHER SAME-REF
'Don't talk to each other about me.'

b. **nosonytxetxkonɨ,   nyamoro**
III-DETRANS-hear-DIST.PAST CONT.COLL III-COLL

rya   rma
TOGETHER SAME-REF
'They were discussing with each other', lit.,
'They were hearing each other.'

In (b), the pronoun phrase with **rye rma** disambiguates the detransitive prefix in the verb by making it specifically reciprocal (see 8.1).

The discourse Prt **rma** 'SAME REFERENT', cooccuring with an R and a double occurrence of **-nye** 'COLLECTIVE', is used in some contexts with a reciprocal meaning:

(142) a. **...,   ketxkonɨ   tɨwyanye**
(direct speech), they-said-it III REFL-to-COLL

rmanye
SAME-REF-COLL
'..., they said to each other.'

Reflexive and Reciprocal Constructions   85

   b. **atxoko,   ohokonye   rmanye**
      take-it-COLL II-concerning-COLL SAME-REF-COLL
      'Each of you take your share.'

If in (142a) the form of the final phrase had been either **tɨwyanye**
or **tɨwyanye rma**, the meaning would have been reflexive: 'they said
to themselves'. (In Derbyshire 1979 (1.7) I wrongly restricted
this kind of sequence to relators with the prefix **tɨ-** 'III REFL';
it also occurs with other possessor prefixes, as seen in (142b)).

9 Additional Constructions

9.1 Comparative and equative constructions

9.1.1 Comparative. Comparative is specifically expressed in many contexts by the relators **yoho** 'bigger than, more important than' and **yosnaka** 'smaller than, less important than' (see 1.4 and the examples given there). The same forms mark the comparative subordinate clause (see 4.4):

(143) **enahrɨ   yoho   rmahaxa   tɨnyahke**
       eating-of-it more-than very-much having-food

   natxow   hamɨ
   they-are DEDUCT
   'It is evident they have much more food than
    they can eat.'

Where these R are not appropriate, there are two ways of expressing the comparative function:

(i) juxtaposition of negative-positive clauses:

(144) **kawohra   naha Waraka. kaw naha Kaywerye**
      tall-NEG   he-is Waraka tall he-is Kaywerye
      'Kaywerye is taller than Waraka.'

(ii) successive positive clauses, in which certain discourse Prt mark some kind of degree: **nyhe** 'more', **rmahaxa** 'very much':

(145) **ohxe naha meku. ohxe nyhe naha yayhɨ. ohxe**
      good it-is monkey good more it-is tapir good

   rmahaxa   naha honyko
   very-much it-is peccary
   'Monkey is good, tapir is better, and peccary
    is best of all.'

Additional Constructions

These discourse Prt are often used to reinforce the comparative marking of the R **yoho** and **yosnaka**:

(146) **kratxatxa   yoho   nyhe naha tukusu**
grasshopper bigger-than more it-is hummingbird
'The hummingbird is much bigger than the grasshopper.'

9.1.2 Equative. Equative is expressed by the R **wyaro** 'like, comparable to' (see 1.4), or by the sequence of R and Prt **me rye** 'same as, equal to, (**me** 'DENOMINALIZER', **rye** 'SAMENESS, TOGETHERNESS'). These forms of equative are often reinforced by the Prt sequence **rmarha** 'likewise':

(147) a. **koso me   rye (rmarha)   naha honyko**
deer DENOMLZR SAME (likewise) it-is peccary
'Peccary is just the same as deer.'

b. **uro ehtxemako,   owya Waraka yohtxemanɨrɨ**
me treat-with-medicine by-you Waraka treating-of

wyaro (rmarha)
like (likewise)
'Treat me with medicine in the same way
you treat Waraka.'

The sequence **me rye** assumes an NP governed by the R (**me**). The particle **rye** can also directly follow an A in an equative expression:

(148) **ohxe rye naha honyko, koso yakoro**
good same it-is peccary deer with
'Peccary and deer are equally good.'

9.2 Possession constructions. Possession is expressed generally by the sets of person-marking prefixes and possession-marking suffixes that occur with N (see 1.2.1; the prefixes occur also with R and derived A) and by possessed NPs (see 2.2). These can occur in any kind of clause and in any constituents of the clause, other than the V in a main clause.

There are two types of construction in which possession is particularly in focus:

(i) a copular clause with a complement that contains as its main constituent a derived A of the form **tɨ-...-ke** 'having, in possession of' (see Appendix G); the stem of the derived form is an N.

(149) a. **totke   wehxaha (tɨ-   otɨ- ke)**
having-meat I-am   (ADVBLZR-meat-having)
'I have meat food.'

b. **tkatxhonke rmahaxa naha Waraka**
having-goods very-much he-is Waraka
'Waraka has lots of things.'

(ii) an equative clause in which the predicate nominal is either a possessed NP or a nominalized form of the derived A described above.

(150) a. **omsamtxemo yoknɨ mokro kyakwe**
girl pet-of that-one toucan
'That toucan is the girl's pet.'

b. **totkem uro (tɨ- otɨ- ke- mɨ)**
one-having-meat I (ADVBLZR-meat-having-NOMLZN)
'I am one who has meat food.'

There does not seem to be any difference of meaning between (149a) and (150b). Another way of expressing the same basic meaning is **rotɨ mosonɨ** 'this is my meat food' (my-meat this-one), but in this case there is emphasis on the person of the possessor. There is no formal distinction between temporary and permanent possession, both types being expressed by any of the constructions described. Temporary possession is involved whether **rotɨ** 'my meat food' or **totke** 'having meat food' is used. Permanent possession is involved in both **ewtɨ** 'his brother' and **towtɨnke naha** 'he has brother(s)'.

Personal pronouns are sometimes used with a possessive meaning:

(151) **uro sohtxoko**
I bring-COLL
'Bring mine.'

The same form could mean 'Bring me'. Only the context will determine which meaning is intended.

9.3 Causative constructions. Causative is marked primarily in the verb by a derivational suffix from one of two sets. One set is applied to intransitive stems and the other set to transitive stems (see Appendix E).

When an intransitive stem is made causative it results in a transitive stem. The subject of the intransitive form becomes the direct object of the corresponding transitive:

(152) a. **horymamye bɨryekomo (∅- horymamɨ-ye)**
he-grew-up boy (IIIS-grow up-DIST.PAST COMPL)
'The boy grew up.'

b. **bɨryekomo horymamnohye wosɨ**
boy she-caused-him-to-grow-up woman

Additional Constructions

```
(∅-        horymamɨ-noh- ye)
(IIISIIIO-grow  up-CAUS-DIST.PAST COMPL)
'The woman raised the boy.'
```

There are two intransitive stems that do not take any causative suffix: **-to-** 'go' and **-omokɨ-** 'come'. For both of these the causative equivalent is the transitive verb **-nyake-** 'send'.

When a transitive stem is made causative, the result is another form of transitive stem, but with an increased valency that permits an added constituent in the clause: causee, which is expressed by a PP governed by the R **wya** 'to, by'. The other possible clause constituents remain the same, with the subject expressing the causer, and the direct object expressing the same referent as in the corresponding (noncausative) transitive:

(153) a. **bɨryekomo yotahahono   wosɨ tɨnyo**
          boy   she-caused-to-hit-him woman her(REFL)-husband

   wya (y-   otaha-ho- no)
   by   (IIISIIIO-hit- CAUS-IMM.PAST)
   'The woman caused her husband to hit the boy.'

Compare this to the corresponding noncausative:

(153) b. **bɨryekomo yotahano   ɨnyo   (y-   otaha-no)**
          boy   he-hit-him her-husband (IIISIIIO-hit IMM.PAST
   'Her husband hit the boy.'

The **wya**-phrase, which expresses the causee relation, is also used to express other functions, including indirect object (adjunct). Stems that can cooccur with indirect object can also be causativized. So far as I know, however, not more than one **wya**-phrase is permitted in the same clause, and this normally expresses the causee function. Should it not be clear from the context, a separate clause is added to express the indirect object:

(154) **kuraha yɨmpoye   Waraka rowya.**
      bow   he-caused-to-give-it Waraka by-me

   wɨmye,   Kaywerye wya
   I-gave-it Kaywerye to
   'Waraka caused me to give the bow to Kaywerye.'

In isolation the first sentence of (154) could mean either 'Waraka caused me to give the bow (to somebody)' or 'Waraka caused (somebody) to give the bow to me.'

A transitive stem that has undergone the causative derivation can then undergo a further process of detransitivization (see

Appendix E). The resulting stem is morphologically of the intransitive type, but the causee relation can still be expressed by the **wya**-phrase:

(155) **nosonyhoye   Waraka kamara wya**
he-caused-to-see-himself Waraka jaguar by

(n-   os-   onye-ho- ye)
(IIIS-DETRANS-see- CAUS-DIST.PAST COMPL)
'Waraka let himself be seen by the jaguar.'

This is as predicted under the usual Relational Grammar account of "clause union." When the cause and see clauses are collapsed, **Waraka**, being a subordinate clause 2, becomes the main clause 2. Then detransitive morphology is determined by the principle mentioned in 8.1, for **Waraka** is now the final 1 of cause to see and also a 2 of that clause at some level. This explains why, when the detransitivizer prefix **-os-** cooccurs with the causative suffix **-ho-**, it always has the reflexive meaning (for other meanings it can have see 8.1).

The causative process expressed by these suffixes can relate to various semantic functions: causing by physical process, commanding to do something, permitting to do something, and indirect causation.

A transitive stem that has been derived from an intransitive stem by the addition of one causative suffix can undergo a further process of causativization by the addition of the other type of causative suffix. Compare the following with (152b):

(156) **bɨryekomo horymamnohpoye   aworu   wosɨ wya**
boy   he-caused-to-raise-him his-uncle woman by

(∅-   horymamɨ-noh- ho- ye)
(IIISIIIO-grow up- CAUS-CAUS-DIST.PAST COMPL)
'His uncle caused the woman to raise the boy.'

9.4 Pseudopassive constructions. There is no true passive in Hixkaryana, but there are means by which the valency of a verb can be decreased, resulting in what I term a pseudopassive form. The means consist of applying one of three different types of derivations to transitive stems. The forms thus derived occur only in constructions in which the underlying subject of the transitive stem is obligatorily not expressed.

(i) The process involving the DETRANSITIVIZER prefix **e-, os-, ot-, as-, at-** (see Appendix E; for the reflexive/reciprocal functions of this prefix see 8.1):

Additional Constructions 91

(157) a. **Waraka ramano yaskomo**
Waraka he-turned-him-round shaman

(∅- rama- no)
(IIISIIIO-turn (TRANS-IMM.PAST)
'The shaman turned Waraka round.'

b. **neramano Waraka** (n- e- rama-no)
he-turned-round Waraka (IIIS-DETRANS-turn-IMM.PAST)
'Waraka got turned round' or
'Waraka turned (himself) round.'

Such sentences should probably be considered vague between the reflexive, pseudopassive, and (where appropriate) reciprocal meanings.

(ii) The derivation **tɨ-...-so** 'ACTION ADVERBIAL', by which an A form is derived (see Appendix G). With transitive stems this derivation relates the action in the verb as a property of the underlying direct object of that verb: **-ono-** 'eat (meat)', **tonoso** 'edible, can be eaten, is to be eaten':

(158) a. **tonoso naha kyokyo**
can-be-eaten it-is parrot
'Parrot can be eaten.'

b. **tarymaxe naha ɨro tho**
to-be-thrown-out it-is that-thing DEVLD
'That old stuff is to be thrown out.'

(The form **-xe** is a phonologically conditioned variant of **-so**.) The derived A can be nominalized by the addition of the suffix **-mɨ**, and in that form also it retains its pseudopassive character: **tonosomɨ** 'thing to be eaten', **thananɨhsomɨ** 'one who is to be taught'. The corresponding negative of both the derived A and its nominalized form is another derived N, applying the derivation **-hɨnɨ** 'NEGATION' (see Appendix F): **tonohnɨ** 'thing that is not eaten'; **arymahnɨ** 'thing that is not thrown out'; **thananɨhpɨnɨ** 'one who is not being taught' (in this negative nominal the 'GENERAL PREFIX' replaces the adverbial prefix **tɨ**---see Appendix B; the prefixal forms that occur with **-ono-** 'eat' are homophonous). It is only the negative nominal, and not the negative adverbial (with the suffix **-hɨra** 'NEGATIVE'), that has the pseudopassive character, as can be seen by comparing the following:

(159) a. **tonohnɨ mokro okoye**
not-to-be-eaten that-one snake
'Snake is not eaten.'

b. **okoye yonohra tehxatxhe**
snake not-eating we(INCL)-are
'We do not eat snake.'

(iii) The derivations **-saho** 'OBJECT (TRANS) OF PAST ACTION' and **-xenyeno** 'OBJECT (TRANS) OF A RECENTLY PERFORMED ACTION', by which N forms are derived (see Appendix F). These are the past action equivalents of the derivations **tɨ-...-so(mɨ)** described in (ii) (the **-xenyeno** forms are not much used):

(160) a. **tonosah**   **me**   **naha kyokyo tho**
     thing-that-was-eaten DENOMLZR it-is parrot DEVLD
     'The parrot has been eaten.'

   b. **arymaxaho**   **ɨro**   **tho**
     thing-that-was-thrown-out that-thing DEVLD
     'That old stuff was thrown out.'

   c. **bɨn**   **kom yaka harha ntotxowɨ,**
     their(REFL)-house COLL to back they-went

     ɨhananɨhxemo komo
     ones-taught COLL
     'The ones who were taught have gone back to their homes.'

The 'GENERAL PREFIX' also occurs with these derivations. The suffix **-xemo** is the collective form of **-saho**, but **komo** 'COLLECTIVE' is also usually added.

PART TWO

SYNTACTIC TYPOLOGY: THE PLACE OF HIXKARYANA

PART TWO

SYNTACTIC TYPOLOGY: THE PLACE OF HIXKARYANA

10 The Basic Order of Constituents: OVS

10.1 Background on word order typology. The starting point for any discussion on basic order of constituents in sentences is necessarily the study by Greenberg (1966). He first summarized the results of his research as follows (p. 76):

> Logically, there are six possible orders: SVO, SOV, VSO, VOS, OSV, and OVS. Of these six, however, only three normally occur as dominant orders. The three which do not occur at all, or at least are excessively rare, are VOS, OSV, and OVS.

This led him to the universal claim (p. 77):

> In declarative sentences with nominal subject and object, the dominant order is almost always one in which the subject precedes the object.

Since the publication of Greenberg's work, typological studies in syntax have, at least until 1976, taken for granted the validity of his claim, and have assumed that only three of the six logically possible orders--VSO, SVO, SOV--actually occur in human languages as the dominant order of constituents. Specific studies on word order led to even stronger claims than Greenberg's, as, for example, Vennemann (1973), who misrepresents Greenberg, by making his universal more absolute than it really was, when he states (p. 27):

> Greenberg observes that of the six possible arrangements ... only three occur as the only dominant pattern of declarative clauses, viz. those in which S precedes O .... This is readily explained.

In 1976, Keenan's work on Malagasy showed that language to have a dominant order of VOS. This shattered the claim that S always precedes O, but did not seem to affect the general assumption that object never occurs sentence initial. In an explicit attempt to extract a language universal from Greenberg's statistical claim, Pullum (1977) made the strongest statement of all that an absolute universal of word order is valid (p. 269):

> Four basic word orders, not three, are found: SVO, SOV, VSO, and VOS. The other two logically possible orders, OSV and OVS, do not occur at all, contra various allusions in the literature on syntactic typology.

Pullum had made a thorough study of the literature concerned with claims that OVS or OSV were basic orders for specific languages, and he was able to account for all of them by constructing a schema which predicted that these two orders would show up as surface orders only as the result of processes of stylistic permutation in specific discourse contexts, and that their basic orders were something different.

I came into contact with Pullum at University College London when his 1977 paper was in press. The immediate result was the writing of two papers (Derbyshire 1977a and 1977b) that set out the relevant facts of Hixkaryana syntax and presented evidence supporting OVS as the basic order (see 10.2).[2] A further consequence was the initiating of a project to investigate other languages of South America, and especially those genetically related to Hixkaryana, for which data (and in some cases descriptions) were available. This has revealed statements and facts pointing to the strong probability that there are other object-initial languages in the Carib language family and in some other languages of that area (see 10.3).

The delimitation to six possible orders assumes, of course, that we are concerned only with verb, subject, and direct object. If indirect object is introduced, it opens up a much larger number of possibilities. Some attempts have been made to predict or constrain the position that indirect object can have in languages, and these are briefly touched on in 12.2.7. Indirect object normally occurs clause-final in Hixkaryana, so it does not affect the object-initial character of the language.

It remains to define what I mean by basic order. It is the order of constituents at the point where linear sequence is first defined in the grammar of a language. This could be identified

---

[2] There was a brief statement on Hixkaryana word order in Derbyshire (1961:233) that seems to have escaped the notice of those who have written on the subject. Referring to the nuclear constituents of transitive sentences, it reads, "When goal and actor tagmemes occur in the same sentence, the goal always precedes, and the actor usually follows, the predicate tagmeme."

with the deep structure of standard transformational theory (Chomsky 1965.123-27; Bach 1975) or, in a Relational Grammar framework, the stage that follows the application of the grammatical-relation-changing rules (Pullum 1977). I assume that this is normally the same as the dominant surface-structure order for simple declarative sentences. Certainly, attempts to argue for a deep structural order that is significantly different from the dominant surface order of SVO for English have proved untenable (Andersson and Dahl 1974, arguing against the proposal made by Ross 1973 for SOV; and Berman 1974, arguing against the proposal of McCawley 1970 for VSO). Statistical predominance, however, may not always be the deciding factor with regard to basic order (cf. Dik 1978.180), especially where there are two or more surface orders that occur frequently. The ultimate test of any hypothesis about the basic order of constituents in a language is that it should permit the optimal generalizations in explaining the conditions under which other surface orders occur.

10.2 Evidence for OVS basic order in Hixkaryana. The evidence presented in Derbyshire (1977b) is here given in summary form. The preferred orders for all five structural clause types are illustrated in 3.1 and discussed in 3.2. OVS is seen to be the underlying dominant pattern. The most common variant order is SOV (intransitive SV and copular S-Comp-Cop). Other orders are extremely rare (the unique case of the pronoun amna 'I+III', which usually occurs as subject immediately before the verb, resulting in OSV, is discussed in 1.2.2).

Before I became aware of word order typology as a live issue in linguistics, I had spent several years in the study of Hixkaryana, hearing and learning to speak the language in many different contexts, and becoming sensitive to the reactions of native speakers to my use of the language. I believe that to a considerable degree I acquired many of their intuitions (though I hasten to add that I am still far from having native-speaker intuitions). I acquired a very strong intuition that OVS is the basic order of constituents in Hixkaryana main clauses.

The statistical evidence provided firm support for the intuition. In considering the statistics, it should be borne in mind that many clauses do not have either subject or direct object NPs (see 3.3). In transitive clauses, where only one NP occurs, and it is the subject, then it can be either preverbal (SV) or postverbal (VS), like intransitives. Such occurrences were included in the sampling.

A random sampling of texts from Derbyshire (1965) showed twice as many clauses with postverbal subject ((O)VS) as those in which subject is sentence initial (S(O)V). Object occurred immediately before the verb in all except three cases of VO. A subsequent check, comparing the Hixkaryana version of the Gospel of Matthew

([Derbyshire]1976) with a modern English version, showed that 91% of transitive clauses had been rendered with OVS order (the translation was done in close collaboration with native speakers, who had the last word on matters of style and naturalness).

The syntactic arguments in favor of OVS as the basic order are concerned with the rules that predict the occurrence of the only other common surface order, SOV. There are two rules that account for all such occurrences: the obligatory question-word fronting rule (see 6.2.2); and the optional emphasis fronting rule (see 7.2), which is applied under discourse-pragmatic conditions that can be stated with a fair degree of precision (see 13.1). These rules apply to adjuncts (including indirect object) as well as subject, but with this significant constraint: not more than one constituent can be fronted in the same clause, so that if a subject is fronted there cannot also be a fronting of an adjunct constituent, and vice-versa. If SOV were assumed to be the basic order, there would be no explanation as to why an adjunct could not be placed before the S, in sentence-initial position, for questioning or emphasis. (S. Dik (1978.180) uses a similar argument for his hypothesis about basic order of constituents in Dutch.)

Discourse-initial sentences are generally (but wrongly, I believe) considered to be free of contextual conditioning and, for that reason, are often cited as instances where the basic order of constituents can reasonably be expected to occur. It is in this position where the Hixkaryana emphasis rule might be expected to apply most often, thus producing the marked order SOV, since highlighting of a newly introduced character often occurs in the case of the subject of the first sentence (see 13.1). In fact, however, the unmarked OVS order occurs more often even in discourse-initial sentences. In the thirty texts of Derbyshire (1965), a subject nominal occurs in twenty-two of the thirty initial sentences (in the others the subject is either in an equative clause or is marked only in the verb prefix). Of the twenty-two, twelve have subject in postverbal position, and ten in initial position (the contexts make it fairly easy to see why some are highlighted and others are not; for discussion see Derbyshire 1977b.596-97).

It has been suggested to me that there might be an alternative to the OVS hypothesis by analyzing the preverbal nominal constituent in transitive sentences as a "syntactic subject," along the lines proposed by some for the absolutive case in ergative languages (cf. Culicover and Wexler 1974, and the discussion in Comrie 1978.330, 343-50). The related Carib languages, Makuchi and Arekuna/Taulipang, with their morphological ergative marking (see 10.3), might provide at least superficial evidence for such an analysis. It is a fact also that Hixkaryana nominalizations follow an ergative pattern, with intransitive subject and transitive object having the same (possessor) form in many of the derivations

The Basic Order of Constituents   99

(see 4.1 and 4.10 for the exceptions). The possibility is ruled out for Hixkaryana, however, by the fact that the subject in an intransitive clause is also postverbal (VS), and thus corresponds to what I have always analyzed as subject in the transitive clause.

In summary, then, all the evidence--intuition, statistics, and syntactic arguments--leads inexorably to the conclusion that the basic order of constituents in Hixkaryana is OVS.

10.3 Other object-initial languages. A preliminary report on object-initial languages was presented to the 1978 Summer Meeting of the Linguistic Society of America (Derbyshire and Pullum 1978). At that time research had produced enough facts to suggest the likely existence of five languages with OVS basic order, and three with OSV. Since then further investigation has added three more OVS languages, and one more OSV language, to the list. These twelve languages are now the subject of a fuller report (Derbyshire and Pullum 1981).

All the languages are found in South America, mainly in the northern Amazonian area. Seven of the OVS languages belong to the Carib family: Apalaí, Arekuna/Taulipang, Bacairí, Hianakoto, Hixkaryana, Makuchi (Makusi, Makúxi), and Panare. The other OVS language is Tupian: Asuriní. The four OSV languages belong to different families: Apurinã (Arawakan), Nadëb (reportedly Macuan), Urubu (Tupian), and Xavante (Gê). The 1981 paper also discusses one other Amerindian language from an entirely different area: Haida (? Na-Dene phylum), which is spoken in the Queen Charlotte Islands (Canada), and in parts of southern Alaska. Some features of the syntax of this language suggest that OSV could be the basic order, but the evidence is inconclusive. Only the seven Carib languages are considered in the rest of this discussion, in which I first summarize the strength of the evidence that was available for postulating OVS basic order in each case, and then go on to compare Hixkaryana with three of the languages which have some notably different syntactic features. Some of these features form the background to the discussion about the diachronic processes that might have been at work in the development of OVS as the basic order for these Carib languages (see 10.4).

For the six languages other than Hixkaryana, the strength of the evidence for OVS basic order varies. Only one source of information was available for each of two languages: Hianakoto (Koch-Grünberg 1908) and Panare (Cauty 1974). In both cases, however, there are explicit statements that the dominant order is OVS, with examples that illustrate the claims. At the other extreme, for Bacairí information comes from three sources, and it is conflicting. Wheatley (1973) reports that the basic order is OVS, but he makes his statement in the context of a discussion of discourse-conditioning factors, and it is not clear if it is intended to apply to transitive clauses in general. His data are also difficult to interpret, since he does not give morpheme glosses, although there are at least two clear examples of OVS clauses. C. de Abreu (1895), on the other hand, gives SOV as the dominant order for Bacairi, with examples that include SOV, SVO, and OVS orders. K. von den Steinen (1892) does not make any statement about the order of constituents, but the data he provides generally support de Abreu. For Apalaí the sources are E. and S. Koehn. They do not make any statement about word order, but S. Koehn (1974) gives a fair number of examples, including some transitive sentences which show a slight preference for OVS over SOV, the only orders that seem to occur. For Arekuna/Taulipang the sources are Koch-Grünberg (1924, 1928), Armellada (1943-44), and Edwards (1977). Armellada states that OVS is the basic order, whereas Koch-Grünberg distinguishes two patterns depending on the type of nominal that occurs as subject: if the subject is a free-form pronoun it is postverbal; and if it is any other kind of nominal it is sentence initial. The relatively large amount of data he supplies in general supports his statement, but there are some sentences that have sentence-initial pronoun subjects, and some with postverbal nominal subjects. Edwards does not make any claim about word order, but has examples of both SOV and OVS.

Finally, for Makuchi both Abbott (1976.235-36) and Willaims (1932.50) make hedged claims for SOV as the basic order. Their data, however, and also that of Hodsdon (1976), suggest that OVS is the dominant order, and that the patterns are very similar to Arekuna/Taulipang. It is these two languages (M and A/T), supported to a lesser degree by Apalaí, that show the features that are particularly relevant to the discussion on the origin of OVS languages in the next section. These features are:

1. In both M and A/T there is a suffix that marks transitive subject, whatever the position in which it occurs, and whether it is a free pronoun or other kind of nominal. In the absence of a free-form subject (by normal process of deletion), the same suffix is postposed to the subject person-marking suffix in the transitive verb. This relates specifically to main clauses and not, as in Hixkaryana, only to subordinate clauses (the **wya** relator, see 4.1). Some examples in Apalaí (S. Koehn 1974) seem to have a subject marker in main clauses, but most do not.

2. The morphological ergativity suggested by the subject-marking suffix is reinforced in two ways: (i) the subject of an intransitive clause and the direct object of a transitive clause are both morphologically unmarked and both normally occur immediately preceding the verb; and (ii) when the subject and object occur as bound affixes in the verb, the same linear sequence is maintained, i.e., intransitive subject and transitive object are prefixes, while transitive subject is a suffix.

3. In clauses other than transitive, the subject precedes the verb. SV for intransitive seems to be absolutely rigid. For copular Comp-S-Cop is preferred, and other orders occur, but none in which S follows the copula (this also appears to be the pattern in Apalaí). The subject-marking suffix does not occur in copular clauses, which fact further identifies the copular with intransitive clauses rather than with transitive. This contrasts with Hixkaryana, where the basic ordering of constituents, with subject postverbal, is the same for all clause types, and where copular clauses are more closely parallel to transitive.

4. In M and A/T quotative clauses the main verb, with the meaning 'say', can occur before or after, or both before and after, the embedded speech direct object clause. If the verb precedes, the subject precedes that verb, with a resulting SVO order, and where the verb follows, the subject follows the verb (OVS). In Hixkaryana the OV sequence in quotative clauses is absolute, and the postverbal position of subject is even less likely to be varied (by either of the fronting processes) than in other types of clause (see 6.2.2 and 7.2).

10.4 A diachronic explanation of the origin of OVS in Carib languages. In the preceding section I have discussed some languages of the Carib family that appear to have OVS as the basic order of constituents. There are other languages in that family for which SOV is claimed to be the basic order. Carib of Surinam (Hoff 1978) and Waiwai (R. Hawkins, personal communication) are two such. Hoff's paper is of particular interest in that he relates the facts of Carib to Vennemann's generalizations, which seek to explain why there is diachronic change in certain basic word order patterns (Vennemann 1975).

These generalizations, at least the two that are relevant to this discussion, take off from Greenberg's universal 41 (Greenberg 1966.96):

> If in a language the verb follows both the nominal subject and nominal object as the dominant order, the language almost always has a case system.

The first generalization elaborates this, in order to pave the way for the second (Vennemann 1975.288-89)[3]:

> 1. (3) Languages with uniform, conspicuous, and dependable Subject-Object marking of a substantive nature (i.e., with a device which makes it clear for every sentence containing

---

[3] In the citation and the discussion I change Vennemann's X to O, to refer to object (his verb complement). In what follows I make similar changes for Hoff's P (my O) and A (my S).

both S and O which one is which, independently of the order in which they appear) tend to be OV languages; languages without such an S-O morphology tend to be VO languages.

2. (4) If an OV language loses its substantive S-O marking system (of the kind characterized in (3)), it changes to VO.

Vennemann applies these generalizations as a partial explanation as to why a language like English should change from SOV to SVO.

Hoff points out that it is extremely unlikely that this particular change would occur in a language like Carib, where the OV sequence is so rigid. Vennemann's principle could, however, operate to move S to the postverbal position, resulting in OVS. Already S moves, under certain pragmatic conditions, to that position in Carib as it is spoken today. (As we have seen in 10.1, Vennemann had excluded the possibility of the existence of OVS languages, so it is not surprising that he did not suggest this as a possible alternative to SVO as the way the change might go.) Hoff sums up the position (personal communication) as follows:

> The neutral position of the Carib (subject) is before (object) and verb. Yet if Vennemann's universal holds good, it will have to drift toward the place after V.

Vennemann's references to "Subject-Object marking" are applied by Hoff to the person-marking prefixes in the Carib verb, and I assume Carib does not have a case-marking system for the subject and object nominals. The case-marking that Vennemann had in mind is, however, found in other languages of the Carib family, as we have seen in 10.3. In Makuchi and Arekuna/Taulipang the subject-marking system is still almost completely intact, and it clearly distinguishes the subject from the object, whether the subject occurs before or after the verb. In these languages no strong case can be made for any single basic order, SOV or OVS (at least from the position of the nominals; the object prefixation and subject suffixation in the transitive verb might be considered as swaying the balance in favor of OVS). There does, however, clearly seem to be a diachronic process of word order change taking place, and the fact that in nontransitive clauses (and often in the quotative) the subject occurs in the initial position would suggest that the (historically) earlier basic order is SOV, so that the direction of the change is toward OVS. In Hixkaryana we see the later stage in this development, where there is still a trace of the subject marker (the **wya**-phrase in subordinate clauses), but where OVS has now become the basic order (even in subordinate clauses the **wya** subject phrase is sometimes moved to a postverbal position--see 7.6).

Vennemann's prediction, that breakdown in the case-marking system is a prime cause of radical word order change, might be accepted if we were considering Hixkaryana in isolation, or if the subject-marking system in M and A/T were already breaking down. But the latter is still largely intact (there are a few examples in the sources of transitive subjects without the marker, but they are rare), although the two languages seem already to have gone a long way in the direction of a fundamental change in basic word order. There must be other forces at work. Hyman (1975.119-21, 124-32) has suggested another explanation for this diachronic change: grammaticalization of afterthought patterns, which has been further elaborated by Vennemann (1975.289ff.). Much of the discussion has been centered on the pragmatic conditions under which afterthought or clarification patterns occur. I do not have sufficient information about M and A/T to determine whether right-dislocated phrases for clarification purposes occur to any great extent, and, if so, under what conditions. Hyman's suggestion does, however, provide the most likely explanation of how the Hixkaryana basic word order has come to change.

Simon Dik first drew my attention to this possibility. In his book (Dik 1978.176-77), he speculates on possible explanations for VOS ordering in languages like Malagasy and Fijian, and refers to historical evidence that in Fijian (Eastern Oceanic subgroup of Austronesian) it "may have arisen through grammaticalisation of a construction with the Subject in right-dislocated position." In a personal communication he directed me to Foley (1976), who gives information about diachronic changes in Fijian (pp. 52-62) that suggests the following hypothesis.

An early pattern of SVO can be adduced for Fijian (by comparison with closely related Nguna, and the retention of this order in current Fijian where S is a first or second person pronoun). At a later stage, the presence of a third person pronoun subject-marker as the initial element in the verb phrase led to the shift of the subject noun phrase from sentence-initial to sentence-final position, giving the order S_{PRO}-V-O-S_{NP}. This noun phrase was probably at first in a right-dislocated position, being added as an "afterthought" for the purpose of clearly identifying the referent of the initial pronoun. The final stage was the disappearance of the sentence-initial third person pronoun (its form has survived as a "clause introducer," but it has lost its distinctive pronominal characteristics) and the incorporation of the rightmost phrase into the main clause intonational group, thus completing the grammaticalization process that results in the present-day basic order of VOS.

In Hixkaryana the subject noun phrase is often right-dislocated (although it also often occurs postverbally as part of the main clause intonation group--see 7.5). In the right-dislocated usage it can be interpreted as an "afterthought," clarifying the referent in the verb prefix (which is the equivalent of the earlier Fijian sentence-initial pronoun). The grammaticalization process has clearly reached a late stage, with OVS established as the basic order, but it may never be as complete as it is in Fijian, for two reasons: right-dislocated phrases are widely used in the language and with varying functions (see 3.4 and 12.2.4); and the anaphoric element occurring earlier in the clause (the verb prefix) is not so likely to be removed, as has happened to the third person pronoun in Fijian. (The parallel with Fijian goes even further: first and second person subject pronouns in Hixkaryana optionally occur preceding the verb.)

This application of afterthought grammaticalization to explain diachronic change in the position of subject goes beyond anything suggested by Hyman or Vennemann. Vennemann, as I noted earlier, was concerned only to explain the change to postverbal position of direct object. Hyman considers that adverbial phrases and oblique objects are most likely to be the first candidates for right dislocation (Hyman 1975.121, 126-27) and subsequent grammaticalization in the postverbal position, but that a similar process for direct objects would naturally follow at a later stage. Neither of them seemed to consider the possibility of subjects undergoing such a change. If the mechanism is also valid for subjects, along the lines proposed for Fijian and Hixkaryana, a further modification of Hyman's explanation is necessary. He suggested that the most natural candidates for afterthought placement are constituents that convey new information. The F and H subjects, however, are constituents that carry given information, i.e., information that can be expressed by pronominal elements because they are recoverable from the preceding context.

The other major modification that may be required concerns Vennemann's prediction that breakdown in the case-marking system is the cause of diachronic change in word order. This prediction may hold in some cases. A comparison of Hixkaryana with related M and A/T, however, suggests that in these cases the breakdown in the case-marking system may follow the change in word order. This would be a natural result of a change in pattern that separated the subject and object nominals in a way that made case markers no longer necessary. It may be possible to demonstrate more conclusively if this is what is happening, by further investigation of Makuchi and Arekuna/Taulipang, for which there are records (most of the early ones, however, seem to be vocabularies only) that go back well over 100 years (see the preface and bibliography in Williams 1932).

11 Correlations between Hixkaryana and Existing Typologies

It has been generally accepted that the most fundamental (syntactic) typological division of languages arises from the position of the verb in relation to its object, resulting in two basic types: VO and OV. These show substantial differences in their syntactic patterning and the types of constructions and processes that occur. The relation of the subject to object and verb has thus far proved to be of only secondary importance, leading to minor subclassification (Lehmann 1978.6, 52-53). (Compare Lehmann's earlier remarks on the minor importance of Subject (1973. 51): "Subjects are by no means primary elements in sentences," and "Typological study accordingly supports this point of view by illustrating that the S in SVO formulae is far less significant than are the categories represented by V and O.") This, however, reflects the fact that the languages studied have been restricted to three basic word order types. SOV have been the only OV languages, so subclassification with regard to subject did not arise. There have been two possibilities for VO: either SVO or VSO. It is here that differences have been noted, but they have been minor compared with the differences between the VO and OV types (Lehmann 1978.15).

The discovery of languages having basic word orders of the other three types (VOS, OVS, OSV) could well reveal more important distinctions, and may necessitate a reevaluation of the basic typological divisions. There are several possibilities as to how the more fundamental oppositions could line up: the relative orders of S and O may prove to be crucial, revealing sharply different patterns for SVO, SOV and VSO, on the one hand, and VOS, OVS and OSV, on the other. The verb may continue to have the decisive role, but with an additional distinct set of patterns emerging for verb medial (SVO, OVS) as against the two that have been assumed so far to be the basic ones, i.e., verb initial (VSO, VOS) and verb final (SOV, OSV). Another possibility is that subject initial (SVO, SOV) and subject final (VOS, OVS) may show different characteristic traits.

In view of the small number of languages affected by the new dimension (S following O), it is not likely that any of the possible divisions just suggested will prove to be as significant as that between VO and OV. The basic patterns of these languages, however, need to be known and compared, so that a proper evaluation can be made. Their importance also needs to be measured against the other dimension that has recently been brought into the typological discussion: the suggested dichotomy between topic languages and subject languages (Li and Thompson 1976). A useful start has been made in both these directions by the publication of <u>Syntactic Typology</u> (Lehmann, ed., 1978), in which there are chapters on a topic-prominent language and on subject-final languages generally.

The rest of Part Two is concerned with evaluating the Hixkaryana contribution to these questions. I discuss first the relation of Hixkaryana syntactic patterns to those of existing typologies (chap. 11). I then present some patterns in Hixkaryana that appear to be sharply different from those found in the existing typologies (chap. 12). This is followed by a discussion of some discourse-related features that have not figured prominently in typological studies, but are being increasingly discussed elsewhere in linguistic literature and which seem, at least in Hixkaryana, to bear some relation to the basic order of constituents in the clause (chap. 13). Part Two ends with a summary of the conclusions to be drawn from the discussion (chap. 14).

Keenan (1978.324) is correct in assuming that Hixkaryana shows a closer correlation with a verb-final typology than with his subject-final languages. This is in keeping with both the relative rigidity of the OV sequence and the diachronic explanation (see 10.4) that OVS has developed from earlier SOV. The properties that relate most closely to those we expect to find in verb-final languages are discussed in 11.2. First, however, I make a brief comparison with the properties of the subject-final languages that Keenan outlines (1978.267-327) (11.1). The other possibility referred to earlier in this section, that verb-medial languages (SVO, OVS) might have similar properties that contrast with both verb-initial and verb-final languages, should not be overlooked. In this regard one interesting correlation between Hixkaryana and English is noted in 12.2.6. A fuller comparison is not, however, considered necessary, since the English glosses of Hixkaryana citations throughout this study draw attention to similarities and differences between the two types. Also, SVO, as a subtype of VO, is covered to some extent in 11.1.

11.1 Properties of subject-final languages. So far as I know, Keenan (1978) is the only general account to date of the syntactic properties of subject-final languages. It is restricted to languages that are not only subject final but also verb initial, i.e., VOS (p. 324), notwithstanding the more general definition given initially in the paper, which suggests that "subject-final" refers to all languages in which subject follows direct object in the unmarked order (p. 267). That definition would also, of course, include OVS and OSV languages. The omission of any discussion of these language types by Keenan was due to the fact that he was unaware of the existence of such languages at the time the paper was written (p. 324). In 10.3 I have referred to the likelihood of the existence of eight OVS and four OSV languages. It would be highly satisfactory to be able here to widen the discussion to include a comparison of both Hixkaryana and Keenan's VOS languages with the properties found in the other OVS and in the OSV languages. This is not possible owing to my lack of adequate descriptive material in these languages. I shall only be able to make an occasional reference to one or two of the languages where information is available to me on some particular property. The rest of this section is primarily concerned with comparing the syntactic properties of Hixkaryana with the generalizations Keenan presents concerning the syntax of subject-final languages, based solely on the VOS type.

The first two generalizations are totally invalidated by the information that has become known since Keenan wrote them, and which he acknowledges in his postscript: subject-final languages are not always verb-initial, nor do they necessarily occur in linguistic phyla in which verb-initial languages are common. With a few exceptions, which I shall discuss later in this section, the rest of the generalizations concern properties that are predicted (by Greenberg's universals or an extension of them by general consensus) for verb-initial languages. This is easily seen by comparing them with the properties listed for Easter Island ('A Characteristic VSO Language') in the same volume (Chapin 1978). The following summary list of these properties, none of which apply in any significant way to Hixkaryana, gives two page number references, the first to Keenan's generalization, and the second to Chapin's description of Easter Island.

(Some of) Keenan's generalizations about VOS languages

- G- 3. SVO is a marked word order (288, 143, cf. Greenberg universal 6).

- G- 7. Prepositions, not postpositions, generally occur (291, 146, cf. Greenberg universal 3).

- G- 9. Subordinate conjunctions occur, and they precede a finite subordinate clause (294, 162).

- G-10. In possessive constructions noun phrase possessors follow the head (the possessed) noun phrase (295, 150, cf. Greenberg universal 2).

G-13. Articles, including usually a definite article, occur in noun phrases (297, 147-48).

G-16. Negative elements precede the verb (299, 157).

G-17. A causative element precedes the root of the causativized verb (299, 159-60).

G-20. There is generally no overt copula (300, 146-47 and 156, by inference).

More specific information on Hixkaryana with respect to some of these generalizations is given in 11.2.

There are four other generalizations relating to properties normally associated with verb-initial languages that do apply in Hixkaryana:

G- 6. Relatively little nominal case marking (289, 168, Greenberg universal 41).

G- 8. Fronting of question word and focused constituent (292-94, 156, Greenberg universal 12).

G-11. In general, nominal modifiers follow the noun they modify (296, 149 and 152, Greenberg universal 17).

G-14. Numerals usually precede the noun they modify (298, 152).

The position of question words and numerals is treated more fully in 11.2. The absence of case-marking in Hixkaryana is directly associated with the diachronic process discussed in 10.4, and so can be considered to be attributable to the subject-final character of the language. Nominal modifiers in Hixkaryana do not exactly parallel Keenan's subject-final languages, since there are no finite relative clauses, but in other respects (nominalized forms and position after the head noun) they are alike. These are discussed more fully in 12.2.4-5.

The exceptions I referred to earlier in Keenan's generalizations are those which are not usually regarded as characteristic of verb-initial languages. They apply to Hixkaryana, as well as to the VOS languages, so they may well prove to be typical of subject-final languages generally (they have, however, been reported for languages of other types, so none of them are unique to the "subject-final" type). There are four such properties (not all are stated by Keenan in the form of a generalization):

1. There is agreement between transitive verbs and their subject and object nominals. Keenan has two generalizations, both of which are somewhat hedged, and the second of which does not apply in Hixkaryana, but the basic pattern is clearly the same. The generalizations are (288):

G- 4. If a language is subject-final, then either transitive verbs of unmarked sentences agree with no full noun phrases in the sentence or they agree with two noun phrases.

G- 5. If transitive verbs in subject-final languages present agreement at all, then they have a prefixal (pre-verb-stem) agreement with the subject noun phrase and a suffixal agreement with a nonsubject.

Two of the languages in Keenan's sample do not have agreement at all; the other six have the agreement described in G-5. The OSV language Apurinã has subject prefixes and object suffixes when the free forms are in the (marked) postverbal position, and when both free forms are postverbal, the subject always follows the object (just as it does when both are in the preverbal position) (Pickering 1973a.1-2). Xavante (?OSV) is reported to have person and number suffixes on the verb that agree with the subject of intransitive clauses, and with both subject and object of transitive clauses (Burgess 1976.3). In Hixkaryana there is an obligatory portmanteau verb prefix that agrees with subject and direct object. In two other OVS languages, Makuchi and Arekuna/Taulipang, the prefix agrees with the direct object, and the suffix with the subject (see 10.3), which is the inverse of the VOS pattern. Verb agreement with subject and object has, however, been reported for other languages that are not subject final, including SOV members of the Carib family, for example, Waiwai (Hawkins and Hawkins 1953.204) and Carib (Hoff 1968.160).

2. Reciprocals (usually) and reflexives (sometimes) are formed by prefixing the verb (310-13). In Hixkaryana both types of construction are primarily formed by the detransitivizing prefix (see 8.1). In verb stem derivations this is the only exception to the regular process of suffixation, which is the normal pattern in verb-final and postpositional languages (Greenberg universal 27; cf. Lehmann 1978.32, referring specifically to reflexive formation).

3. Headless relatives and nominalizations usually substitute for finite relative clauses and subordinate clauses in the four Amerindian languages of Keenan's sample (294-97). Nominalization is almost exclusively the form of both subordination (see chap. 4) and relativization (see 12.2.5) in Hixkaryana. I regard derived A as pseudonominals, at least those which function in subordinate clauses, inasmuch as they can be preceded by possessor NPs in the same way as derived nominals—see 1.3 and 4.3. The relative clause reported for the (?OSV) language Xavante (McLeod and Mitchell 1977.103, 160-62), appears to be essentially a headless relative or nominalized form.

4. Direct objects which are expressed by "heavy" constructions are usually moved to the rightmost position in the languages Keenan describes. This results in a marked order VSO (316-17). There is a parallel process in Hixkaryana resulting in any of the marked orders VO, SVO, or (rarely) VSO (see 7.4).

While nothing definitive in the way of subject-final properties has emerged from this comparison of Hixkaryana and VOS languages, the common characteristics noted can be used to supplement the distinctive patterns and processes described in chapters 12 and 13 for Hixkaryana, and thus provide a basis for further empirical testing. A necessary prerequisite, if that testing is to be sufficiently exhaustive, is the investigation and description of other subject-final languages. This should include OSV languages, for which as yet no single adequate description is available, as well as other OVS languages, and also further work on those VOS languages for which Keenan notes lacunae in the descriptions presently available.

11.2 Properties of verb-final languages. There are a number of syntactic properties that show the strongly OV character of Hixkaryana. In discussing them I will again make a comparison with another language, this time with one that is characteristically OV: Japanese. My references will once more be from Lehmann's volume (Kuno 1978).

11.2.1 Adpositions, genitive, and standard of comparison. There are three properties that fulfill, without any qualification, the predictions of Greenberg universals for SOV languages:

> Universal 4: With overwhelmingly greater than chance frequency, languages with normal SOV order are postpositional.
>
> Universal 2: In languages with prepositions, the genitive almost always follows the governing noun, while in languages with postpositions it almost always precedes.
>
> Universal 22: If in comparisons of superiority the only order, or one of the alternative orders, is standard-marker-adjective, then the language is postpositional....

The facts concerning these properties are given in Part One: postpositions (R) in 1.4 and 2.4; genitives (possessed NP) in 2.2; and comparisons in 4.4 and 9.1. Like Japanese (78), Hixkaryana adpositions are all postpositional. With regard to genitives, there is one feature that is different from Japanese (90-91) and from many other SOV languages: the morphological marking is on the head noun (possessed item), not on the genitive or by means of a separate particle, e.g., **toto yowanɨ** (man his-chest) 'the man's chest', the head noun being marked by the prefix **y-** 'III' and the suffix **-nɨ** 'POSSESSION' (see Appendix C for fuller discussion of possessor and possession morphemes). In another feature, however, Hixkaryana is closely parallel to Japanese: complex left-branching constructions permit expansions of the genitive by clausal constituents. It differs from Japanese only in that no finite relative clauses occur, but the nominalized subordinate clause is possible:

(161) **oroke   omohxemo   komo kanawarɨ**
      yesterday ones-who-came COLL canoe-of
      'the canoe of the people who came yesterday'

The whole genitive construction is often the nucleus of a subordinate clause. In such cases the head noun (possessed item) is a derived nominal; the genitive (possessor) is either the subject (intransitive) or direct object (transitive) of the nominalized verb; and there can be other clausal constituents (see chap. 4):

(162) **xaro   rowya rohetxe yoknɨrɨ**
      to-here by-me my-wife bringing-of
      'my bringing my wife here'

11.2.2 Suffixation. There is another Greenberg universal that applies with just a few qualifications to Hixkaryana and reflects its basically OV character:

> Universal 27: If a language is exclusively suffixing, it is postpositional....

There is only one general exception (there are a few other idiosyncratic ones) to the rule in Hixkaryana that derivations are suffixal: the detransitivizing prefix that functions, among other things, as reciprocal and reflexive (see 8.1 and 11.1; and, for derivations generally, Appendixes E-H). Inflectional morphemes are also mostly suffixes, the notable exception being the person-marking prefixes which occur with all four major word classes: V, N, A, and R (see Appendixes B-D). The extension of this universal, that OV languages undergo final morphophonemic modification (Lehmann 1978.23), also holds generally for Hixkaryana (see Appendix A).

11.2.3 Numerals. There is one close correlation between Hixkaryana and Japanese that is not particularly associated with the verb-final characteristic: numerals can be used as prenominal modifiers, as nouns, and as adverbs (91-92):

(163) a. **asako Wayway komo wenyo**
         two   Waiwai COLL I-saw-them
         'I saw two Waiwai.'

b. **Wayway komo wenyo,   asakon(o) komo**
   Waiwai COLL I-saw-them, two-NOMLZN COLL
   'I saw Waiwai, two of them.'

c. **Wayway komo wenyo,   asako**
   Waiwai COLL I-saw-them, two
   'I saw Waiwai, two.'

11.2.4 Nominal modifiers. The characteristic of numerals just noted is related, of course, to the whole question of nominal modifiers, and here Hixkaryana diverges from Japanese and from what is generally predicted for verb-final languages. There are a number of Greenberg universals that bear on this question (they are listed in Kuno, p. 82), but none which directly predicts the position of the modifier in relation to the noun. Greenberg's statistics, in fact, show that SOV and postpositional languages are about equally divided between those that have modifiers before the noun and those which have them after the noun (Greenberg 1966.85). Notwithstanding these facts, Lehmann has developed a principle stating that any modifier is "placed between the modified constituent and the sentence boundary," which leads him to the conclusion that "nominal modifiers precede nouns in OV languages" (19-20; cf. Lehmann 1973, where he says the principle applies to "consistent OV" languages, and cites from Japanese, Turkish, Quechua, and Tamil (Sanketi) in support). Japanese certainly follows this principle, according to Kuno (82-83): "Descriptive adjectives, demonstratives, numerals, and relative clauses all precede their head noun, without exception." The facts of Hixkaryana are somewhat complicated by the general lack of NPs in which simple adjectives occur as modifiers (see 1.3). Numerals are the one exception and, as noted above, they occur before the N, but even they occur more frequently as adverbial adjuncts (see 2.2 and cf. (163a) and (163c) above). But N can be modified, and it is usually by means of another nominal that has been derived from a V stem or an A. Such modifiers nearly always follow the N they modify, in a paratactic construction (see 12.2.4 and 12.2.5). (Equative clauses also have two NPs, often in a head-modifying relationship, and in this case the unmarked order has the modifier first, followed by the head. I regard these constructions, however, as primarily copular, the first NP being the predicate nominal and the second the subject. In this way they match exactly the (overt) copular clause, in which the predicate complement precedes the copula, which in turn precedes the subject--see 3.5 for a comparison of equative and copular clauses.) The position of nominal modifiers is thus the opposite of genitives, relative to the head noun in each case, and is inconsis tent with (although not directly opposed to) another Greenberg universal concerning verb-final languages:

Correlations   113

> Universal 5: If a language has dominant SOV order and the genitive follows the governing noun, then the adjective likewise follows the noun.

Nominal modifiers also follow their head noun in the OSV language Urubu (Kakumasu 1976.179-81) and in (?OSV) Xavante (McLeod and Mitchell 1977.103-4).

11.2.5 Subordinate verb forms and auxiliary verbs. Hixkaryana copular clauses follow the predictions of two Greenberg universals as they apply to verb-final languages:

> Universal 13: If the nominal object always precedes the verb, then verb forms subordinate to the main verb also precede it.

> Universal 16: In languages with dominant order SOV, an inflected auxiliary always follows the main verb.

The only item that could be viewed as an "auxiliary" in Hixkaryana is the copula, if one regards its complement in certain cases as desentential. The copula is inflected and follows what is semantically the main verb, but the latter is a subordinate derived form N or A. This is most clearly seen in a negative sentence (164b), comparing it with its positive counterpart (164a):

(164) a. **namryekyako   Mahxawa oroke**
         he-went-hunting Mahxawa yesterday
         'Mahxawa went hunting yesterday.'

   b. **amryekhɨra   nehxako Mahxawa oroke**
         not-hunting he-was Mahxawa yesterday
         'Mahxawa did not go hunting yesterday.'

The semantically contentful predicate element **amryekhɨra** is a derived A (see Appendix G), which can be regarded as a reduced, nonfinite subordinate clause. The (syntactic) main verb is the inflected copula **nehxako**, which is semantically contentless. Not to regard **amryekhɨra** as a main verb at some level would be to fail to relate negative and positive sentences at all. Regarding **nehxako** as a superordinate "auxiliary" verb, on the other hand, reveals a pattern consistent with both Universal 13 and Universal 16. (In other ways Hixkaryana sentence negation violates certain principles which have been proposed as universally applicable--see 12.2.6).

There is another construction that patterns according to Universal 13: the main verb is an inflected form of **-e(rye)-** 'make, do, fix' and it is preceded by a subordinate form marked by **-no** 'GENERAL NOMINALIZATION' (see Appendix F):

(165) ahxemtono   yeryeye   Waraka
       feeding-of-people he-did-it Waraka
       'Waraka provided a feast for the people.'

In other constructions, subordinate forms derived from verb stems may precede or follow the main verb of the clause, depending on whether their syntactic function is subject, direct object, or adjunct. Those which normally follow the main verb in the unmarked order, i.e., subject and adjunct, are often moved to the sentence-initial position by the Emphasis Fronting rule or by virtue of being a "heavy" construction (see chap. 4 and 7.2-3).

11.2.6 Question-word preposing. In Hixkaryana, question words are <u>always</u> moved to sentence-initial position (see 6.2.2). This is inconsistent with an absolute claim made for verb-final languages by Greenberg, and does not parallel Japanese, where the question word can be preposed to the initial position, but does not have to be (93):

> Universal 12: If a language has dominant order VSO in declarative sentences, it always puts interrogative words or phrases first in interrogative word questions; if it has dominant order SOV in declarative sentences, there is never such an invariant rule.

11.2.7 Passivization. Lehmann (1978.22) notes:

> Passivization is prominent in SVO languages, but not at all in OV languages ....

This generalization is not followed in Japanese, which has two types of passive, both of which have an underlying agentive and passive marking in the verb (108-9). (Keenan's subject-final VOS languages also have passive forms (300), as do some VSO languages, though not Easter Island (167)). Hixkaryana does not have a regular passive, only the nonagentive derivations I call pseudo-passives (see 9.4). One of those derivations, the DETRANSITIVIZER prefix, occurs in one construction where the gloss might suggest an agentive passive. It is the detransitivizing of a causative construction, however, and the agentive relates to the causee of that construction (see 9.3):

(166) nataymompotxowɨ   bɨryekomo
       IIIS-DETRANS-put in-CAUS-IMM.PAST COLL boy

       komo tuna kwaka, Waraka wya
       COLL water into Waraka by
       'The boys have been ducked in the water by Waraka.' (lit.,
       'The boys let themselves be ducked in the water by Waraka.')

Correlations

11.2.8 Movement of subordinate clause constituents to postverbal position. Hixkaryana is like Japanese in that it permits rightward movement of subordinate clause constituents (60-64; cf. 4.5 and 7.6), but with two significant differences:

(1) In Japanese the moved constituent cannot remain in the subordinate clause immediately to the right of the verb of that clause (63-64). In Hixkaryana this is permitted for the (underlying) subject of a transitive verb (and, less frequently, for the (possessor) subject of an intransitive—see 7.6):

(167) a. **owya   Waraka yonyetoko, onɨ   tɨmko ɨwya**
by-you Waraka when-seeing this-thing give-it to-him
'When you see Waraka, give this to him.'

b. **Waraka yonyetoko owya, onɨ tɨmko ɨwya.**

(167a) is the unmarked order in the subordinate clause, but (167b) is also acceptable. Strictly speaking the underlying subject is not moved <u>immediately</u> to the right of the verb of the subordinate clause, <u>but to the</u> right of the subordinating element, which in the case of (167) is the derivational suffix **-toko** 'SIMULTANEOUS ACTION'. Thus, when the subordinating element is an R, the subject can be to the right of that R, but cannot occur between the (derived N) verbal element and the R:

(168) **wewe yamanɨrɨ   ke   rowya, amryekhɨra wahko**
tree felling-of because by-me not-hunting I-was
'Because I was felling trees, I did not go hunting.
(But not *****wewe yamanɨrɨ rowya ke, ...)**

This does not, however, affect the difference between Japanese and Hixkaryana at this point.

(2) Where the constituent is moved to the right of the main clause verb, as is permitted in Japanese, Kuno argues convincingly for an "afterthought" analysis of such nonverb-final sentences. This avoids violating the Ross constraint which states that rules which adjoin elements to the right of variables are upward bounded (Kuno, 61-63; Ross 1967). The subordinate clause constituent can also be moved to the right of the main clause in Hixkaryana, but with two differences: it is to the right not only of the main verb, but also of the main clause subject noun phrase (if any); and the conditions that Kuno attaches to the application of his afterthought analysis do not always apply, so that there does not seem to be any way of avoiding violation of the Ross constraint:[4]

---

[4] Ross (1967:5.123) states the rightward bounding condition in terms of the notion of command:

(169) **Manawsɨ hona ronyaknyɨr xe   nehxako Waraka**
Manaus to   sending-me desirous-of he-was Waraka

Kaywerye wya
Kaywerye by
'Waraka wanted Kaywerye to send me to Manaus.'

The phrase **Kaywerye wya** is the subject of the subordinate clause and could occur as part of that clause in the form **Manawsɨ hona Kaywerye wya ronyaknyɨr xe (nehxako Waraka)**. The order given in (169) is, however, the preferred pattern when the subordinate clause is the complement of the copula (see 4.5). The frequency of the afterthought pattern in Hixkaryana by way of right-dislocated paratactic constructions (see 12.2.4) would suggest that this could be the explanation here. That this is not so can be seen by

> In all rules whose structure index is of the form ... AY, and whose structural change specifies that A is to be adjoined to the right of Y, A must command Y.

It is clear that in (169) the phrase **Kaywerye wya** does not command either the verb (**nehxako**) or subject (**Waraka**) of the main clause. The underlying structure can be represented as:

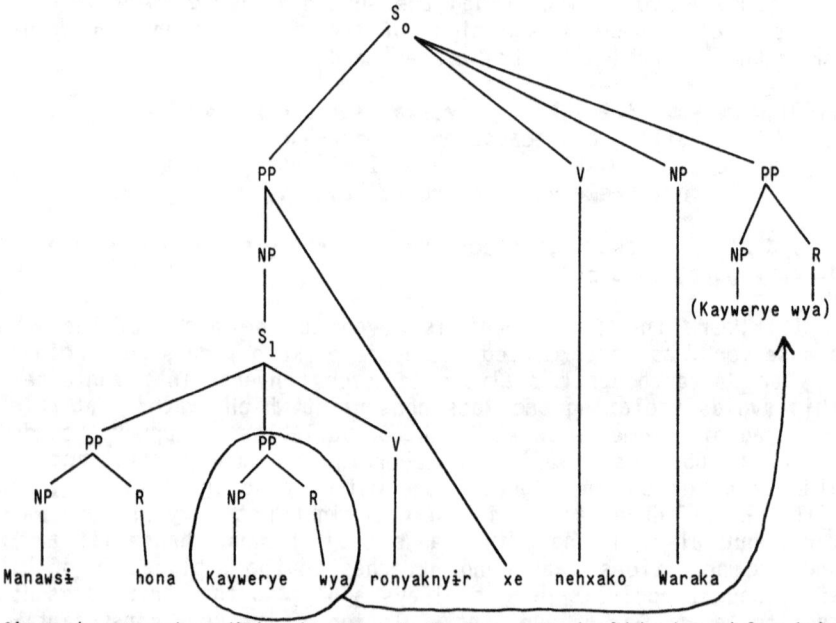

Since the command condition is not met, **Kaywerye wya** should be barred from being moved to the right of the higher clause, but it is, in fact, well-formed there.

Correlations   117

trying to apply Kuno's conditions that must be met if the
afterthought analysis is to prove a viable alternative to a rightward movement rule. The conditions are in the form of two predictions that the afterthought analysis should be able to make (62):

(i) Postverbal elements are either discourse-predictable (or
rather, the speaker assumes that they are) or supplemen-
tary; therefore, the sentences should have made sense
without them.

(ii) Elements that would change the interpretation of the first
part of the sentence cannot appear postverbally.

It is the second of these predictions which (169) crucially fails
to meet. If the phrase **Kaywerye wya** is omitted, the sentence makes
good sense, but with a different meaning: 'Waraka wanted
to send me to Manaus'; i.e., an obligatory rule of Equi-NP
deletion applies when the subject of the subordinate clause is the
same as that of the higher clause (see 4.10 and cf. especially
(63a) and (63b)). This appears to be a clear case of a rightward
movement rule that is not upward bounded, and one that is closely
associated with the postverbal position of subject in Hixkaryana
clauses.

11.2.9 Interrogative particle. The only specifically interrogative
particle is **katɨ** 'ALTERNATIVE' (see 6.2). It is not specified in
position by reference to the sentence as a whole (see condition in
Greenberg universal 9), so it is not of the sentence-final type
that Kuno says "is a characteristic of postpositional languages"
and does not parallel Japanese at this point (80, 93). It does,
however, follow the more basic patterning of postpositional
languages, since it occurs phrase final (only other particles can
follow it, and this happens only infrequently). (See discussion in
12.2.3 on phrase orientation of particles in general.)

11.2.10 Sentence negation. Sentence negation in Hixkaryana does
not pattern like Japanese or most other languages. It is treated
fully in 12.2.6.

**11.2.11 Causative constructions and the marking of secondary
agent.** The use of the dative marker to express the secondary agent
function in a number of different constructions in Japanese
corresponds closely to the use of the indirect object marker **wya**
in Hixkaryana (see 3.4 and, for fuller discussion, 12.2.7).

This marker is used to express the causee function in constructions where a transitive stem is made causative (see 9.3), just as
it is in Japanese (113). It is never used, however, when the
causative is formed from an intransitive stem, as it sometimes is
in Japanese (110-12). In this case the underlying subject of the
intransitive verb always becomes the object of that verb stem
after it has been causativized, which is the pattern in the other
form of intransitive-causative construction in Japanese.

11.3 Conclusions on the relation of Hixkaryana to other typologies. Hixkaryana clearly has many of the characteristics of verb-final languages, as seen in 11.2. This was predictable from the rigidity of the OV sequence in Carib languages generally and the diachronic explanation proposed for the origin of OVS in Hixkaryana in 10.4.

The more interesting conclusions that result from the comparison made with the two different typologies in this section are those that reveal syntactic patterns which are not characteristic of verb-final languages, and which in some cases correlate with Keenan's generalizations on subject-final languages. Some of these may be merely idiosyncratic departures from the type, such as is common in most languages with regard to one or more particular features. There are, however, at least four patterns in Hixkaryana that appear to be more or less directly associated with its subject-final character (the first two perhaps more strongly so than the others):

(1) It is necessary to postulate a rightward movement rule that is not upward bounded and which, therefore, violates the Ross constraint (11.2.8).

(2) Nominal modifiers follow the head noun they modify (11.2.4). This pattern is also found in Keenan's subject-final languages (11.1). The modifiers usually take the form of nominalizations (as in some of Keenan's languages), and the sequence is a paratactic construction (see 12.2.4 and 12.2.5), so that in the case of the postverbal subject constituent the noun-modifier sequence fulfills Lehmann's principle, which predicts that a modifier will be placed between the modified constituent and the sentence boundary (Lehmann 1978.19). (The adjunct, which would normally follow the subject, rarely occurs in a sentence with a subject that consists of a paratactic sequence of this kind; when it does, it usually occurs between the verb and the subject.) This would seem to have dictated a similar sentence-final pattern when the object constituent is modified in this way. One of the exceptions to the fairly rigid rule that the object precedes the verb is the case of "heavy" (including paratactic) constructions, which can result in either (i) the whole object constituent being moved into the postverbal and sentence-final position, or (ii) the head noun phrase being placed before the verb and the modifying noun phrase after, again in sentence-final position (see 7.4 and 12.2.4). It is of some interest that in Makuchi, according to Williams (1932.57), the "adjective precedes or follows the word it qualifies"; this could be interpreted as further evidence that the language is in a transitional stage from basically SOV to OVS (see 10.3), but more data would be needed to justify this conclusion.

(3) There is no agentive passive construction in the language (11.2.7). The absence of a "distinct passive voice" is also re-

ported by Williams (1932.85) for Makuchi. The fact that direct object is sentence initial obviates the need for a passive construction; it is the subject that has to be fronted for special "topicalization" or contrastive emphasis (see 7.2 and 13.1). This cannot be regarded as generally true of subject-final languages; indeed, Keenan generalizes that all subject-final languages have passive constructions, but he was speaking only of VOS languages. The crucial factor appears to be the sentence-initial position of the object, so it should apply to OSV as well as OVS languages, and the evidence available confirms this: there is no passive voice in Urubu (Kakumasu 1976.196); there is no passivizing mechanism in Xavante (Burgess 1976.2); and Apurinã does not have an agentive passive, although it seems to have some way of passivizing the verb, perhaps parallel to the Hixkaryana pseudopassive described in 9.4 (Pickering 1973a.5).

(4) Question words are obligatorily placed in sentence-initial position (11.2.6). This also appears to be the rule in Arekuna (Edwards 1977.45). Keenan (1978.293) links question-word fronting with other kinds of fronting: "focused, or relatively new, information is fronted," and this is exactly what is included in the Hixkaryana emphasis-fronting rule (see 7.2 and 13.1).

This chapter (11) has been concerned only with the patterns and constructions common to languages that fit easily into the existing typologies. Hixkaryana has other distinctive patterns, described in chapters 12 and 13. Some of these are extensions of properties listed in this summary. Others may prove to be even more characteristic of subject-final languages than anything I have discussed in this chapter (see the final summary in 14.1).

12 Major Differences between Hixkaryana and Existing Typologies

12.1 Constructions and processes that are lacking in Hixkaryana.
Certain types of construction and process have been generally assumed to occur in languages and usually receive a good deal of discussion in individual language descriptions. Some of these are notably missing in Hixkaryana, although in most cases there is some form of substitute for the underlying semantic configuration. The substitutes are discussed in detail in 12.2. First, I summarize the common constructions and processes that are lacking, with a brief mention of what compensates for them. I shall also refer in a number of cases to the OSV language, Apurinã, which is strikingly similar to Hixkaryana in a number of features, as reported in two unpublished papers by Pickering (1973a, 1973b), but is genetically quite unrelated to the Carib family.

(1) There is no special form for indirect statements, questions and commands (such as the English he said that he is going, you know where I am going, and he told you to go). Apurinã has "no indirect discourse .... (It) is expressed either as a nominalized construction or as direct quotation" (Pickering 1973b.3). Hixkaryana has a number of ways of compensating for this lack: direct speech (see 12.2.1), the "hearsay" verification particle (see 12.2.3), nominalizations (see 12.2.5), and rhetorical questions, which sometimes function as indirect questions (see 12.2.2).

(2) There are no finite complement clauses, subordinate clauses, or relative clauses. The complement-marking particle that occurs in many languages to introduce an embedded finite clause (e.g., English that, Portuguese que, Hindi ki) is completely lacking. There are no finite elements to mark tense/aspect in subordinate clauses, and there are no relative pronouns. Apurinã also lacks relative pronouns and any "relative clause in English would be expressed as a nominalized construction in Apurinã functioning as a noun phrase" (Pickering 1973b.3). Nominalizations are also the most general form of substitute in Hixkaryana for all three types of embedded finite clause (see 12.2.5, also chap. 4), but there are other ways in which the complements of cognitive processes like think and know can be expressed:

Major Differences

(i) direct speech (see 12.2.1);

(ii) an ordinary finite main clause, followed by another with an inflected form of the verb -**hutwa**- 'think, know', with no formal connection between the two clauses, and with the intonation patterns of separate sentences; the following example is taken from Derbyshire (1965.46):

(170) **nomokno mɨ.   uhutwehe,   ketxkon**
　　　he-came DEDUCT I-know/think-it they-said-it

　　　hatɨ, kamarayana   komo
　　　HSY   jaguar-people COLL
　　　'"I'm sure somebody has come," said the jaguar people.'

(iii) the addition of a dative experiencer phrase to a finite main clause (the "cognizer function" of **wya** 'to, by'--see 12.2.7):

(171) a. **ehonomnɨ   me   rmahaxa   naha   yaskomo,**
　　　　　important-one DENOMLZR very-much he-is shaman

　　　　　totokomo wya
　　　　　people   to
　　　　　'The people think the shaman is a very important person.'

　　　b. **onok haxa   ryhe omoro, owya**
　　　　　who CONTR EMPH you   to-you
　　　　　'Who do you think you are?'

The same possibilities that express indirect statements and questions can also be used for cognitive processes (see (1) above). These include verification particles (see 12.2.3) and rhetorical questions (12.2.2).

(3) There is no formal means for expressing coordination at the sentence, clause, or phrase levels. There are no exact equivalents for conjunction particles like English and, but, or, although some discourse particles can be used to supplement the more general means by which coordination is expressed, i.e., juxtaposed clauses and phrases in paratactic relationship (see 6.4 and 12.2.4). The or type of coordination is usually expressed by means of constructions in which the particle sequence **hana** 'UNCERTAINTY' occurs, and often involves rhetorical questions (see 12.2.2). One (?)OSV language, Nadëb, lacks coordinating conjunctions and uses juxtaposed phrases and clauses (Helen Weir, personal communication), while Pickering says: "It is not clear ... that Apurinã has conjoined sentences in the usual sense" (1973a. 3), and later in the same paper (p. 4): "Noun phrase conjunction occurs, but neither verb phrase nor sentence conjunction occurs except as juxtaposed independent clauses."

(4) There is no class of adjective and, apart from numerals and the small set of modifying particles (see 2.2), there is no form of modifier that occurs within the noun phrase (see 11.2.4 and 11.3). There are two forms of noun phrase modification that substitute: (i) adverbs, which function as the complement of the copula or as adjunct in any type of sentence (see 1.3, where there is fuller discussion on the absence of a distinct adjective class; a simple example of an adverbial complement that modifies a noun in a copular clause is (35c) in 3.1); and (ii) sequences of noun phrases in paratactic constructions with a head-modifier relationship (see 12.2.4).

(5) There is no regular passive, only the nonagentive pseudo-passive derived forms (see 9.4 and 11.2.7). Apurinã also lacks an agentive passive, and two other OSV languages, Urubu and Xavante, are reported not to have any passive construction (see 11.3).

(6) There are no clause-internal processes that change grammatical relations, such as Passive or Dative. Other processes which are necessarily completely absent are those which relate to conjoined clauses: Right-Node Raising (which occurs in Japanese, Kuno 1978.132) and Gapping (lacking in Japanese, ibid.). Pickering states, "Apurinã appears not to exhibit any gapping behavior" (1973b.1), and goes on to propose a hypothesis which is supported by the facts in Hixkaryana (1973b.3): "Any language that is devoid of overt markers for sentence conjunction will not exhibit gapping behavior."

There are other syntactic processes which do occur in Hixkaryana, and which are described in various sections: Equi NP Deletion occurs in a number of constructions where the subject of a subordinate clause is the same as that of its superordinate clause (4. 10); Subject Raising occurs in relation to the negative subordinate clause (12.2.6); Pronominalization and NP Deletion are common (13.5); VP Deletion does not occur with respect to conjoined clauses, but the copula is often omitted in negative answers to yes-no questions, and the verb phrase can also be deleted in answers to questions in which a question-word is used (6.6.1); and there are various movement processes (chap. 7 and 11.2.8).

12.2 Patterns and processes that are characteristic of Hixkaryana.
The seven syntactic features discussed in this section are not unique to Hixkaryana. All have been reported for other languages. They are, however, characteristic of Hixkaryana in the sense that they are pervasive, have a wide range of function, and they compensate for the lack of constructions that are common in other languages (see 12.1). This is especially true of the first five, which account for a number of underlying semantic relations that are often expressed in other ways. The last two, sentence negation

and the functions of **wya**, give rise to questions concerning proposals that have been made with respect to language universals, and they have some properties which, so far as I know, have not been reported for other languages.

12.2.1 Direct speech. Direct speech is embedded as the direct object in a quotative clause. The syntax of that clause type and of the more complex constructions arising from it is discussed in chap. 3, 5.3, and 6.5. The discussion here concerns the extensive usage of direct speech in narrative and reporting.

The quotative verb -**ka**- 'say' is the only verb which can have direct speech embedded as its object or complement of any kind. There are verbs with the meanings 'cried (out)', 'whispered', 'called', 'answered', etc., but they are either intransitive (e.g., -**kowonta**- 'cry out') or transitive forms that can have only human objects (e.g., -**oyuku**- 'answer (someone)'). The verb -**ka**- is the only one that can signal the performance of a speech act. There are no special forms to express the meaning of illocutionary acts such as 'assert', 'question', 'command', 'request', 'promise', 'warn', etc. These concepts are expressed by a quotative sentence in which -**ka**- 'say' is the main verb. The semantic distinctions in the speech acts are signalled in the direct speech, either by the use of an interrogative or imperative sentence (see 6.2 and 6.3), or by the use of certain particles, or simply by the use of a semantically appropriate verb:

(172) a. **mon   hona arko   kanawa kano   Waraka rowya**
       over-there to take-it   canoe he-said-it Waraka to-me
       '"Take the canoe over to the other side," said Waraka
       to me' or 'Waraka ordered me to take the canoe over
       to the other side.'

   b. **kamara mpɨnɨ   oyoskeno,   kekonɨ**
      jaguar warning it-bite-you-NONPAST-UNCERT she-said-it

      notxwakomo tɨmryerɨ wya
      old-woman   her-son   to
      '"Be careful lest the jaguar bite you," said the old
      woman to her son' or 'The old woman warned her son
      that the jaguar might bite him.'

   c. **wɨmyaha owotɨ   kano   owto   yohɨ**
      I-give-it your-meat he-said-it village chief-of

      hawana wya
      visitor to
      '"I will give you meat," said the chief to the
      visitor' or 'The chief promised to give the
      visitor meat.'

In (172a) the command speech act is signalled by the imperative direct speech sentence. In (172b) the warning is signalled by the nonpast uncertainty suffix in the verb and the verification particle **mpɨnɨ** 'warning'. In (172c) the promise is expressed by the form of the verb alone. The second gloss in each case indicates the force of the illocutionary act and also reflects the fact that the Hixkaryana quotative sentence is the natural (and in many cases the only) way to express indirect statements and commands (and also questions). In some cases indirect statements and commands can be expressed by means of verification particles as an alternative to the use of direct speech (see 12.2.3).

Direct speech is often used to express the content of cognitive processes, and the **-ka-** verb then has the meaning 'think, know'. The degree of certainty is indicated by a particle in the direct speech, and this is the only way of expressing distinctions like 'doubt', 'be sure', 'believe', and 'not believe':

(173) a. **awanaworo kamryekyaha kekonɨ Waraka**
tomorrow I-go-hunting he-said-it Waraka

(**tɨwya rma**)
(to-himself SAME)
'"I'll go hunting tomorrow," said Waraka to himself' or 'Waraka thought/decided he would go hunting the next day.'

b. **roxehra nay hamɨ Kaywerye ɨkekonɨ**
not-liking-me he-is DEDUCT Kaywerye I-said-it
'I said (to myself), "Kaywerye evidently doesn't like me"' or 'I was sure Kaywerye didn't like me.'

The parenthetical phrase in (173a) can be added to make more explicit the fact that the person is speaking to himself, but it is not necessary in order to convey that meaning. This use of direct speech substitutes for a large group of finite clauses that occur across languages as the complement of cognitive verbs.

These functions of direct speech appear to be general in Carib languages, and not restricted to those which are subject final. Waiwai, reported to be SOV (personal communication from Robert Hawkins), corresponds exactly to Hixkaryana in its use of direct speech (R. Hawkins, 1962.164-66). I have not found any specific description for other languages in the family, but the data in the various sources suggest the same basic pattern.

12.2.2 Rhetorical questions. The rhetorical question is the only type of indirect speech act in Hixkaryana, but it is used very frequently and for a variety of purposes. It takes the form of one of the regular question words, which is usually followed by a particle that clearly marks it as rhetorical, although the particles that can have this function (with the exception of **horo**) are also used in other ways: they are **hana** 'UNCERTAINTY', **haryhe** 'FRUSTRATIVE', **harha** 'back again', **komo** 'COLLECTIVE', and **horo** 'MEMORY RECALL'. The rhetorical question phrase may occur alone, in which case it has an exclamatory function (see below), or it may be part of a normal sentence. Incomplete sentences are also quite frequent. The normal interrogative intonation pattern does not occur with rhetorical questions, but the peremptory pattern is frequent, as it is with genuine questions (see 6.2 and Appendix A.3.4).

The primary purpose of the rhetorical question, as distinct from a normal question, is to convey information rather than to ask for it. It has a number of specific functions:

(1) There are two general discourse functions related to the flow of information. First, it adds an element of redundancy in many cases, since the same information could be given more directly, and this contributes to the slowing down of the rate at which new information is introduced (see 13.6). Second, it has the effect of drawing special attention to an item of new information, and can be regarded as a marked form of thematic prominence (cf. 13.5.2 (2)). A more direct, nonrhetorical construction would convey that the item was only secondary or background information. Both these discourse functions can be seen at work when the rhetorical device is used to reinforce the information given in a subordinate clause. This can be done by means of either complete (174a) or incomplete (174b) sentences:

(174) a. **ɨsok tawro hana amryekhɨra nehxak ha,**
how doing UNCERT not-hunting he was INTENSFR

Waraka. amryekhɨra nehxako, bararɨn
Waraka not-hunting he-was his(REFL)-field

hoko tesnɨr ke hatɨ
occ.-with his(REFL)-being because HSY
'Why didn't Waraka go hunting? He didn't go hunting, I am told, because he was working on his field.'

b. **amryekhɨra nehxako Waraka, ɨsok tawro hana,**
not-hunting he-was Waraka how doing UNCERT

bararɨn hoko tesnɨr
his(REFL)-field occ.-with his(REFL)-being

ke hatɨ
because HSY
'Waraka didn't go hunting. Why? Because, I am told, he was working on his field.'

(2) A rhetorical question is the regular means used to express an indirect question:

(175) **henta ya na ɨten ha. ɨsna ɨtohra manaha**
where to UNCERT I-go INTENSFR to-there not-going you-are
'Where am I going? You can't go there' or 'You cannot go where I am going.'

This use is often closely related to the cognitive verb **-hutwa-** 'think, know', which may also be expressed in the total construction (176a) or may only be implied (176b):

(176) a. **henta hana nay ha, oyeheryanɨ.**
where UNCERT it-is INTENSFR your-sickness

ɨro ryhe hutwehe
that-thing EMPH it-knows-it
'Where is your sickness? That (X-ray machine) will know' or 'That machine will know (or, find out) where your sickness is.' (From the journal of a Hixkaryana man who went to a city hospital.)

b. **ɨsokentok hana wenyan ha, rowtɨ**
when UNCERT I-see-him INTENSFR my-brother

ha
INTENSFR
'I don't know when I will see my brother.'

(3) Disjunction (the or coordination) can be expressed by a rhetorical question (see 6.4 for other ways of expressing it):

(177) a. **twahak hana nehxakon ha, ɨmoxenonɨ**
how-much UNCERT it-was INTENSFR its-distance

kuknomatxho, 5 kerometrus hana, 6 kerometrus hana
measuring-of 5 kilometers UNCERT 6 kilometers UNCERT
'Its distance was about five or six kilometers.'

b. **henta nyero hana nomokyak ha, karaywa.**
where from UNCERT he-came INTENSFR non-Indian

henta ya hana nten ha. uhutwahra
where to UNCERT he-goes INTENSFR not-knowing-it

tehxatxow hamɨ
we(INCL)-are DEDUCT
'It is evident we do not know where the non-Indian has come from or where he is going.'

(4) Rhetorical questions also function as exclamations, when they can express some kind of emotion or reaction to a circum-

Major Differences

stance, such as surprise, frustration, or annoyance. Here, the minimal form of the question phrase alone often occurs (178a, b), but it may also be a complete sentence (178c).

(178) a. **ɨsok tawro harha**
how doing back-again
'What's going on?'

b. **henta haryhe**
where FRUST
"Where on earth is it?'

b. **ɨsok ma ryhe kahataken ha**
how ABNORMAL EMPH I-come-out INTENSFR
'However can I get out?' or 'There's no way out.'
(from a folktale, spoken by a character who had
been swallowed by an anaconda, see Derbyshire 1965.68)

12.2.3 Verification particles and the phrase orientation of particles. The properties of postpositional particles in general, and of verification particles in particular, are described in l. 5. The verification set is listed, with examples, in Appendix K. Verification particles (often referred to in the literature as "evidentials") function primarily to express the attitude or relationship of the speaker to what he is saying, including the degree of certainty and the authority for making the assertion. They have been reported for numerous other South American languages, e.g., Waiwai (R. Hawkins 1962.167), Inga (Quechuan) (Levinsohn 1975), and Nambikuara (Lowe 1972). One type of verification particle described here, the hearsay particle, has also been reported for Malayo-Polynesian languages in the Philippines (Ballard 1974).

The particle **(ha)tɨ** 'HEARSAY' is used whenever the speaker is reporting what someone else has told him, events he did not witness himself. When those conditions are met it is obligatory. If it is not used, there is an assumption that the speaker witnessed what he is reporting (unless he uses another member of the verification set that indicates a different relationship or attitude). The particle is used, therefore, in telling folktales and in retelling personal experiences first told by someone else, and in such narratives the particle is repeated in almost every clause. It is also used in everyday conversation when giving information or passing on commands that have come from another person. It then functions as a form of indirect statement or indirect command (see Derbyshire 1978 for fuller discussion). It also effectively places the responsibility for the assertion or command on someone other than the speaker:

(179) a. **naryak hatɨ Waraka oroke**
he-took-it HSY Waraka yesterday
'(I am told--either by Waraka or by someone else)
Waraka took it yesterday.'

b. **naryan   hati Waraka**
      he-take-it HSY Waraka
      'Waraka will take it (I am told--most probably by
      Waraka himself, but it could be someone else).'

   c. **arko   hati**
      take-it HSY
      '(Someone told me to tell you to) take it.'

In each case, the words in parentheses give the force of **hati** and show that the source of the information is ambiguous; in (a) and (b) it could be Waraka, the participant in the action reported, but it could be someone else, or just general hearsay. If information as to the source is important, the only way to disambiguate (assuming that the context does not do so) is to use direct speech (see 12.2.1). The corresponding direct speech sentences might be as follows:

(180) a. **waryako   oroke   kano   Waraka rowya**
         I-took-it yesterday he-said-it Waraka to-me
         'Waraka told me he took it yesterday.'

   (or) **naryako   Waraka oroke,   katxowi   totokomo rowya**
        he-took-it Waraka yesterday they-said-it people   to-me
        'People told me Waraka took it yesterday.'

   b. **waryaha   kano   Waraka**
      I-take-it he-said-it Waraka
      'Waraka said he will take it.'

   c. **arko   hati kasko iwya   kano   Kaywerye rowya**
      take-it HSY say to-him he-said-it Kaywerye to-me
      'Kaywerye told me to tell you to take it.'

Other information conveyed in the direct speech sentence, which is not in the indirect (**hati**) construction, concerns the time when the reporter first heard the information; this is contained in the tense-aspect suffix in the quotative verb **kano** (**-no** 'IMM. PAST' indicates that it was the same day). Although it supplies much less information, the **hati** construction is used more than the direct speech form in everyday reporting of this kind.

Both **(ha)ti** and some of the other verification particles have a secondary function of representing, in effect, a higher clause verb, in relation to which the rest of the clause in which they actually occur is the complement. Considered in this way they compensate for a number of constructions that contain finite complement clauses in other languages:

(181) a. **ton   hati Waraka**
         he-went HSY Waraka
         'They say Waraka has gone' or 'It is reported
         that Waraka has gone.'

Major Differences   129

   b. **yaworo mɨkan   hamɨ**
      truly   you-said-it DEDUCT
      'It is evident you are telling the truth' or
      'I'm sure you are telling the truth.'

   c. **kana yanɨmno   hana**
      fish he-lifted-it   UNCERT
      'I don't know if he caught any fish' or 'I doubt he
      caught any fish' or 'Maybe he caught some fish.'

   d. **awanaworo nomokyaha hampɨnɨ**
      tomorrow   he-comes CERTAINTY
      'It is certain he will come tomorrow' or
      'I'm sure he will come tomorrow.'

The particle **(ha)na** 'UNCERTAINTY' occurs very often in rhetorical questions (see 12.2.2) and to express disjunction (see 6.4; also 12.2.2). The particles **(ha)mɨ** 'DEDUCTION' and **(ha)tɨ** 'HEARSAY' are also common in rhetorical expressions; they occur in the response clause following the rhetorical question clause in which **hana** usually occurs (see (174a, b) and (177b) in 12.2.2).

Hixkaryana particles are phrase oriented syntactically, although some of them have a wider semantic scope: verification particles usually relate to the whole clause; and discourse particles normally relate the head of the phrase in which they occur to some other part of the discourse. Verification particles are mutually exclusive and only one occurs in a clause. It is often placed in the verb phrase, which may or may not be the initial phrase of the sentence; however, when a subject or adjunct phrase is fronted for emphasis, the verification particle is usually placed in that initial phrase (see 7.7). The particles thus follow the postpositional character of the language, by following the head word(s) in the phrase, but there is a complete lack of the (specifically) sentence-final particles that frequently occur in postpositional languages.

12.2.4 Paratactic constructions. A paratactic construction is here defined as a sequence of phrases, clauses, or sentences in juxtaposition. Each phrase, clause, or sentence in the sequence constitutes a distinct intonation group; that is, it is phonologically dislocated from the rest of the sequence. This is one of the most characteristic features of Hixkaryana. Clause and sentence parataxis is described in 6.4, and there is further discussion on one particular type of sentence sequence, the "sentence cluster," in 13.6. In this section only phrase sequences are in focus.

Simon Dik has proposed a universal schema for the ordering of constituents in a sentence (LIPOC, i.e., Language-Independent Preferred Order of Constituents), which allows for a right-dislocated "Tail" constituent (Dik, 1978). Hixkaryana paratactic constructions are mostly right-dislocated and generally fit the pattern of this "Tail," but their functions extend beyond the "afterthought" clarification function attributed to this constituent by Dik. It is the normal means for expressing modification and coordination in the language.

There can be right-dislocation of a noncomplex kind, i.e., without paratactic sequences. Thus, a simple noun phrase may occur as subject, or an adverb phrase as adjunct, in a dislocated position after the verb. It is this pattern which I have suggested is historically the cause of the emergence of OVS as the basic order of constituents (see 10.4). A high proportion of postverbal constituents are still intonationally dislocated in all types of Hixkaryana discourse. In most cases they take the form of complex phrase sequences I call paratactic constructions.

Syntactically the whole sequence of phrases constitutes a single grammatical relation in the clause. (In the case of the adverbial sequence function--see (1) below--it might be argued that there is a sequence of two or more adjuncts, but in other functions there is only one relation.) Paratactic constructions rarely, if ever, occur in subordinate clauses; they are restricted to main clause constituents (there can be a sequence of subordinate clauses which function as a single constituent of the main clause--see chap. 4). This is a natural consequence of the predominantly (nominalized) verb-final character of subordinate clauses (only the subject constituent, usually a **wya**-phrase, can be moved to the postverbal position, and so far as I know, this is always a single, noncomplex phrase--see 7.6).

Occasionally there is a left-dislocated paratactic construction. This occurs when "heavy" constructions functioning as subject or adjunct are fronted for emphasis and also dislocated (see 7.3, from which the example (122c) is repeated here as (182)):

(182) **ɨwahathɨyamo, aknyohnyenhɨyamo   tho, oske**
     his-killers   ones-who-had-burned-him DEVLD thus

    nketxkonɨ
    they-said-it
    'His killers, the ones who had burned him, said thus.'

Mostly, however, left-dislocated constituents are single phrases or subordinate clauses. The dominant pattern for paratactic constructions is right-dislocated sequences of phrases or subordinate clauses.

Any nonverbal constituent of the clause can take the form of a paratactic construction. This includes: Subject NP (183a); Direct object NP (183b); Adjunct AP (183c); Adjunct PP (183d); Adjunct

Major Differences   131

subordinate clause (183e); a mixed Adjunct complex, i.e., of AP
and PP, or one of these and a subordinate clause (183f, g); and
Complement of the copula (183h) (but in the case of the copular
complement it is usually discontinuous parataxis, in which the
first phrase or subordinate clause precedes the copula and the
other(s) follow(s)--see below):

(183) a. **wayehyako nor heno, horykomo tho heno,**
      he-died   he   dead   chief-man DEVLD dead

    owto   yohɨ   ymo
    village chief-of AUG
    'He has died, the old man who was the village chief.'

  b. **arko   Waraka hyaka, ɨro   ha,   karyehta**
     take-it Waraka to   that-thing INTENSFR notebook
     'Take that notebook to Waraka.'

  c. **nomokyan hatɨ Kaywerye, amnye, kokonye**
     he-comes HSY Kaywerye soon   in-the-afternoon
     'Kaywerye said he will come later, in the afternoon.'

  d. **nomokno Nonato, Manawsɨ hoye, thetx   yakoro**
     he-came Nonato Manaus from his-wife with
     'Nonato has come from Manaus with his wife.'

  e. **ohxe harha wehxaha, Nonato wya rohtxemanɨr ke,**
     good again I-am   Nonato by treating-me because

    ɨwya   rathonɨr   ke
    by-him injecting-me because
    'I am well again because Nonato treated me
     with an injection.'

  f. **ɨnomyako ɨto, Waraka mɨn   yawo**
     I-left-it there Waraka house-of in
     'I left it there in Waraka's house.'

  g. **amna   nahatakeko, owto   hona, ɨsna   ɨpaha**
     we-EXCL came-out   village to   to-there let's-go

    katxhɨr   hona amna   wya
    saying-it-PAST to   we-EXCL by
    'We arrived at the village, at the place we
     said we were going to.'

  h. **hawana komo ryhe nehxatxkonɨ, ohxehra, ekeh**
     visitor COLL EMPH they-were   not-good sick-one

    me
    DENOMLZR
    '(It was) the visitors (who) were not well,
     (who were) sick.'

There are two basic discourse functions that paratactic constructions usually have: (i) they introduce some degree of redundancy and thus slow down the rate of new information (compare one of the functions of rhetorical questions described in 12.2.2); and (ii) they clear up possible ambiguities in the preceding discourse. They also fulfill more specific functions and substitute for other types of construction that occur in many languages. There are at least four such functions:

(1) They permit a sequence of APs in a single clause. It is in this function that they could be said to have more than one grammatical relation in that clause. (I regard the constituent as a single complex adjunct, but it could be argued that the separate phrases form a sequence of two or more distinct adjuncts.) One example of this function is seen in (183d), and another is the following:

(184) **waywɨ yeryeye   toto, warata hona, karye**
      arrow he-put-it person shelf onto high
      'The man put the arrows on the shelf, high up.'

Although this kind of sequence is well-formed, there is a preference to have two separate sentences and to repeat the verb:

(185) **waywɨ yeryeye   toto, warata hona. karye neryeye**
      arrow he-put-it person shelf onto high he-put-it
      'The man put the arrows on the shelf.
       He placed them high up.'

Any type of adverbial, including PPs and subordinate clauses, may occur in this adverbial phrase function.

(2) This is the primary means of phrase coordination. Certain Prt may also be used, e.g., **xarha** 'ADDITIVE', **komo** 'COLLECTIVE'; and the R **yakoro** 'with, accompanying' may be added. But none of these is obligatory. The mere juxtaposition of phrases can be used to express the coordinating relationship:

(186) a. **towenyxa nehxakonɨ, ɨyonɨ,   ɨmryerɨ, noro ymo**
         one   it-was   his-mother her-son he   AUG
         'It was one (family), the mother, her son,
           and the big bad (jaguar-man).'

      b. **namryehtxowɨ   Waraka komo, Kaywerye xarha,**
         they-went-hunting Waraka COLL Kaywerye also

         Mahxawa xarha
         Mahxawa also
         'Waraka, Kaywerye, and Mahxawa have gone hunting.'

c. **ɨto   rye   rma   nehxatxkonɨ, Wanawa heno,**
there TOGETHER SAME they-were   Wanawa dead

Txawa yakoro
Txawa with
'The late Wanawa and Txawa used to live together.'

d. **amnyehra htxero haka ɨtoye, Mutuma hona, Kasawa**
past   first   then I-went Mutuma to   Kasawa

hona (xarha)
to   (also)
'Long ago that very first time I went to
Mutuma and to Kasawa.'

(3) The head-modifier relationship can be expressed. This often includes a phrase with a derived nominal functioning as a relative clause (see 12.2.5). It also includes simple NPs and adverbials:

(187) a. **romɨn   hoko   rakoronometxoko, hawana komo,**
my-house occ.-with they-helped-me visitor COLL

enyhoru komo
good-one COLL
'Those good visitors helped me build my house.'

b. **oyoro   ɨnyahtxoko, mokyamo,   temenyem   komo**
from-here send-them those-people one-who-steals COLL
'Send those people who steal away from here.'

c. **Fumasa hona ntetxoko, karyhe, ɨhorohpɨra**
Fumaça to   they-went fast   not-stopping
'They went to Fumaça quickly, without stopping.'

(4) Each successive phrase in the sequence may add a degree of specification concerning the entity in focus. This is the function of clarification often associated with afterthought pat- terns. It is also similar to the head-modifier function just discussed, but it can usually be distinguished from it by the following characteristics: (i) the specification often moves from anaphors to fuller identifying expressions; (ii) synonyms or near synonyms are frequently used; and (iii) in other cases the progression is from general to more specific expressions of reference:

(188) a. **wewe yamaxe   nɨnyahtxowɨ, noro, horykomo,**
tree PURP-to-fell he-sent-them he   adult-man

owto   yohɨ
village chief-of
'The chief (referred to earlier) has sent them
to fell trees.'

b. **naryako   ɨsna,   nɨmno ymo yaka, ohsamnohno**
   he-took-it to-there house AUG to   people-gathering

   ytxoho   yaka
   do-'PLACE' NOMLZN to
   'He took it there, to the big house, the
   place where people meet together.'

c. **wɨmyako, ɨwya, Waraka wya, ɨsna   anɨr   horɨ,**
   I-gave-it to-him Waraka to   to-there taking-it PURP

   Manawsɨ hona rokaryehtanɨ yanɨr   horɨ
   Manaus   to   my-letter   taking-of PURP
   'I gave it to him, to Waraka, so he could take
   it, my letter, to Manaus.'

In (188c) there are three distinct sequences relating to different referents: **Waraka** further specifies the prefix **ɨ-** in **ɨwya**; **Manawsɨ** identifies the prefixal element in **ɨsna**; and **rokaryehtanɨ** specifies the prefix **∅** in **anɨr** and also the direct object element in the portmanteau prefix **w-** 'lSlllO' in the main verb **wɨmyako**. All these examples illustrate how this pattern of specification results in a considerable amount of backward anaphora (see 13.5).

Grimes (1975.92-93) has proposed a generalization, based on a pattern that is frequent across languages:

> An identification span consists of a series of identifications of the same participant, not necessarily in contiguous clauses, in which no identification is stronger than the one before it. Strength of identification is a ranking that goes from proper names like <u>George Washington Carver</u> to explicit descriptives like <u>the mechanic who fixed our generator in Arkansas</u> to common <u>nouns like the teacher</u> to nouns used generically like <u>the fellow</u> to pronouns like <u>him</u>, and from there to reference without identification.

The generalization that "no identification is stronger than the one before it" clearly does not apply in Hixkaryana, where the ranking often goes the other way, as seen in the foregoing examples (it also often applies across sentence boundaries, i.e., from less specific to more specific forms of identification--see Derbyshire (1977c) for fuller discussion, and see 13.6).

Discontinuous paratactic constructions also frequently occur, where either (i) the first phrase in a paratactic sequence of Subject noun phrases, or Adjunct adverbial phrases, is fronted for emphasis, and the other phrase(s) in the sequence remain in the postverbal position, or (ii) the first phrase in a Direct Object or (copular) Complement sequence of phrases remains in the normal preverbal position, and the other phrase(s) in the sequence are placed after the verb (see 7.4):

(189) a. **noro mah   tɨ   nawotoy   ha,   tukusu**
       he ADVERS HSY he-cut-it INTENSFR hummingbird
       'But he cut it, the hummingbird.'

   b. **oroke   nomokyako,   royarɨhnawo**
      yesterday   he-came   in-my-absence
      'He came yesterday when I wasn't here.'

   c. **hawana heno komo yonyekon   hatɨ,**
      visitor dead COLL he-ate-them HSY

      amryehxemo   komo
      ones-that-went-hunting   COLL
      'He (jaguar-man) used to eat the visitors
       who had gone hunting.'

   d. **kuraha tho   tɨ   hnɨnkaye   waywɨ heno komo**
      bow   DEVLD HSY he-put-it-down arrow set COLL
      'He put down the bow and set of arrows.'

   e. **tawasnye roro nehxakonɨ, ɨkokmampɨra**
      light   PERM it-was   not-getting-dark
      'It was light all the time, never getting dark.'

The same range of functions applies to discontinuous as to other paratactic sequences. Thus in (189c) there is a head-modifier relationship, in (189d) a coordinate relation, and in the others an increasing degree of specification. Burgess (1976) reports an almost identical pattern of discontinuous parataxis for (?OSV) Xavante. She describes it in terms of new and given information: new primary information normally occurs clause initial, but it can occur in a discontinuous sequence, with one phrase in the initial position and a right-dislocated phrase in clause-final position, for purposes of coordination, modification or additional specification; given information which takes the form of an anaphor in the early part of the clause may also have a full identifying phrase in a right-dislocated, clause-final position.

The modification and specification functions are also sometimes expressed by a special type of paratactic construction that crosses clause and sentence boundaries: the subject of one clause may be modified or further identified by an equative clause that immediately follows that first clause, either alone, or as the embedded subject of a copular clause (the embedded construction is described in 5.2):

(190) **nemokotoye omɨnɨthɨrɨ.   horyetho ymo monɨ (nehxakonɨ)**
      it-fell   your-house-PAST big-one AUG that (it-was)
      'That great big old house of yours collapsed.'

12.2.5 Nominalizations. The language is rich in derivational morphology resulting in either full nominals, i.e., N (see Appendix

F), or pseudonominals, i.e., A (see Appendix G), which function as Adjunct or (copula) Complement but have some of the properties of N, e.g., the same set of person-marking prefixes. Many of these forms are derived from V stems and then their primary function is as the nuclear constituent of a nonfinite subordinate clause (see chap. 4). A few of the derivations, both full nominals and pseudonominals, also function as pseudopassives (see 9.4).

There are two other general ways in which full nominals function to substitute for constructions that are lacking in the language:

(1) They replace finite complement clauses, including indirect statements and the complements of cognitive verbs:

(191) a. **tɨtonɨrɨ yokarymano rowya**
his-going he-told-it to-me
'He told me about his going' or
'He told me he was leaving.'

b. **monyero karyeno ymo yomoknɨrɨ wenytxehe**
from-over-there high-thing AUG coming-of I-hear-it
'I hear the airplane coming from over there.'

c. **ekeh me ryehtxoho muhutwehe**
sick-one DENOMLZR my-being-'THING' NOMLZN you-know-it
'You know about my being sick' or
'You know that I am sick.'

d. **Waraka totho hutwahra wahko**
Waraka his-going-'THING' NOMLZN not-knowing I-was
'I did not know that/when/where Waraka was going.'

The foregoing are examples of object complements. Derived nominals also function as subject complement clauses:

(192) **Mahxawa wya owto yoh yameryekanɨrɨ, ryeryehokehe**
Mahxawa by village chief-of disputing-with it-troubles-me
'That Mahxawa is disputing with the chief bothers me.'

There are other examples of this complement function of derived nominals in 4.4.

(2) They replace finite relative clauses and also function in a more general way as nominal modifiers. In this function they usually form part of a paratactic construction, following the noun they modify:

Major Differences   137

(193) a. **tɨywero natxow   hamɨ   bɨryekomo komo,**
          clever they-are DEDUCT child   COLL

   ɨhanánɨhxemo   komo
   ones-who-were-taught COLL
   'The children who have been getting taught
    are evidently clever.'

  b. **kuryetxetxe xe   wehxaha, tutxuryemɨ**
      seed-bead   desirous-of I-am   red-thing
      'I want red seed beads.'

  c. **woto tɨmko   rowya, onwothɨrɨ**
      game give-it to-me   thing-shot-by-you
      'Give me (some of) the meat you shot.'

  d. **nomohtxownɨ Wayway komo. Ewka nɨnyaketxko rma**
      they-came   Waiwai COLL Ewka one-sent-by SAME

   mokyamo (nehxatxkonɨ)
   those   (they-were)
   'Some Waiwai came who were sent by Ewka.'

In (193d), there is another example of the use of the paratactic equative clause that can occur alone or as the embedded subject of a copular clause (see 12.2.4, last paragraph). Derived nominals also frequently occur as headless relatives, often as the predicate nominal in an equative clause, but also as any other clause or phrase constituent where a noun phrase can occur:

(194) a. **ronɨnyaknyɨrɨ   mosonɨ**
          one-being-sent-by-me this-one
          'This is the one I am going to send.'

  b. **ɨnyahmatxoko, wewe yamanyenhɨyamo**
      feed-them   tree ones-who-have-felled
      'Feed the men who have been felling the trees.'

  c. **kanawa yakatxho   xe   nay   hatɨ**
      canoe thing-for-hollowing-out desirous-of he-is   HSY
      'He says he wants the adze for canoe making.'

12.2.6 Sentence negation. In 11.2.5 I cite an example of a negative sentence to show how Hixkaryana generally follows the pattern predicted by Greenberg's universals 13 and 16, relative to the position of subordinate verb forms and inflected auxiliary verbs in (S)OV languages. In other ways Hixkaryana negative sentences seem to provide counterexamples to some hypotheses recently proposed as language universals. I begin this discussion with a simple sentence involving the negation of a transitive verb (195b), with its positive counterpart first shown in (195a):

(195) a. **apaytara yarɨye   wekoko**
chicken he-took-it hawk

(y-   arɨ- ye)
(IIISIIIO-take-DIST.PAST COMPL)
'The hawk took the chicken.'

b. **apaytara yarhɨra   nexeye wekoko**
chicken not-taking it-was hawk

(y- arɨ-hɨra n-   exe-ye)
(III-take-NEG IIIS-be- DIST.PAST COMPL)
'The hawk didn't take the chicken.'

The essential changes in the negative construction are: the main verb **-arɨ-** 'take' has the form of a derived A with a nominal POSSESSOR prefix **y-** 'III', and the derivational suffix **-hɨra** 'NEGATIVE'; and finite elements are in the inflected copula **nexeye**, to which the derived A and its (object) possessor **apaytara** function as complement.

Dahl (1979) makes a number of generalizations based on a study of negative constructions in 240 languages. Some of them fit the pattern of Hixkaryana sentence negation, but two of them significantly do not. First, he states (p. 85):

> [The 'Dummy Auxiliary'] construction can ... be exemplified from English ... the Neg particle not [and] an auxiliary verb does which does not appear in the affirmative sentences. This construction is not very frequent, but it does occur in a few other languages .... No language seems to use this as the only way of constructing negative sentences.

The Hixkaryana copula, with its marking of the finite elements, is equivalent to the "dummy auxiliary" (other similarities between English and Hixkaryana negative constructions are discussed later in this section). In Hixkaryana, however, unlike English and the other languages to which Dahl refers, this dummy auxiliary construction is the only way to form a negative sentence.

Dahl goes on to discuss an example from Japanese of an irregular negative formation (the form he cites is **kaimasen desita**), where a nonfinite verb form with the negative suffix is followed by a finite form of the copula. With reference to this he makes a statement which he evidently intends to support another generalization (pp. 9-10):

> The resulting form is unusual in that the Neg morpheme does not adhere to the word which is most naturally regarded as the finite element. It is hardly motivated, however, to regard this as a separate Neg 'construction'; rather it seems

Major Differences   139

that tense-marking operates on something that has already
been marked as negative. Similar examples can be found in
other languages.

The central claim here seems to be that a negative morpheme attaches to the finite element of the sentence (like English didn't
go, etc.). Hixkaryana is also a counterexample to this claim,
since the negative morpheme is obligatorily tied phonologically to
the nonfinite element. It is the subject of morphophonological
rules which apply only to morpheme boundaries within the word--
see Appendix A.4.

I am indebted to Geoffrey Pullum for suggesting the lines of
enquiry that result in the following additional observations on
negation (see also Pullum 1980 for more detailed discussion, with
exemplification from Hixkaryana).

The Hixkaryana negative sentence is the exact mirror image of
the equivalent English sentence. In view of the many possibilities
available for negative formation (per Dahl, and others) this is a
rather striking reflection of the mirror image relation of their
respective basic word orders: OVS and SVO. In the surface negative
forms the relationship can be obscured by the fact that the
negative morpheme attaches to the nonfinite verb in Hixkaryana,
and is either a separate particle or attaches to the finite
auxiliary in English. It is more clearly seen in the underlying
structures, which can be represented simply as follows:

(196) Hixkaryana: chicken - take -   NEG - V finite - hawk
      (195b)
      English: hawk -   V finite - NEG - take -   chicken
      'The hawk did not take the chicken.'

A more elaborate formulation of the underlying structure shows
that a Subject-to-Subject Raising rule is at work in Hixkaryana:

(197) [NEG [[apaytara -ari- wekoko] -exe-]]
           (chicken) (take) (hawk) (be)

To that deep structure the following rules are applied: S-to-S
Raising moves the subject **wekoko** into the higher clause, to the
right of the verb of that clause; the NEG morpheme is placed after
the leftmost verb in the sentence and attached to it morphologically; the tense-aspect suffix is attached to the verb in the
higher clause; and agreement rules apply in both clauses to add
the person-marking prefixes to their verbs. The following structure results:

(198) [[$_S$**apaytara y-ari-hira**] **n-exe-ye** [$_{NP}$**wekoko**]]

The proposed "trace theory of movement rules" (Chomsky 1977) would insert a trace (t) in the position occupied by **wekoko** before it was moved. The resulting linear relationship between the trace and the moved constituent is the reverse of that in the SVO languages to which trace theory has been mainly applied, and one might expect that the constraint regarding position of traces and moved phrases would be that the trace must <u>precede</u> the moved phrase in Hixkaryana. (This would parallel anaphoric constructions in the language like reflexives and Equi clauses, where the null anaphor <u>precedes</u> the antecedent.) That this is not so is seen by considering the application of the Question Word Fronting rule:

(199) a. [$_S$Q **apaytara yariye** [$_{NPx}$**onokɨ**]]
       chicken it-took-it   what

    b. [$_S$[$_{NPx}$**onokɨ**] **apaytara yariye** [$_{NPx}$t]]

    c. **onokɨ apaytara yariye**
       what   chicken it-took-it
       'What took the chicken?'

The trace in (199c) <u>follows</u> the moved phrase **onokɨ**, as shown in (199b). In fact, in a <u>negative</u> interrogative sentence one can see two traces of a single moved phrase, both following it:

(200) [$_S$[$_{NPx}$**onokɨ**] [$_S$ **apaytara yarhɨra** [$_{NPx}$t]] **nexeye** [$_{NPx}$t]]

This underlies the surface form shown in (201):

(201) **onokɨ apaytara yarhɨra**   **nexeye**
      what chicken not-taking it-was
      'What didn't take the chicken?'

Not only is the <u>NP ... trace</u> configuration of English nonuniversal, but no linear configuration can be universal given the Hixkaryana facts.

One further point concerning WH-Movement more generally is that Hixkaryana can be added to other languages that have been noted as undermining the proposed universal: "Move wh-phrase to COMP" (Chomsky 1977.72). In languages that do not have any kind of complement-marking particles (see 12.1 (2)) it seems strange to relate any WH-Movement rule to a COMP node. Cf. Epée (1976) on Duala and Bresnan's comment (1976.363) that it is "somewhat peculiar (to presuppose) the universality of a minor category of clause-marking particles not found in all languages."

12.2.7 Functions of wya and the status of indirect object. The relator **wya** 'to, by' marks the indirect object in a clause, but it also has other functions. The main purpose of this discussion is to suggest that the combined functions of **wya** indicate that, at least for Hixkaryana, there is a more fundamental grammatical relation involved than that of indirect object. This leads to consideration of the validity of the status of grammatical prime given to indirect object in the theory of Relational Grammar. Since, however, the position of indirect object has also been generally considered of some importance in the matter of the basic order of constituents, I first show what Hixkaryana has to contribute to this question.

As a subtype of adjunct (see 3.4), the normal position of indirect object is after the subject, so that the basic order is OVSI. Hixkaryana is, therefore, unlike Malagasy, whose unmarked order has subject in absolute clause-final position and indirect and oblique objects occurring between the object and the subject, i.e., VOXS (Keenan 1978.270; cf. Keenan 1976). This property of having subjects in absolute sentence-final position also pertains to several other VOS languages in Keenan's sample, but he describes two (Batak, p. 272; Gilbertese, p. 279) that have indirect object occurring after subject, just as in Hixkaryana.

The OSV language Apuriná also has indirect object in the clause-final position, which distinguishes it from more rigidly verb-final languages like Japanese and some other SOV languages.

The preferred final position of indirect object in Hixkaryana and some other subject-final languages is evidence against the restrictive theory of word orders proposed by Culicover and Wexler (1974), who predict (p. 19):

> In every language the syntactic subject must appear normally or strictly to the left of the indirect object, direct object and the verb, or to the right of all three.

Like other adjuncts (and also the subject), the indirect object can be placed in the clause-initial position by operation of the Emphasis Fronting rule (see 7.2 and 13.1). It also sometimes occurs between the verb and subject; in these cases the subject is usually a "heavy" construction:

(202) **nekarymetxkoni   Waraka wya, Ewka ninyaketxho komo**
they-were-telling-it Waraka to   Ewka one-sent-by COLL
'The ones sent by Ewka were telling Waraka about it.'

With reference to the status of indirect object as a grammatical prime, I suggested in 3.4 that there is no good reason for setting up indirect object as a separate clause constituent in Hixkaryana. The **wya**-phrase, when it functions as indirect object, has all the properties of any adjunct (which includes all PP, as well as AP and subordinate clauses). There are, however, many other functions that **wya**-phrases express, and it is difficult to analyze all of them as adjuncts. In particular, when they occur in transitive subordinate clauses to express the underlying subject role, they have special properties that do not apply in general to adjuncts: in Relational Grammar terms they represent an initial 1. (In the remainder of this section I use the R.G. notations 1 = subject, 2 = direct object, and 3 = indirect object.) These **wya**-phrases can trigger **tɨ**- reflexivization (see 8.2). They can be moved to the right of the (nominalized) verbal constituent of the subordinate clause (see 7.6). They can cooccur with another adjunct in the same subordinate clause (more often than in the case of 3 and other adjunct in a main clause), and then there is a preferred ordering pattern: A - **wya**S - O - (NOMLZD)V (see 4.5). Equi-NP Deletion rules operate to delete the **wya**-phrase when there is identity of reference between the 1 of the main and subordinate clauses (see 4.10).

A closer look at the various functions of **wya** suggests, in fact, the following hypothesis:

(203) In all occurrences, **wya** marks an initial 1.

It is most clearly seen in the marking of the 1 of a transitive subordinate clause (as noted above) and the causee in a transitive-causative construction. These two functions are discussed more fully in chap. 4 and 9.3 respectively, and illustrated below in (204a) and (204b). The other examples that follow cover the whole range of **wya** functions, and most of these are discussed and/or exemplified in other parts of this description, as follows: (204c) recipient function (3.4); (204d) addressee function (3.4); (204e) source (or ultimate cause) function (3.4, (39c)); (204f) cognizer function (12.1 (2)); and (204g) benefactee function (see also 1.4 for examples of most of these functions):

(204) a. **rowya wewe yamatxhe,   ɨtehe harha owto   hona**
by-me tree after-felling I-go back village to
'After felling the tree I will go back to the village.'

b. **tkaryehtanɨ yarhoye   Kaywerye rohetxe wya**
his-letter   he-caused-to-take-it Kaywerye my-wife by
'Kaywerye had my wife take his letter.'

c. **otweto yɨmyakonɨ   rohetxe totokomo wya**
hammock she-gave-it my-wife people   to
'My wife used to give hammocks to the people.'

d. **awanaworo tamryekyatxhe kekonɨ   Kaywerye**
tomorrow we-INCL-hunt   he-said-it Kaywerye

towtɨ   komo wya
his-brother COLL to
'"We will go hunting tomorrow," said Kaywerye to his brothers.'

Major Differences   143

> e. **namotohyaha romuru atunano wya**
>   he-is-weak my-son fever by
>   'My son is weak with fever.'
>
> f. **ɨsoke ryhe weryano owyanye**
>   how EMPH I-fix-it by-you-COLL
>   'What do you think I should do?'
>
> g. **baf txe,   kay   hatɨ, waywɨ, ɨwya**
>   flight-of-arrow it-did-it HSY   arrow for-him
>
>   **kahe hoko**
>   sky occ.-with
>   'The arrows flew through the air and hit the sky
>   for him' (i.e., to make a path for him). (From
>   a folktale, Derbyshire 1965.24)

In each case, it is at least conceivable that the NP marked by **wya** could be analyzed as an initial 1. This is fairly clear in the case of (a) because it is part of a complete (subordinate) clause. It is possible to clarify the nature of the semantic relation involved in each of the other sentences, by adding a subordinate clause of which the **wya**-phrase is a constituent:

(204) b' ... **rohetxe wya anɨr   me**
              my-wife by taking-it DENOMLZR
          '... my wife taking it'

   c' ... **totokomo wya ahosnɨr   me**
              people   by taking-hold-of-it DENOMLZR
          '... people receiving it'

   d' ... **towtɨ   komo wya enytxanɨr   me**
              his-brother COLL by hearing-it DENOMLZR
          '... his brothers hearing it'

   e' ... **atunano wya tahosnɨr   ke**
              fever   by taking-hold-of-him because
          '... because the fever caught him' (This is the
              natural Hixkaryana idiom, equivalent to the
              English he caught a cold.)

   f' ... **owyanye   uhutwanɨr   me**
              by-you-COLL thinking-it DENOMLZR
          '... in your thinking'

   g' ... **ɨwya   akmehtxoho   me**
              by-him PURP-of-stepping-on DENOMLZR
          '... for him to step on'

The subordinate clauses in (204b'-g') are all natural extensions of the **wya**-phrases in (204b-g), and seem to capture the underlying semantic content in each case. The **wya**-phrase in each clause represents an initial 1 relation, which in turn reflects a semantic relation "agent" (in Hixkaryana culture this includes certain personified inanimate concepts like **atunano** 'fever', as in (204e')). This is in keeping with a principle formulated in one treatment of Relational Grammar (Frantz 1979.67) as:

Universality of initial termhood: Initial GR's are predictable from semantic relations.

(Frantz (1981.77) subsequently modified this by adding: "Apparently much too strong".) For a discussion on the importance of this principle, see Rhodes (1977.508-10) and for its application to a specific hypothesis, Perlmutter (1978.185).

Relational grammar also, however, assumes that 3 is a universal grammatical relation, on a par with 1 and 2 (Perlmutter and Postal 1977.402). In most RG treatments these three are considered the most central relations, often referred to as the term relations (i.e., only 1, 2, and 3 are terms). Two reasons (among others) given for this basic assumption are that these three relations "most radically subcategorize verbs and are most frequently referred to by rules of grammar" (Frantz 1981.1). In Hixkaryana both claims hold for the 1 and 2 relations, but neither applies to the 3. There are other languages in which the relation sometimes referred to as "secondary agent" appears to be more significant than that of 3. Thus, for Japanese, Kuno states (1978.109):

... the **ni** used both as a dative marker and as a passive agentive marker has the characteristic that it marks a secondary agent.

He goes on to show that the same marker is also used in causatives and certain other constructions where it clearly represents secondary agent. And Faltz (1978) has argued that the syntactic category corresponding to the traditional concept of indirect object is "not a uniform syntactic category for all languages." The notion of 3 as a basic primitive for Hixkaryana syntax certainly seems unmotivated.

Even for English, some analysts (e.g., Postal) would probably be prepared to posit an initial-stratum 1 relation for every case of a **wya**-phrase in (204). In (204c), for example, the verb 'give' would be analyzed into CAUSE and HAVE, with **totokomo wya** the initial 1 of HAVE.

For the moment I leave open the question whether the **wya**-phrase in Hixkaryana calls for a separate final grammatical relation (i.e., 3) distinct from adjunct. I regard it certainly as representing an initial 1 relation, but am content (though not entirely satisfied) to regard the surface form as a subtype of adjunct, which corresponds to a (nonterm) oblique object in Relational Grammar.

13 Discourse-related Phenomena

In this chapter I discuss other characteristic features of Hixkaryana relating to the discourse and pragmatic conditions that govern the occurrence of particular syntactic patterns and processes. In doing so I shall, in effect, be attempting to describe the "systematic constraints [that] exist across sentence boundaries" (Chafe 1970.95). Some of the processes, such as topicalization, deletion, and pronominalization, have been described in typological studies (see, for example, Lehmann, ed., 1978.25, 127-37). Other phenomena have not been prominent in works on typology, but are receiving increasing attention in other areas of the literature: the concepts of "new" and "given" information; the rate at which new information is introduced into a discourse; focus and thematic prominence; primary (foreground) and secondary (background) information; the function of repetition in discourse (see among others, Chafe 1976, Grimes 1975, Halliday and Hasan 1976, Longacre (ed.) 1976b and 1977, Pickering 1977). The ways in which these processes and phenomena are realized in Hixkaryana seem to be related, in varying degrees, to the basic order of constituents in the sentence, and especially to the final position of the subject. In some cases they provide counterexamples to generalizations that have been proposed on the basis of studies that have not included any object-initial/subject-final languages.

13.1 Focus and emphasis. I specify here the discourse-pragmatic conditions under which the Emphasis Fronting rule operates (see 7.2). In Derbyshire 1977b I referred to this rule as a Topicalization Fronting rule, using the term most frequently found in the literature to refer to this process. I have changed the term, primarily because I use the term topic in another sense (see 13.3), but also because it seems to me that topicalization is a misnomer for something that relates to both new and given information and is primarily a matter of focus or emphasis. I use these latter two terms interchangeably. The term emphasis is most prominent in Derbyshire 1979; but focus is the term more generally used for the phenomenon I describe here (e.g., Keenan 1978.293; Chafe 1976). Chafe's distinction is particularly relevant: "the status focus of contrast is different from the status new" (1976.38). This applies in Hixkaryana, where the fronted constituent can be either given or new information, and where new information (as well as given) can also occur later in the clause, i.e., in postverbal, and even right-dislocated, position. Thus, for example, the subject normally occurs after the verb and may contain either given (see 13.2) or new information (as in many discourse-initial sentences, see 10.2 and fuller discussion in Derbyshire 1977b.597), but if that information is being given any sort of focus it is moved to the sentence-initial position. There is no special stress or intonation on constituents that undergo this process.

Adjuncts as well as subjects can be fronted for emphasis. It is possible to specify four pragmatic or discourse-related conditions under which this fronting process operates:

(1) New information highlighting. This frequently occurs in the discourse-initial sentence, but can occur elsewhere when a new item is introduced, or when an item previously introduced is reinstated as the item in focus. (Many of the examples in this sentence are taken from Derbyshire 1965 and [Derbyshire] 1976, where the fuller discourse context in which they occur can be seen; references that follow the citations are to these two works.)

(205) a. **murha tɨ natakɨhtoye, kɨrɨ hyaka**
frog HSY it-was-made male for
'The frog was made to become (a wife) for the man.' (1965.100)

b. **kurumyana   komo, xofrye heno**
buzzard-person COLL sloth dead

yanotometxkonɨ
they-made-a-servant-of-him
'The buzzard people used to make a slave of the sloth.' (1965.28)

c. **meku   tɨ nomokye ha,   ɨhyaka**
species-of-monkey HSY it-came INTENSFR to-her
'A monkey came up to her.' (1965.44)

d. **ɨnyo   tɨ nenyakon   ha**
her-husband HSY he-was-seeing-it INTENSFR
'Her husband was watching it.' (1965.45)

In (205), examples (a) and (b) are discourse initial and (c) and (d) are discourse medial. In (c), **meku** is a newly introduced character, while in (d) the referent of **ɨnyo** has been introduced earlier, but is out of focus in the immediately preceding context.

(2) Anaphoric focusing. This occurs when an anaphor is fronted for emphasis and its antecedent (or another anaphor of it) is in

Discourse-related Phenomena

the immediately preceding sentence. The anaphor most commonly functioning in this way is **noro** 'III NONDEICTIC'. The anaphoric particle **rma** 'SAME REFERENT' also often occurs in a fronted phrase with this function:

(206) a. **ɨto tɨ nehxakon ha kamara yohɨ. noro tɨ**
there HSY he-was INTENSFR jaguar chief-of he HSY

nonyetxkon ha. hawana heno komo yonyetxkonɨ
he-ate-them INTENSFR visitor dead COLL he-ate-them
'The jaguar chief was there. He used to eat them. He used to eat the visitors.' (1965.109)[5]

b. ... **mana yonahyatxkon hatɨ, ohoryen heno komo.**
manna they-ate-it HSY your-ancestor dead COLL

mana yonahneynhɨrɨ rma, wayehtxownɨ hatɨ
manna one-who-had-eaten-it SAME they-died HSY
'Your ancestors ate manna. Those same manna-eaters died.' (1976.476)

Where the pronoun **noro,** or its collective counterpart **nyamoro,** occurs in the normal subject position, i.e., after the verb, the antecedent does not occur in the preceding sentence (at least as subject of that sentence), but in an earlier part of the discourse. These two contrasting positions of the third person pronoun indicate whether or not the same character is in focus as in the preceding sentence.

Certain link words and phrases, whose normal position is sentence initial, can also be regarded as examples of anaphoric focusing. These include **oske** 'thus', **ɨro ke** 'because of that, therefore', **onɨ wyaro** 'like this', **ɨto** 'there'. These sentence constituents are syntactically adjuncts, and the more typical position for adjuncts is sentence final:

(207) **oske tɨ nenɨhtotxownɨ**
thus HSY they-got-them-down
'That is how they got them down.' (1965.14)

Sentence connectives of this kind frequently refer to a sequence of sentences in the preceding context (or in the following context where **onɨ** 'this' is a part of the connective phrase), and not just to the preceding sentence (see 13.4).

(3) Contrastive emphasis. The contrast may be either with something in the preceding context or of a more general kind, where the focus is placed on one of a set of possible candidates. Parti-

---

[5] In the text as published there was an error to which my informant, Kaywerye, drew my attention later: the printed text shows the verb in the second sentence as **yonyetxkonɨ**, but it should be **nonyetxkon(ɨ)** as shown above.

cles such as **haxa** 'CONTRAST' and **ryhe** 'EMPHASIS' often occur in phrases fronted for this purpose:

(208) a. **enytxahra   nehtxownɨ ... yɨrɨsɨ   nenytxay**
not-hearing-it they-were ... cricket   it-heard-it

  ha
  INTENSFR
  'They (people) didn't hear it .... The crickets heard it.' (1965.25)

  b. **Moyses henohnɨ   nɨmyakonɨ, nyamoro heno wya. Royɨm**
  Moses dead-NEG   he-gave-it them   dead to   my-father

  haxa uyuru   komo yɨmyakonɨ
  CONTR their-bread COLL he-gave-it
  'It was not Moses, but my Father, who gave them their bread.' (1976.474)

When a nominal constituent has the suffix **hɨnɨ** 'NEGATION', as in (208b), it is always fronted for contrastive emphasis, so both sentences in that example have constituents fronted under the same conditions.

(4) Redundancy emphasis. This involves repetition of the same word, or a synonym, in the special redundancy unit I call sentence cluster (see 13.6). It consists of a sequence of two or more sentences, each of which contains the same information. One item may be singled out for emphasis by fronting it in the second (or subsequent) sentence of the sequence:

(209) a. **tomyarke rma tɨ nehxakonɨ, watma hnɨnkahra.**
carrying SAME HSY he-was   club not-putting-it-down

  watma hnɨnkahra   nehxakonɨ
  club not-putting-it-down he-was
  'He was still carrying it, not putting down the club. He did not put down the club.' (1965.112)

  b. **noseryehyakon mak   hatɨ, ɨhona.   tehurkanɨr**
  he-was-afraid ADVERS HSY   towards-it his-falling

  hona   nenyakonɨ
  towards he-saw-it
  'He was afraid of (falling). He was watching out lest he fall.' (1965.13)

The direct object, which normally occurs before the verb, can be considered the unmarked form of emphasis. This is consonant with the fact that a noun phrase object usually occurs only when it is being highlighted or is introducing new information, and is omitted at other times, leaving only the person marker in the verb (see 3.3). A direct object noun phrase can also be marked for emphasis by having one of the appropriate particles added:

(210) **yawaka ryhe wimyako, Waraka wya**
 axe   EMPH I-gave-it Waraka to
 'It was the axe I gave to Waraka.'

Constituent emphasis in Hixkaryana combines two separate functions which Dik has postulated as part of the predication proper in his Functional Grammar model (1978.127ff.), i.e., Topic and Focus, both of which are closely associated with the clause-initial position (p. 178). (There are two other pragmatic functions in Dik's model: left-dislocated Theme, which is equivalent to my "frame-of-reference" topic (see 13.3) and right-dislocated Tail, which is similar to some uses of right-dislocated paratactic constructions in Hixkaryana (see 12.2.4).) Dik distinguishes Topic and Focus (p. 130):

> A constituent with Topic function presents the entity 'about' which the Predication predicates something in the given setting. A constituent with Focus function presents the relatively most important or salient information with respect to the pragmatic information of the Speaker and the Addressee.

In Hixkaryana, Topic (in the Dik sense) does not seem to have any syntactic significance except when it is fronted for emphasis, and it is then (syntactically) identical with Focus. (Topic in this sense does not seem to have any relevance at all in the grammar; either it is fronted, in which case it merges with Focus, or it is not fronted, in which case it is normally the same as the Subject constituent and does not give rise to any special function--see 13.2.)

The constituent that is fronted for emphasis may be left-dislocated (see 7.3 and some of the examples earlier in this section), and this also distinguishes it from Dik's Topic and Focus functions. Hixkaryana does, however, correspond with what Dik terms the "general pattern" for fronted constituents, i.e., that where a designated category of constituents (e.g., question word) is fronted, there is no possibility of fronting any Topic or Focus constituent (pp. 178-79). In discussing question-word fronting for subject-final languages, Keenan also speculates that there is this close link between focused constituents and question words, and suggests a generalization that would embrace both types of constituent (Keenan 1978.293):

> ... focused, or relatively new, information is fronted.

Subject-final Hixkaryana certainly fulfills that prediction, and the implication it contains (made explicit by Dik) that a sentence will not have both a question word and a (nonquestion) focused constituent.

The Focus constituent in subject-final (VOS) Mezquital Otomi (drawn to my attention by Keenan's summary (Keenan 1978.282; Hess 1968.80-81)) seems to be very similar to the Hixkaryana fronted constituent:

> Focus indicates to the listener by a shift of the item from postnuclear to prenuclear that the speaker is shifting attention to something not already calling for special attention in the preceding clauses.

There is an implication that this constituent may be given or new information, as in Hixkaryana, and it can apply to any major noun phrase.

Burgess (1976) reports a complex system of information and topical structure for Xavante (?OSV), but there are some marked similarities with Hixkaryana. The unmarked position for new information is clause initial; a constituent which establishes a new topic for the following discourse takes precedence over other new information in the clause-initial position; that position may also be occupied by a constituent that is given information, if it reintroduces a topic or situation already mentioned; and new information can also occur following the verb, under stated conditions (see also 12.2.4 and 13.2).

Subject-fronting for emphasis in object-initial languages is to some extent the counterpart of object-fronting devices like passivization in verb-initial and subject-initial languages. There is no need to front the object, since it is already clause initial in the unmarked pattern. This accounts for the lack of passive constructions in object-initial languages (see 11.3).

13.2 Theme-rheme (given-new information). In this section I show that Hixkaryana provides a direct counterexample to those theories standardly attributed to the "Prague School" which assume that thematic elements of "given" information occur before "rhematic" elements of "new" information in the unmarked sentence. A short sequence from a Hixkaryana text is given to demonstrate how thematic constituents interact with the focused constituents described in the preceding section.

It was an axiom of the early Prague School that languages generally make thematic material initial and rhematic material final in sentences, and by thematic material was meant that which conveys "known" or "given" information (see Firbas 1966 for a summary of the work of some linguists of that school). Firbas has introduced more flexibility into the whole theme-rheme concept by his principle of communicative dynamism (CD) (see, for example, his 1971 paper), including degrees of thematicity and rhematicity, and another element between theme and rheme called "transition." He also recognizes that thematic material is not always first in the sentence, but he evidently regards placement of rhematic material initially (and the consequent placement of thematic material later) in the sentence as a deviation from the norm. This is reflected in his statements about "the basic distribution of CD" (1971.138, 143):

> A sequence showing a gradual rise in degrees of CD (i.e., starting with the lowest degree and gradually passing on to the highest degree) can be regarded as displaying the basic distribution of CD. I also believe to be right in assuming that this conclusion is quite in harmony with the character of human apprehension.
>
> ... the tendency towards the basic distribution of CD is borne out by the described interplay of means of FSP, which either permits the basic distribution of CD to assert itself, or prevents it from functioning but signals the deviations.

Halliday (1967) uses the theme-rheme concept rather differently from the Prague School (including Firbas), by separating it completely from the given-new distinction (p. 205). For him "the theme is what comes first in the clause." Gundel (1974) proposes a "topic-comment" distinction, in which the topic is "known" information and is the "starting point of the sentence," i.e., the conceptual starting point, which is frequently, but not necessarily, the first constituent in surface structure. Lyons (1977) sums up these emphases on the relation of theme and topic to sentence-initial constituents (p. 507):

> The theme ... is the expression used by the speaker for what he announces as the topic of his utterance .... Not surprisingly there is a very high correlation, not only in English, but in all languages, between occupying initial position in the utterance and being thematic.

The influence of such work is seen in the assumptions that are made in typological studies. For example, Kuno says about Japanese (1978.58):

> Ordinarily, constituents that represent older information precede those that represent newer information.

In the same volume Keenan, seeking to explain the scarcity of subject-final languages, concludes (1978.305):

> Subjects usually come first because they are the topics of the least-marked sentences in a language. And topics in gen-

eral come first because they determine the relevance of what is said for the addressee.

Hixkaryana displays a completely different basic pattern with respect to the interplay of theme-rheme (topic-comment) and given-new information. The constituent that primarily carries unmarked theme is the subject, and this normally follows the verb (and object). In Firbas's terms, the greatest degree of communicative dynamism is carried in Hixkaryana by constituents that normally occur at the beginning of the clause; the basic distribution of CD is rheme-transition-theme, the reverse of what Firbas believes to be "in harmony with the character of human apprehension."

The factor that most influences both the thematic and syntactic ordering of constituents in Hixkaryana (and in all other OVS and OSV languages for which I have seen data and/or descriptions) is the subject and object agreement in the verb affix system. This allows null realization of pronominal subjects and objects in many sentences in all types of discourse. The important consequence with regard to thematic patterning is that the unmarked theme or topic is often expressed only in the verb prefix. (This is always "known" or "given" information in that it relates to either first or second person referents, which are clearly shared information on the part of speaker and addressee, or third person referents, which are usually recoverable from the discourse context, but may be shared information on other grounds, in the sense that it is "activated" in the consciousness of the addressee; see Chafe 1976 and Gundel 1977.)

Thematic patterning cannot be separated from the focus/emphasis process discussed in 13.1. The constituent fronted for emphasis is often "new" information, and therefore rhematic. But it may also be "given" information, and sometimes with a high degree of thematicity. In this latter case it is clearly a case of marked theme. The interplay of these patterns and process is in the following sequence from a text in Hixkaryana (from [Derbyshire] 1976.499, a translation of parts of verses 11 and 12 of chapter 10 of the Gospel of John. For clarity of exposition, some clauses and sentences which convey only background information have been omitted and the sentences are numbered for ease of reference):

(211) 1. **enyhoru ryhe, kahneru yonye ro rma,**
good-one EMPH sheep one-who-watches HABIT SAME

nosoxanomkahnohyan hamɨ, twayehso ro,
he-rejects-himself DEDUCT dying until

toknɨ kurunhonɨr horɨ
his-animal protecting-of PURP
'The good shepherd disregards himself to the point of dying in order to protect his sheep.'

Discourse-related Phenomena 153

2. **noro yanoto kom haxa ryhe, osoxanomkahnohpɨra**
   III servant-of COLL CONTR EMPH not-rejecting-self

   natxow hamɨ
   they-are DEDUCT
   'But his employees, in contrast, do not disregard themselves.'

3. **anatoko kamara yonyatxow hana**
   another-time jaguar they-see-him UNCERT
   'Perhaps they see a predator.'

4. **tɨwyanye xenyetxhe, nekahtɨmyatxhe**
   by-them after-seeing-it they-flee
   'When they see it, they flee.'

5. **kahneru tho komo nomyatxhe**
   sheep DEVLD COLL they-leave-them
   'They leave the sheep.'

6. **ɨro ke, kahneru tho yahohsaha, kamara**
   that because-of sheep DEVLD it-grabs-it jaguar
   'So the predator grabs the sheep.'

7. **natakhahyatxhe, kahneru tho komo, nyamoro**
   they-are-scattered sheep DEVLD COLL III-COLL

   yokahtɨmrɨ ke mak ha
   fleeing-of because-of ADVERS INTENSFR
   'The sheep are scattered because they fled when they shouldn't.'

The following analysis is largely restricted to main clause subject and object constituents. In every main clause except (2), the verbal element conveys relatively new information. In (1) the NP subject is new, emphatic, and a marked theme (it is also a complex paratactic construction). In (2) the NP subject (of a copular clause) is new, with contrastive focus and a marked theme. In (3) the subject is unmarked theme and is expressed only in the verb prefix, the noun phrase **(noro y)anoto komo** 'his employees' being omitted; the direct object NP **kamara** is expressed, being new information and the unmarked form of emphasis. In (4) the subject is again the same unmarked theme and is expressed only in the verb prefix (the whole subordinate clause is fronted for anaphoric focus, linking up with the immediately preceding main clause). In (5) the subject is the same unmarked theme and is again expressed only in the verb prefix. The direct object NP **kahneru tho komo** is expressed, being the unmarked form of emphasis (it is "given" information, having occurred earlier in the passage, but it is being reintroduced here). In (6) the subject is an NP after the verb; it is clearly given information and unmarked theme, but the identifying NP is added to the verb prefix to avoid possible ambiguity (which is a potential problem here, where there are four different third person referents in these two verses, and several others in the preceding context). The direct object in (6) is also expressed as a full NP to avoid ambiguity (it is also given information and can be regarded as a mild form of contrastive emphasis). In (7) the subject NP following the verb is again the unmarked theme.

Burgess (1976.1) shows that Xavante is strikingly similar to Hixkaryana in fundamental ways:

> The unmarked position for new information in the clause is the initial position. This affects the analysis of topical structure in that topic cannot be defined as the starting point of the clause if part of its definition is that it is given information and anaphoric in reference to which new information is attached by the comment.

Given information normally occurs within the predicate (p.7) (the predicate is defined as "that part of the clause which begins with the person-aspect proclitics and ends with the verb," p. 3). Given information can also precede the predicate when "reintroducing a topic or situation already mentioned but from which the narrator has digressed" (p. 8).

The placement of unmarked theme in the verb prefix and (optionally) in the NP subject that follows the verb supplements the evidence in 13.1, which shows that clause-initial constituents usually express new information or a marked theme (i.e., given information that is emphasized for some reason). The Xavante facts suggest that this unusual ordering of thematic elements may be characteristic of object-initial/subject-final languages.

13.3 Topic as "frame of reference". A different concept of topic from that referred to in 13.2 has received some attention in the literature and is, indeed, the central feature of another dimension that has been brought into typological discussions (Li and Thompson 1976). The best definition I have seen is that of Chafe (1976.51): "the frame within which the sentence holds," and he enlarges on it as follows (p. 50):

> What the topics appear to do is to limit the applicability of the main predication to a certain restricted domain .... Typically, it would seem, the topic sets a spatial, temporal, or individual framework within which the main predication holds.

Li and Thompson are mainly concerned with what they call "topic-prominent" languages in contrast with "subject-prominent" languages. A topic-prominent language is one in which the normal grammatical relation subject of is less significant than another relation: topic-comment. Topic-prominent languages include Chinese, Lahu, and Lisu. A few languages, including Japanese, are listed as both subject-prominent and topic-prominent.

Hixkaryana is not a topic-prominent language. A very large proportion of its sentences have only the normal grammatical relations of subject, direct object, and adjunct (including indirect object), without any separate (syntactic) categories such as topic or comment. There are some sentences, however, which have this "frame-of-reference" topic, a separate nominal phrase in a right-dislocated position, not having any normal grammatical relationship to the rest of the sentence:

(212) a. **txokororowe,   txokororowe   kekon   hatɨ,**
stomach-gurgling stomach-gurgling it-did-it HSY

    kamarayana   hosotɨ,   uhutwanɨr hatɨ
jaguar-person stomach-of knowing-it HSY
'(As an indication of their) knowing (the fact that someone was around), the jaguar people's stomachs were gurgling.' (The "knowing of it" is the topic established in the preceding discourse, and the rest of the sentence tells how the knowledge is expressed.) (Derbyshire 1965.46)

b. **ɨsna   rma txko tyufa   nkekonɨ,   oseryehrɨ**
to-there SAME DIMIN spitting she-did-it her-being-afraid
'(As an expression of) her being afraid, she was spitting into the little (pot).' (Derbyshire 1965.47)

    c. **koseryehyakonɨ, romryenɨ**
I-was-afraid   my-boyhood
'(With reference to) my boyhood, I used to be afraid.' (Derbyshire 1965.168)

The fact that Hixkaryana has this kind of topic construction is not surprising in view of the statement by Li and Thompson (1976.459): "All the languages we have investigated have the topic-comment construction." What is different about the Hixkaryana construction is the position the topic occupies. Nearly all who have discussed this question seem to be agreed that it invariably occurs in the sentence-initial position, e.g., Li and Thompson (1976.465):

It is worth noting that the surface coding of the topic in all languages we have examined always involves the sentence-initial position.

Nigel Vincent, in a paper presented at the Linguistic Association of Great Britain meeting at University College London in November

1977 ("Some issues in the theory of word order"), contrasted topic and subject properties, one of them being that, whereas subject is found in a number of different sentence positions, topic is "always sentence-initial" (from the handout). Dik's pragmatic function Theme includes occurrences where it "cannot be regarded as being part of a predication," and is thus equivalent to the concept of topic being discussed here; it always occurs in a left-dislocated sentence-initial position (Dik 1978.132ff.). Haiman (1978), after specifically referring to Chafe's notion of topic (p. 564), draws attention to: "the frequently noted characteristic of topics, and one which distinguishes them from subjects, is their tendency to occur sentence-initially" (p. 572). He then goes on to make a further observation:

> Contrastive topics tend to occur not only as the first constituents in their sentences, but as left-dislocated constituents.

The term contrastive topics tends to confuse the two notions I have tried to keep separate (and which Chafe distinguishes, 1976. 49-50): contrastive focus or emphasis (which includes marked theme) and "frame-of-reference" topic. In Hixkaryana, the contrastive focus constituent does occur sentence initial and is often left-dislocated, but the topic constituent being discussed in this section is always right-dislocated and sentence final. In this latter respect it cuts across a generalization that has seemingly come to be regarded as a universal characteristic of languages.

The VOS language, Mezquital Otomi, appears to have a frame-of-reference topic, which Hess (1968.81) describes as a focused topic:

> Topic is a special filler of focus in that the topic is composed of words and phrases that would not otherwise occur on the clause level.

There are, however, two major differences between Otomi and Hixkaryana: the Otomi topic is fronted, this being a characteristic of the Focus constituent; and, from an example cited by Hess, it seems that a modifier phrase can be extracted from a complex NP subject and moved to the Focus position with this topic function. The extraction of a constituent from a complex NP for the purpose of fronting as topic is also possible in Japanese (Kuno 1978.135).

13.4 Anaphora: sentence connectives and discourse particles. The form of sentence connectives and the function of discourse particles are primarily anaphoric. They are distinguished from other types of anaphora (see 13.5), however, since they also have non-anaphoric functions: both sentence connectives and discourse particles function as conjunctions, and discourse particles often have a more general pragmatic function.

13.4.1 Sentence connectives. Sentence connectives are the link words and phrases referred to in 13.1 (2). They usually occur sentence initial, and in most cases have as their anaphoric elements either a free form inanimate pronoun as the head word or a third person prefix in the head word: **ɨro wyaro** (III-NONDEICTIC-INANIMATE like) 'like that'; **ɨtoko** (III-SIMULTANEOUS) 'when it, at that time' (this is a highly idiosyncratic form, combining the third person nominal prefix with a derivational suffix--see Appendix G). Forms without any specific anaphoric element are the locative adverb **ɨto** 'there (medial-deictic)' (see 1.3) and **oske** 'thus, in that manner', which is formally related in an idiosyncratic way to the question word **ɨsoke** 'how?, in what manner?'. Their antecedents can be in the immediately preceding sentence:

(213) a. **nomokyaknano tuna heno. ɨro ke**
it-was-coming rain QUANT that because-of

   romararɨn hokohra wehxaknano
   my-field not-occ.-with I-was
   'It was raining heavily. Therefore I did
   not work on my field.'

b. **manhetxkonɨ totokomo. ɨtoko rma**
they-were-dancing people at-that-time SAME

   nomohtxownɨ hawana komo
   they-came visitor COLL
   'The people were dancing when the visitors arrived.'

c. **romɨn yawo amna nohsamnohyako. ɨto**
my-house in I+III gathered there

   amna nosonytxeko
   I+III heard-each-other
   'We met in my house and discussed things there.'

Often, however, these connectives refer back to cover a whole sequence of sentences in the preceding discourse. The following examples are from Derbyshire (1965):

(214) a. **oske rma nahayehkaye**
thus SAME he-caused-it-to-drop
'That's how he caused (the river level) to drop.'
(1965.29; this is sentence 29 in the text, and
oske refers back to the whole sequence from 19 to 28.)

b. **ɨro wyaro tɨ nehxatxkonɨ, kanye**
   that like HSY they-were   one-who-says-it

   mokɨ   nexey heno
   that-one he-was dead
   '"They were like that", (my) late (father) was the
   one who said it.' (1965.20, where the sentence
   comes at the end of a story and relates back to
   the whole preceding text.)

The deictic pronoun **onɨ** 'this thing' occurs in these link
phrases, and always has a forward reference, i.e., to something
that comes later in the discourse. (It can also occur sentence
initial with a normal deictic usage, when it refers to something
in the speaker-hearer situation, and not in the text itself.)

(215) **onɨ wyaro haxa neyukye   hatɨ, Txesusu**
      this like CONTR he-answered-him HSY Jesus
      'Jesus answered him like this.' ([Derbyshire] 1976.68;
      this sentence occurs in verse 48, and anticipates all
      the direct speech that follows in a sequence of sen-
      tences that continues through to verse 50.)

Some of these link phrases occur in formulaic clauses that often occur at intervals through a discourse and function at a
higher level to signal paragraph or episode breaks in the discourse. (See Grimes 1975.109-110 for a brief discussion of the
kind of signals used for such higher level divisions in discourse.) The most common of these formulas, which can be found
frequently in Derbyshire (1965) and (1976), are:

(216) a. **onɨ wyaro nkekonɨ**   b. **ɨro wyaro nkekonɨ**
         this like he-said-it   that like he-said-it
         'This is what he said.'   'That is what he said.'

      c. **ɨto   nehxakonɨ**   d. **ɨro wyaro nehxatxkonɨ**
         there he-was   that like they-were
         'There he was.'   'That is how they were.'

      e. **ɨro tɨ on(ɨ) ha**
         that HSY this INTENSFR
         'That (which precedes leads to) this (which follows).'

There are minor variations that add (or exclude) particles like **tɨ**
'HEARSAY' and components with the 'COLLECTIVE' meaning. The word
oske 'thus' seems to be interchangeable with **ɨro wyaro**. But
oske is more often used in each of a sequence of sentences, all
referring back to the preceding discourse. See, for example, such
sequences in Derbyshire 1965.13, 14; **oske** is also often used when
a nominalized form follows, as in the formula: **oske kanye mokɨ**

Discourse-related Phenomena   159

nexeye (thus one-who-said-it that-one he-was) 'he was the one who said thus.'

There is one other form that is used almost exclusively to signal a higher-level discourse break: **taa** 'O.K., let's move on.' It occurs sentence initial, but otherwise is more like a discourse particle in function. Some speakers use it much more often than others, and the informant who provided the texts for Derbyshire (1965) uses it sparingly; even so, examples can be seen on pp. 14, 19, 24, 30, 31, 39, and elsewhere. The same form **taa** is even more frequent in Waiwai discourse and with a similar function, described (in notes sent to me by courtesy of Robert Hawkins) as "a paragraph introducer and an event-line progression indicator."

13.4.2 Discourse particles. Discourse particles constitute one of the three groups of postpositional particles (see 1.5). They are an optional, peripheral element of the phrase (see chap. 2), always follow a head word of one of the four major word classes, V, N, A, or R, and can occur in particle sequences, in which case they usually follow modifying particles and precede verification particles (there can also be sequences of discourse particles). There is a complete list, with examples, and including some commonly recurring sequences, in Appendix J. Like verification particles (see 12.2.3), they have a general pragmatic function, but are distinct from both other sets of particles in that they most often have a discourse function, linking together sentences that may be juxtaposed or may be widely separated in the discourse, and sometimes, like sentence-connective phrases (13.4.1), signalling higher level divisions in the discourse. Their linking function may be either conjunctive (see 6.4) or anaphoric. One particle, **rma** 'SAME REFERENT', is primarily anaphoric (see 13.1 (2)), and can also have a reflexive function (see 8.3).

This type of particle has been receiving increasing attention in the literature. The problems relating to their meaning and function have led to such epithets as "mystery particles" (Longacre 1976a, whose paper is designed to show that they are not so mysterious when approached from a discourse perspective) and "pesky little particle" (Grimes 1975.93). Grimes describes them more fully:

> Most languages have particles whose use seems to be related to gluing the parts of discourses together but which are never easy to pin down. In English they are words like now, either, moreover, when used to relate more than one sentence. In Huichol they include both words like **mérɨ+kʌʌte** 'well, then' and postfixes (suffix-like forms that follow enclitics) like **-rɨɨ** 'definitely'.

Halliday and Hasan (1976.267-71) say a little more about six of the words and phrases in English that function in this way (now,

of course, well, anyway, surely, after all), but they confess that
they regard this group as "a residual category of the usual
'miscellaneous' type." A more thorough and enlightening study of a
similar set of such English discourse function words has been
undertaken by Diane Brockway (1981) in the framework of a particular theory of pragmatics (Sperber and Wilson, forthcoming).[6]

As with verification particles, there is a preferred pattern of
placing discourse particles in the phrase that has been fronted
for emphasis, but (different) members of this set (unlike the
verification set) can occur in successive phrases in the clause
(see 1.5 and 12.2.3). The examples that follow illustrate both the
general pragmatic function (**ryhe** in (217a) and **haxa** in (217b)) and
some of the more specific discourse functions. (**rma** in (217a, d,
e) is anaphoric, either to the immediately preceding sentence, a
single constituent in an earlier sentence, or to a larger chunk of
the earlier discourse; **haxa** in (217c) shows a contrastive link
with a constituent of the preceding sentence; and **harha** in (217e)
shows a relation with an event that is described several sentences
back in the story.)

(217) a. **yaskomo foryeni rma uro ryhe**
shaman chief-of SAME I EMPH
'I am still the chief shaman.' (1965.199)

b. **ɨto wehxakoni huhyaye, romryen haxa**
there I-was downriver my-boyhood CONTR
'With reference to my boyhood (in contrast to my
present manhood), I used to live there, downriver.'
(1965.168)

c. **Kaywerye katɨ nomokno. Waraka haxa nomokno**
Kaywerye ALT he-came Waraka CONTR he-came
'"Did Kaywerye come?" "Waraka (not Kaywerye) came."'

d. **ɨro rma narymaye, masku rma**
that-thing SAME it-threw-him dysentery SAME
'The dysentery (I've been talking about)
killed him.' (1965.201)

e. **nomokye harha tɨ, ɨramampɨra rma**
he-came back HSY not-delaying SAME
'He came back, still not delaying.' (1965.111)

There is one particle that has proved particularly difficult to
analyze: **ha** 'INTENSIFIER'. In Derbyshire (1979) I assigned it

---

6 I have experienced the same difficulty with regard to Hixkaryana discourse
particles as Brockway finds with the English set of words, namely, to decide
whether they have truth conditional properties. One factor that suggests they do
not is that they seem in general to be outside the scope of negative suffixes.

tentatively to the verification set, but after further reflection I now feel convinced it properly belongs to the discourse set of particles. Its functions are varied, but include some which are discourse (not merely sentence) oriented. It can occur preceding verification particles (see 12.2.3) and certain other discourse particles (see Appendix J). It also often occurs alone and following other discourse particles, and it then always precedes an intonational pause. This can be sentence oriented, as when it occurs in imperative sentences (see 6.3, exs. (99) and (104)), in rhetorical questions (see 12.2.2, most of the examples), and in the verb phrase in sentence-final position when verification particles are moved to a fronted phrase constituent (see 7.7); (**ha** itself never occurs in a preverbal phrase unless it is dislocated). Its more specific discourse function relates to sections of the discourse which contain background information that is not part of the main theme line of the discourse. (See Grimes 1975. 55ff. for the types of information that frequently constitute background, or athematic, material, and some of the grammatical devices used to signal such sequences.) The particle **ha** often occurs in the final phrase of a sentence, or a sequence of sentences, that conveys such background material; this may be the verb phrase or a following subject NP:

(218) **waywɨ yarymekonɨ,   txa txa txa. ɨto   tɨ nehxakonɨ**
      arrow he-was-shooting-it shooting   there HSY he-was
      noro ha,   kamara ha,   ɨmɨhto.   tomyarke rma
      III INTENSFR jaguar INTENSFR near-him carrying SAME

   tɨ   nehxakonɨ, watma hnɨnkahra
   HSY he-was   club not-putting-down
   '(The hero) was shooting arrows. The jaguar was close by.
   (The hero) was still carrying (his weapon), not putting
   down the club.' (1965.112)

This is an example where the background material is a single sentence (the second of the three sentences.) It is often a sequence, in which **ha** usually occurs in the sequence-final position, but can also occur in earlier sentences of the sequence. When it occurs in an NP, as in (218), it places focus on a participant who is not at that point in the foreground of the narrative.

Two (?) OSV languages have particles whose form, as well as function, is similar to Hixkaryana **ha**: Xavante -**hã** (Burgess 1976. 22) and Nadëb -**hë** (Weir, personal communication). The closely related Carib language Waiwai has an identical form **ha**. (I am indebted to Robert Hawkins for notes on the Waiwai particle that led me to a better understanding of the functions of **ha** in Hixkaryana.)

13.5 Anaphora: deletion and pronominal elements. Deletion and pronominalization are processes based on recoverability of items from the context. This is not always true of discourse particles, which may have a more general pragmatic function (see 13.4).

13.5.1 Deletion. Hixkaryana does not have the type of verb phrase deletion process found in English. This is not surprising, since the standard VP constituent in English is V (NP) (PP) and is clause final. There are, however, several other kinds of deletion process in Hixkaryana:

(1) Deletion of elements in interrogative sentences. This takes various forms, which are described in 6.2. A question word or phrase may occur alone, without any other sentence constituents. The copula can be deleted in expressions like **henta ohetxe** (where your-wife) 'Where is your wife?'. Where the question word occurs in a subordinate clause, the main clause can be deleted (which is evidence that wh-words never escape from their initially dominating clauses, as they do, for example, in English, where the wh-word may be moved to a higher clause and the subordinate clause deleted, as in I don't know who (we should send)). In yes-no echo questions all elements other than the verb phrase can be deleted.

(2) Deletion of elements in answers to questions. There are various possibilities here also, all of which are described in 6.6.1. Response particles may occur alone. The copula can be deleted in negative answers. Verb phrases and other constituents can be deleted in answers to question-word questions.

(3) Deletions in rhetorical questions. Any constituent other than the question word or phrase may be deleted in the main clause (see 12.2.2).

(4) Deletion of the main (quotative) verb **-ka-** 'say' and all constituents other than the embedded speech direct object in a quotative clause (see 3.1 for a description of the constituents of this type of clause). The effect of this deletion is to leave a direct speech "island" in the middle of a narrative discourse. It is rare, but when it occurs, two factors combine to identify it as direct speech: (i) the semantic ties between it and the surrounding context, and (ii) the application of the Lowe rule, which identifies the referents of person markers in direct speech sentences. (The Lowe rule states that the subject of the quotative main clause is coreferential with first person in the embedded speech clause; the indirect object (addressee) in the main clause is coreferential with second person in the embedded speech clause; and any other person referred to in the main clause is coreferential with third person in the embedded speech clause (Lowe 1969)). The following is taken from Derbyshire (1965.121):

(219) **nosenymay**   **tɨ noro hoko.**   **toto mokɨ**
he-protected-himself HSY III concerning person that-one

yenyemekonɨ.   **karyhe ryehtxoho me**   **haka**
it-protected-him-against strong my-being DENOMLZR IMP

kosenymaxe.   **ekeh**   **hokutho me**   **tesnɨr**
I-protect-myself dead-one child-of DENOMLZR his-being

ke   **nehxakonɨ**
because-of it-was

'He protected himself (by keeping the food taboos) concerning (game meat). It protected him against that man. "So that I will be strong let me now protect myself." It was because he was the child of a dead man.'

The third sentence in (219) is direct speech without the usual margin containing the verb **-ka-** 'say'.

(5) Deletion of the nominal head in the case of modifying particles (see 1.5) when these occur in a V or A phrase. Where the particle is in a VP its immediate antecedent is the verb prefix that marks the person of the referents; this is usually the subject-marking element of the prefix. There is always a full nominal antecedent in the preceding discourse:

(220) a. ...   **kekon**   **heno hatɨ**
(direct speech) he-said-it dead HSY
'"...," he, the one now dead, said.' (1965.187, etc.)

b. **nehurkaye**   **ymo hatɨ**
he-dropped-down AUG HSY
'He, the big bad (jaguar), dropped down (from a tree).' (1965.112)

In (220a), the particle **heno** refers to the prefix ∅-'IIIS' in **kekon**, and in (220b) **ymo** refers to the prefix n- 'IIIS' in **nehurkaye**. In both cases there are fuller identifying noun phrases earlier in the discourses.

13.5.2 Pronominal elements. Lehmann(1978.23) generalizes that "OV languages are poor in pronouns," but this is hardly true of Hixkaryana, where there are full systems of both person-marking prefixal elements and also free pronouns.

(1) Person-marking prefixes. These are obligatory in finite verb forms (see Appendix B for the complete set), and another set operates for nouns, relators, and derived adverbs (see Appendix C). The latter are obligatory with certain nouns and derived adverbs, but also occur frequently with other forms. The antecedent of any pronominal prefix may be in the same clause (221a), in a

superordinate clause (where the prefix occurs in a subordinate clause (221b)), in a subordinate clause (where the prefix is in another subordinate clause in the same sentence (221c)), or in another sentence (221d):

(221) a. **thetxe**   **yaryako**   **Waraka**
III REFL-wife-POSSN IIISIIIO-take-REC.PAST COMPL Waraka
'Waraka took his wife.'

b. **yawaka wɨmyako**   **Waraka wya,**
axe   ISIIIO-give-REC.PAST COMPL Waraka to

ɨxe   **esnɨrɨ**   **ke**
III-desirous-of III-being because-of
'I gave the axe to Waraka because he was wanting it.'

c. **ɨhoko**   **ɨmenhoye**   **ɨhyaka,**
III-concerning ISIIIO-write-DIST.PAST COMPL III-to

ɨsna   **ɨtotho**   **me,**   **Waraka totho**
to-there III-going DENOMLZR Waraka III-going

me,   **Manawsɨ hona ɨtotho**   **me**
DENOMLZR Manaus to   III-going DENOMLZR
'I wrote to him about it, so that he, Waraka, would go there, to Manaus.'

d. **tukusu**   **yakɨhtoye**   **Mawarye.**
hummingbird IIISIIIO-create-DIST.PAST COMPL Mawarye

herywo yawotoye   **xarha**
vine   IIISIIIO-cut-DIST.PAST COMPL also
'Mawarye created a hummingbird. He also cut a vine.'
(1965.63)

Example (221a) is from section 8.2, where there are other examples of anaphora within the sentence, involving the reflexive prefix **tɨ**- 'III REFL'. Backward anaphora is common (see (221a), (221c), and the first sentence of (221d)). This is necessarily characteristic of an OVS language in which the subject is coded in the verb, but it relates primarily to anaphora within the sentence. (For an example of backward anaphora across sentence boundaries, involving a free pronoun, see later in this section.) In addition to the antecedent in the same sentence, pronominal prefixes (and free forms) usually have antecedents in one or more earlier sentences. The pattern of increasing specification of a referent (see 12.2.4 (4)) is closely associated with backward anaphora.

As noted in 3.3, pronominal subjects and objects are often phonologically unrealized, leaving only the verb prefix to signal those grammatical relations and the person of the referents. Thus, in (221c) the prefix **ɨ**- 'ISIIIO' is the only form for both subject

Discourse-related Phenomena

and object, while in the second sentence of (221d) the subject NP (Mawarye) is deleted. The significance of subject NP omission for thematic patterning is discussed in 13.2. It is also related to the hypothesis concerning the diachronic process that moved the subject NP from clause-initial to postverbal position, since the option involved in that process was either complete omission of the NP or its introduction as an afterthought (see 10.4).

(2) Free pronouns. Both deictic and nondeictic third person pronouns are used anaphorically (see 1.2.2 for the complete set of pronouns). The nondeictic forms are most generally used in this way: **noro** 'III, ANIMATE'; **nyamoro** 'III, ANIMATE, COLLECTIVE'; and **iro** 'III, INANIMATE'.

A speaker has three basic options in determining how to refer to an entity: pronominal prefix, free pronoun, fuller identifying NP. The factors that condition his choice appear to be a combination of focus and thematicity. By focus I mean the same phenomenon described in 13.1, i.e., emphasis, contrast, the entity that is being given the primary attention at that point in the discourse. By thematicity I mean something rather different from what is discussed in 13.2. Here it relates to discourse prominence, whether that section of the discourse is dealing with primary information that is on the main event line of the total discourse (thematic), or with secondary information of an explanatory or background nature (athematic) (Callow 1974.52; I am here following Callow's use of "theme" and "thematic," but not her distinction between "focus" and "emphasis").

Wheatley (1973) describes a complex system for (?OVS) Bacairi (Carib) that has distinct thematic, athematic, focal, and nonfocal pronouns. Hixkaryana does not have different forms, but uses the pronouns it has in different ways to express these discourse functions. This is best seen in the most generally used of the pronouns in this way, the nondeictic form **noro**. There are three ways in which **noro** is used: (i) in sentence-initial position it is focused and thematic (222a); (ii) cooccurring with the particle **ha** (see 13.4) in the postverbal position it is focused and athematic (222b); (iii) in other postverbal occurrences it is thematic with a mild degree of focus (222c):

(222) a. **kunoro   nemimtoye,   txow.**
   red-macaw he-made-himself-a-house threading-leaves

   noro ti wenyhera nehxakoni. xahe
   III HSY not-lazy he-was   blue-and-yellow-macaw

   tho   wenywakoni haxa
   DEVLD he-was-lazy CONTR
   'The red macaw threaded leaves together to make himself a house. That one was not lazy. But the blue and yellow macaw was lazy.' (1965.90)

b. **nomokye harha tɨ, ɨramampɨra   rma,**
   he-came back HSY not-delaying SAME

   ɨhpo.   ɨmahyaka nexey
   arriving-at-village-clearing behind-him he-was

   ha,   noro ha,   kamara ymo
   INTENSFR III   INTENSFR jaguar AUG
   '(The hero) came back, still not delaying, and arrived
   at the village clearing. The jaguar was behind him.'
   (1965.111)

c. **nomokye hatɨ ɨhoko.   kowontekon   hatɨ noro**
   he-came HSY occ.-with-him he-was-crying-out HSY III
   '(The jaguar) came attacking him. (The hero) was
   crying out.' (1965.112)

When it occurs sentence initial, as in (222a), **noro** is usually anaphoric to an antecedent that is the subject (and topic) of the immediately preceding sentence. The fact that it is already the established topic (but one that is marked with focus by being fronted) explains why the pronoun and not a fuller identifying noun phrase occurs. In the postverbal position, **noro** always has some degree of focus. In this way it contrasts with a sentence in which only a pronominal prefix is used. The pattern of increasing specification of an entity (see 12.2.4(4)) often involves a pronoun in a postverbal sequence (as in 222b), and it also helps to see how the system of speaker options works out:

(223) **xofrye heno yanotometxkonɨ,**
      sloth dead IIISIIIO-make-a-slave-of-DIST.PAST CONT.COLL

      kurumyana   komo. ɨtoko, ketxkon   hatɨ. omoko,
      buzzard-person COLL go   they-said-it HSY   come

      mararɨ taknyohnye,   ketxkon   hatɨ, ɨwya,
      field let-us-INCL-burn-it they-said-it HSY   III-to

      noro heno wya, xofrye heno wya ha
      III dead to   sloth dead to INTENSFR
      'The buzzard people used to make a slave of the sloth.
      "Go," they used to say. "Come, let's burn the field,"
      they used to say to him, to the sloth.' (1965.37)

The narrator of the story can be seen to be changing his options as he adds each postverbal phrase in the paratactic sequence at the end of the last sentence: the first phrase **ɨwya** contains only the pronominal prefix to signal the third person referent, and this would leave it completely nonfocused. He decides this is not enough, so he adds the pronoun **noro** in the next phrase, bringing in a degree of focus, and by the use of the particle **heno** more clearly identifying the entity as the one introduced in the first

Discourse-related Phenomena 167

sentence. The addition of the final phrase gives the full identification, but probably does not add anything in the way of focus. The whole sequence is clearly thematic, since it is primary information that contributes to the development of the main theme of the first part of the story.

This pattern involving a changing of options by the speaker is a way of resolving the tension that results from two possibly conflicting aims of a discourse, what Kantor has called brevity and perceptibility (Kantor 1977:36-37):

> Deletions, pronominalizations ... reduction of clause structure, and insertion of lexical items, are the mechanisms in language which ... satisfy the <u>brevity function</u> of language.
>
> Among the other <u>functional considerations</u> that a language must satisfy is <u>perceptibility, that is</u>, a language must be able to be understood .... The desire for brevity may be attained with a concomitant loss of information, thus hindering perceptibility. This is exactly the problem that may arise with the use of personal pronouns.

In the last sentence of (223), the aim of brevity would best be attained by uttering the one phrase **iwya** (even that might be omitted). The speaker judges, however, that this may not be adequate for comprehension by the hearer, so he adds, first **noro heno wya**, and then, because he is still not sure that the goal of perceptibility has been reached, the phrase **xofrye heno wya ha**. He has taken pains to avoid uttering what Kantor calls an "inconsiderate discourse."

The pattern of increasing specification is closely associated with backward anaphora within the sentence, as can be seen in (223). When pronouns occur, however, there is usually an antecedent earlier in the discourse, as is also the case in (223), where the antecedent is in the first sentence. Occasionally, however, the pronoun occurs first and the antecedent in a following sentence. Example (224a) is a discourse-initial sequence, and (224b) occurs discourse-medial, and in both the pronoun occurs in the first sentence of the sequence, with the antecedent in the next sentence:

(224) a. **tinotxhiri   yaheye,   noro. toy**
      his-own-sister he-seduced-her III   he-went

      hati, kohsaya, nuno
      HSY   at-night moon
      'He seduced his own sister. The moon (man) went at night.' (1965.23)

b. **noro tho xaxa xe wehxaha.**
   III DEVLD SUPERLATIVE desirous-of I-am

   ohetxenhɨrɨ xe xa wehxaha,
   your-wife-PAST desirous-of CONTR I-am

   kekon hatɨ
   he-said-it HSY
   '"She is the one I really want, it is the one who has been your wife I want," he said.' (1965.69)

The deictic pronouns are also sometimes used anaphorically. The remote-deictic forms, **mokɨ** 'III, ANIMATE', **mokyamo** 'III, ANIMATE, COLLECTIVE', and **monɨ** 'III, INANIMATE', are nonfocused and athematic, nearly always occurring in an equative clause that contains explanatory, background material (see 5.2 and 12.2.4 (4)). The medial-deictics, **mokro** 'III, ANIMATE', **mokyamo** 'III, ANIMATE, COLLECTIVE', and **moro** 'III, INANIMATE', are focused and are neutral as to thematic status; they also frequently occur in equative clauses. The near-deictics (except **onɨ**--see below) only rarely occur with an anaphoric function, and their focus-theme status is not clear to me:

(225) a. **ɨtono monɨ, okoymo**
        there-NOMLZN that-thing anaconda

   hkotothɨrɨnhɨrɨ, kanye
   part-that-had-been-cut-in-two one-who-says-it

   mokɨ nexeye heno, rowya
   that-one he-was dead to-me
   '"The part of the anaconda that had been cut in two is over there", (my) late (father) was the one who told it to me.' (1965.91)

b. **kɨhrohomanye mokro, txakaryma.**
   one-that-can-harm-us that-one night-monkey

   osonyhenɨ mak mokro ha
   one-not-to-be-seen ADVERS that-one INTENSFR
   'The night monkey, that is a creature that can harm us. It is one that should never be seen.' (1965.104)

In (225a) both **monɨ** and **mokɨ** are used anaphorically, in a sequence that is off the main theme line of the story, and both are nonfocused constituents of equative clauses. In (225b) **mokro** is also a constituent of an equative clause in each sentence, but is more emphatic, and occurs in a discourse-initial sequence that is establishing the theme of the text.

The third person inanimate pronouns **ɨro** (nondeictic) and **onɨ** (near-deictic) are widely used with an anaphoric function in sentence connective phrases (see 13.4.1).

13.6 Discourse redundancy. There is a high degree of redundancy in a typical Hixkaryana discourse. The forms this redundancy takes are described in some detail in Derbyshire (1977c) and are only summarized here. I concentrate mainly on the construction I call "sentence cluster."

Discourse redundancy is common in all languages, functioning primarily to give cohesion and unity to a discourse, and thus distinguishing it from a randomly chosen set of unrelated sentences (Halliday and Hasan 1976). Another general function is to slow down the rate of information. In Hixkaryana this rate seems very slow in comparison with most other languages. A sentence that has one or more items of new information is often followed by several sentences that do not add anything new. This is effected mainly by repetition of lexical items (frequently exact repetitions of words and phrases, and elsewhere the substitution of synonyms and near-synonyms in a succession of sentences) and the interacting of the various types of anaphora (see 13.4 and 13.5). Certain patterns and constructions contribute significantly to the redundancy: rhetorical questions (see 12.2.2 (1)); paratactic constructions, especially in their function to add an increasing degree of specification with respect to a constituent (see 12.2.4); ideophones (see 1.6); the complex quotative sentence in which there is repetition of the direct speech clause before and after the verb **-ka-** 'say' (see 6.5, exs. (111a) and (111b)); and the constant repetition of such forms as the tense-aspect suffixes, members of the three sets of particles (see 1.5; 12.2.3; 13.4.2; and 13.5.1 (5)), the quotative verb phrase (**-ka-**) (see 6.5), and the formulaic clauses that signal higher-level breaks in the discourse (see 13.4.1).

One function of repetition of a clause or sentence is to mark the boundaries of an embedded section of discourse which gives secondary, background information; the repeated clause is on the main theme line, and it occurs before and after the embedded sequence:

(226) **kohsaya toy hatɨ, horykomo, Txesusu hyaka.**
at-night he-went HSY important-man Jesus to

Nekoknemusu noro hatɨ, esotɨ. Farysew komo kukuru
Nicodemus III HSY his-name Pharisee COLL member-of

rma mok nehxakon hatɨ, Xuknewyana yoh komo
SAME that-one he-was HSY Jew-people chief-of COLL

kukuru rma hatɨ. noro rma toy hatɨ, Txesusu
member-of SAME HSY III SAME he-went HSY Jesus

hyaka, kohsaya hatɨ
to at-night HSY

'A leading man went to Jesus at night. His name was
Nicodemus. He was one of the Pharisee group, one of
the leaders of the Jewish people. That same one went
to Jesus at night.' ([Derbyshire] 1976.453).

Another function of a sequence of repeated identical clauses is
to indicate successive occurrences of the same action:

(227) **bo,**   **amna nomokye. amna nomokye.**
      dropping-into-hammock   I+III came   I+III came

      amna nomokye. amna nomokye. bo,
      I+III came   I+III came   dropping-into-hammock

      amna nomokye ha
      I+III came   INTENSFR
      'We journeyed each day, stopping to sleep at night.'
      (From an unpublished text)

The sentence cluster is a redundancy unit consisting of a sequence of two or more sentences with complete, or near complete, identity of forms. It is the maximal form of repetition of lexical items. It is similar in both form and basic functions to the paratactic sequences of phrases and subordinate clauses that occur within a single sentence (see 12.2.4), but it differs in that the verb phrase (and thus the whole of a main clause) is repeated.

The most general function of sentence clusters seems to be emphasis: either of the whole sentence, where the constituents are not only identical (or nearly so), but also in the same order in each sentence (228a); or of one particular constituent, which is fronted in the second sentence of the sequence (228b):

(228) a. **meya xaxa mah tɨ tetxkon ha.**
       far   SUPERL ADVERS HSY they-used-to-go INTENSFR

       meya xah tɨ mah tɨ ntetxkon ha
       far   MISF HSY ADVERS HSY they-used-to-go INTENSFR
       '(The hunters) used to go really far away; it was
       their misfortune to have to go further than you can
       imagine (because they were living at a time when
       the sun never used to set).' (1965.16)

    b. **nomokyatxkon hatɨ hawana. hawana me**
       they-used-to-come HSY visitor visitor DENOMLZR

       nomokyatxkonɨ
       they-used-to-come
       'Visitors used to come. They used to come visiting.'
       (1965.109)

Discourse-related Phenomena   171

They also function in ways that are closely parallel to the paratactic constructions that occur within a sentence (12.2.4): coordination in the case of repeated occurrences of the same action (229a); modification of one of the constituents, with substantial identity of the rest (229b); and increasing degree of specification of one or more of the constituents (229c):

(229) a. **narymay   xarha tɨ, txa,   txe,**
   he-fired-it ADD   HSY firing hitting-target

   eryetwo.   narymay   xarha tɨ,
   in-the-pointed-end-of-it he-fired-it ADD   HSY

   txa,   txe   neryetɨkrahxakonɨ
   firing hitting it-was-piercing-the-pointed-end-of-it

   hatɨ. neryetɨkrahxakonɨ
   HSY   it-was-piercing-the-pointed-end-of-it
   'He fired one arrow after another into the tail end of each preceding arrow.' (1965.24)

   b. **rotahanɨr   xe   mak   manatxhe.**
   killing-of-me desirous-of ADVERS you-COLL-are

   yaworon   xaxa   yokarymanye   rma yotahanɨr
   true-NOMLZN SUPERL one-who-tells SAME killing-of

   xe   manatxhe
   desirous-of you-COLL-are
   'But you are wanting to kill me. You are wanting to kill the one who tells you the truth.' (1976.490)

   c. **noseryehyakonɨ mak   hatɨ. noseryehyakonɨ mak**
   he-was-afraid ADVERS HSY   he-was-afraid ADVERS

   hatɨ, ɨhona.   tehurkanɨrɨ   hona   nenyakonɨ
   HSY   towards-it his-own-falling towards he-was-seeing-it
   'But he was afraid, afraid of it, afraid of (lit., watching against) his falling.' (1965.13)

14 Conclusion

My final conclusions with regard to Hixkaryana and syntactic typology fall into two categories: first, a summary of what I tentatively regard as the characteristic features of Hixkaryana syntax that relate more or less directly to its object-initial, subject-final character (14.1); second, a suggestion that there is some support for an "areal" typology that might be especially conducive to word order change in the direction of producing languages with object-initial word orders (14.2).

14.1 Characteristic features of Hixkaryana syntax. In 11.3, following a comparison of Hixkaryana with both OV and VOS languages, I noted four patterns that appeared to be especially appropriate to a language that is both object initial and subject final. I summarize them here as part of a longer listing of characteristic features of the language:

(1) Rightward movement of constituents (especially the subject in subordinate clauses) is not upward bounded.

(2) Nominal modifiers normally follow the head noun they modify.

(3) There is no agentive passive construction.

(4) Fronting rules for question words (obligatory) and focused constituents (optional) provide the mechanism for marked orders in which the subject is emphasized (or "topicalized").

Chapters 12 and 13 contain a more detailed treatment of certain aspects of patterns (2) to (4) above, and also introduce several other features that seem to be particularly compatible with the basic order OVS. These are summarized here:

(5) The closely related patterns of paratactic phrase sequences and nominalizations, which provide the principal means for modification and coordination within the clause, are mostly expressed as right-dislocated constructions, and are primarily associated with the subject constituent.

Conclusion 173

(6) The Subject-Raising rule associated with sentence negative constructions is clearly related to the position of subject in the clause, and when considered along with the Question-Word-Fronting rule shows that the final position of subject has negative implications for any theory of a universal linear configuration between a moved constituent and its "trace."

(7) The proposal that **wya**-phrases represent an initial 1 (i.e., underlying subject) relation is to be linked with the fact that such phrases (as adjuncts) normally occur in the postverbal position, as subjects also do.

(8) The pattern of "communicative dynamism" that results from the relative ordering of new and given information is the reverse of what has been generally predicted: given information, primarily associated with the subject constituent, occurs at the end of Hixkaryana clauses.

(9) The "frame-of-reference" topic, consisting of a nominal phrase that does not have any grammatical relationship with the main predication of the sentence, also occurs in sentence-final position, again the reverse of what has been generally predicted.

(10) Backward anaphora is a prominent feature in the language.

14.2 Towards an Amazon-area typology. In this chapter I have referred to a number of other languages of the Amazon area on which I have at least some information. They can be classified in terms of two parameters: genetic affiliation, either Carib or non-Carib; and basic word order types, either object-initial or not. (In some cases the classification is tentative, through lack of adequate data and facts.) I now list these languages (including Hixkaryana for completeness, but excluding the other three extant languages referred to in 10.3 as probably OVS--Apalaí, Asuriní, and Bacairí--for which I have no information concerning specific syntactic properties):

	Affiliation	Object initial
Apurinã	non-Carib (Arawakan)	Yes (OSV)
Xavante	non-Carib (Gêan)	Yes (OSV)
Nadëb	non-Carib (? Macuan)	Yes (OSV)
Urubu	non-Carib (Tupian)	Yes (OSV)
Makuchi	Carib	Yes (OVS)
Arekuna/Taulipang	Carib	Yes (OVS)
Hixkaryana	Carib	Yes (OVS)
Waiwai	Carib	No (SOV)
Carib (Surinam)	Carib	No (SOV)

The map shows the approximate locations of these languages.

Syntactic Typology

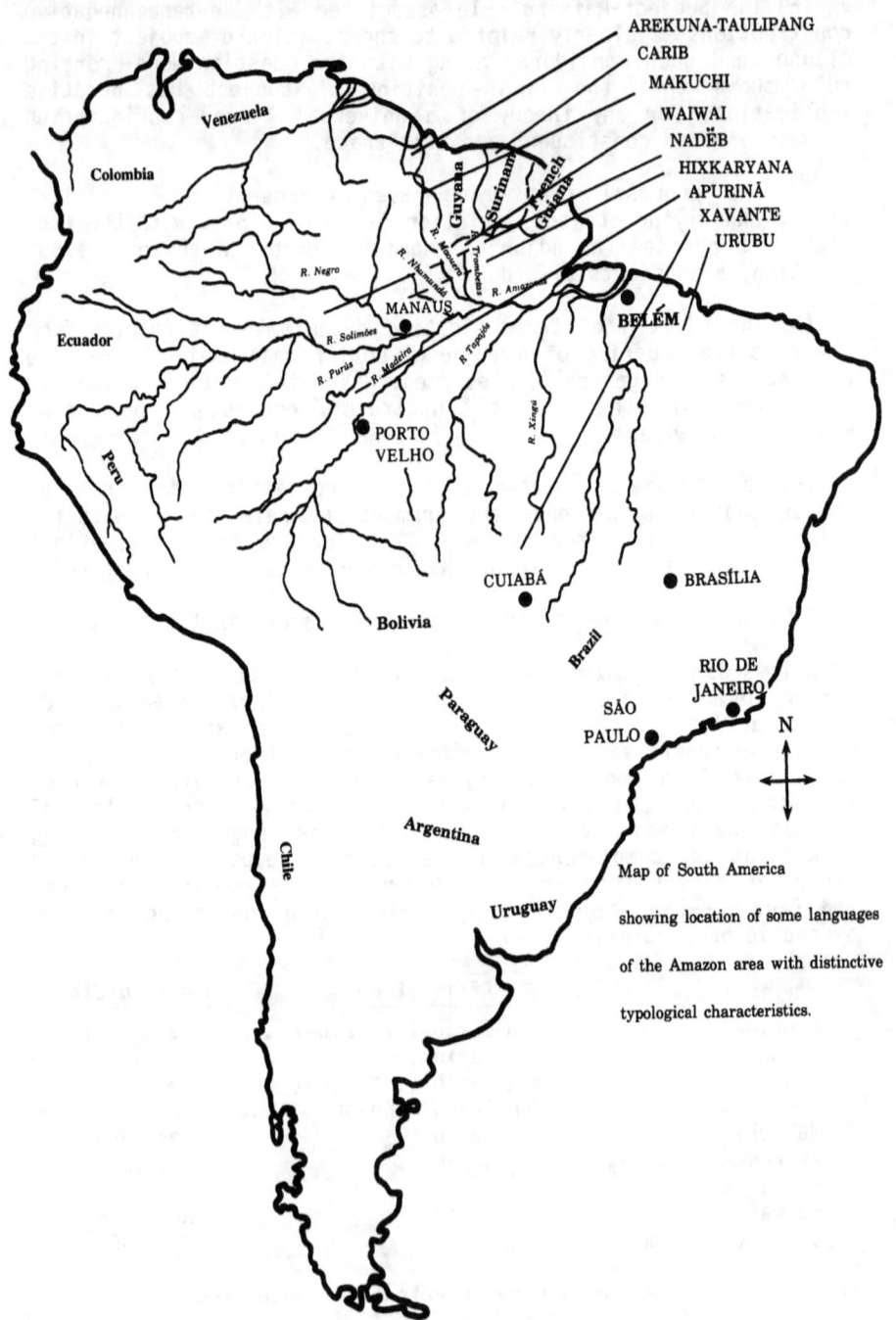

Map of South America showing location of some languages of the Amazon area with distinctive typological characteristics.

Conclusion 175

Although data and descriptive statements are flimsy for most of these languages, there is some evidence that they have in common a number of syntactic features that are by no means common (at least as an interrelated set of features) in the world's languages as a whole. These include: (1) verb agreement with subject and object; (2) substitution of nominalizations for relative clause constructions; (3) nominal modifiers following their noun heads; (4) lack of an agentive passive construction; (5) direct quotation replacing indirect statements; (6) absence of coordinating conjunctions; (7) use of right-dislocated paratactic constructions; and (8) use of phrasal discourse (and possibly verification) particles. The evidence is uneven, so that it is not possible to affirm that all the languages in question have all these properties, but I can say that each property shows up in at least three of the languages, and there are no languages for which I have seen negative statements relating to any one of these properties.

This leads me to the tentative conclusion that we have here a set of language traits that may well be regarded as characteristic of Amazon-area languages. If this holds true, it has some interesting implications:

(1) It would seem to strengthen the case for area-based typologies. Emeneau (1964) has defined "linguistic area" as meaning

> an area which includes languages belonging to more than one family but showing traits in common which are found not to belong to the other members of (at least) one of the families.

I have been mostly concerned here with the positive part of that definition, that is, traits that are common to languages that cross family boundaries. Further research is needed to show that at least some of these traits are lacking in other languages in one or more of the families represented here.

(2) It may be reasonable to suggest that the set of syntactic traits listed above (plus possibly others) can be regarded as particularly appropriate for languages with object-initial basic word orders. This entails the inference that languages with these traits which do not have such a basic order may be susceptible to word order change in that direction (this has already been predicted as a distinct possibility for Carib; Hoff 1978). It also implies that OVS and OSV (the types in which the initial position of object is absolute) may have more in common with each other than with either the other OS order (VOS) or with other verb-final languages. This conflicts with Kakumasu's statement that (OSV) Urubu has the grammar of verb-final (SOV) languages (Kakumasu 1976.172). He does not, however, supply any solid supporting

evidence for this statement, and the few specific syntactic characteristics of Urubu that he presents tend to place it in some doubt: in Urubu, nominal modifiers follow, whereas genitives precede, their noun heads (see discussion in 11.2.4); there is no passive in the language (which is characteristic of some verb-final languages, but not of Japanese, which is the example Kakumasu gives of an SOV language; see 11.2.7 and 11.3); and the first Phrase Structure rule which Kakumasu gives for his transformational-generative treatment is S   (NP) (NP) V (p. 171), which differs from the usual first rule of T-G grammars (S   NP VP) and highlights the fact that the standard VP constituent containing the verb and the direct object does not make sense for an OSV language, although it is easily applied to SOV languages (VP   (PP) (NP) V).

(3) The possible existence of an object-initial area suggests an urgent need for research in two directions. First, thoroughgoing historical and comparative studies are needed to substantiate (or refute) the conjecture I have made. There will be no written records going back hundreds or thousands of years, such as were available to Emeneau and others in their work which has established India as a significant linguistic area for historical study (Emeneau 1964.650). Such records as there are go back not much more than 200 years and they are likely to provide little in the way of syntactically relevant data or description. Others (scholars in the North America areas, for example) have shown, however, that reconstructions from the comparative study of languages as they are spoken today can throw considerable light on areal traits and the nature of the diffusion that produces those traits. Such comparative studies are still possible for the languages discussed here, and for a number of others in the Amazon area, and can be expected to lead to the formulation of a more definitive statement on the syntactic typology of the area.

APPENDIX A[7]

PHONOLOGY

A.1 Phonological units (segmental)
The distinctive segments are: p, t, tx, k, b, d, dy, f, s, x, h, m, n, ny, r, ry, w, y, e, a, i, u, o.

A.1.1 Plosives and affricate
(Voiceless) p labio-labial, t apico-alveolar, tx lamino-postalveolar [tʃ], k dorso-velar; (voiced) b labio-labial, d apico-alveolar, dy lamino-postalveolar [ɖ].

Voiceless segments are lengthened when they occur syllable final preceding syllable-initial h. In the case of the affricate, it is the stop component that is lengthened: *ahakheno* [æhæk̟ːhɪnɔ] 'my dead father', *tamutho* [tæmʊtːhɔ] 'grandfather', *sokitxhe* [sɔku̇tːʃhi] 'after bringing it'. In some idiolects the t and k contrast is neutralized to a glottal closure preceding a voiced nasal (or its plosive alternant): *kosenyetno* [kɔseːɲitnɔ] or [kɔseːɲiʔnɔ] or [kɔseːɲitdɔ] or [kɔseːɲiʔdɔ] 'I dreamt', *komokno* [kɔmɔknɔ] or [kɔmɔʔnɔ] or [kɔmɔkdɔ] or [kɔmɔʔdɔ] 'I came', *wetmano* [wɪtmænɔ] or [wɪʔmænɔ] or [wɪtbænɔ] or [wɪʔbænɔ] 'I gave him meat', *nemtakmano* [nɪmtækmænɔ] or [nɪmtæʔmænɔ] or [nɪmtækbænɔ] or [nɪmtæʔbænɔ] 'he took a meal', *titxenotnye* [tu̇tʃiᵊnɔtɲi] or [tu̇tʃiᵊnɔʔɲi] or [tu̇tʃiᵊnɔtɖi] or [tu̇tʃiᵊnɔʔɖi] 'cold', *naknyohno* [nækɲɔhnɔ] or [næʔɲɔhnɔ] or [nækɖɔhnɔ] or [næʔɖɔhnɔ] 'he burnt it'. The velar plosive k is fronted when it precedes [j] or the close front vowel, and backed when it precedes the back unrounded vowel [ɯ]: *kyakwe* [k̟jækwe] 'white-throated toucan', *keko* [k̟eːkɔ] 'he said it', *kiri* [k̠ɯːrɯ] 'male'. Elsewhere the voiceless plosives and affricate have their normal phonetic realizations: [p] *epepe* [ɪpeːpe] 'older brother', *timpira* [tʊmpɯræ] 'not giving it'; [t] *tuna* [tuːnæ] 'water', *fotwo* [ɸɔtwɔ] 'species of banana'; [tʃ] *atxowowo* [ætʃɔːwɔwɔ] 'wind'; [k] *kana* [kæːnæ] 'fish', *arko* [ærkɔ] 'take it'.

The voiced plosives are closely related to the nasals and contrast with them only in phrase-initial position, as the following pairs show: *banhono* [bænhɔnɔ] 'I danced' and *manhono* [mænhɔnɔ] 'he danced', *datiri* [dætɯːrɯ] 'our (incl.) plants' and *nati* [næːtɯ] 'seed, plant', *dyahri* [ɖæhrɯ] 'our vegetable food' and *nyahi* [ɲæːhɯ] 'vegetable food'. The same phonetic realizations, [b] [d] [ɖ], occur as alternants of the corresponding nasals in the speech of some people in phrase-medial position following any voiceless nonsyllabic other than h (the rule applies vacuously following p). For examples following t and k see the preceding paragraph; following other nonsyllabics: *wahosno* [wæhɔsnɔ] or [wæhɔsdɔ] 'I caught it', *baxme* [bæʃme] or [bæʃbe] 'silver-beaked tanager', *txuf moni* [tʃʊɸ mɔnɯ] or [tʃʊɸ bɔnɯ] 'that (is) grass'.

A.1.2 Fricatives
f labio-labial [ɸ], s apico-alveolar, x lamino-postalveolar [ʃ], h glottal. The glottal fricative h has the quality of the preceding vowel where the h is syllable final and of the following vowel where it is syllable initial; the other fricatives have their normal realization in all occurrences: *foru* [ɸɔːrɯ] 'plantain', *xofrye* [ʃɔɸri] 'sloth', *soko* [sɔːkɔ] 'bring it', *romsiri* [rɔmsɯrɯ] 'my daughter', *exexwa* [ɪʃiʃwæ] 'rope', *honye* [hɔːɲi] 'piranha (fish)', *nahko* [næhkɔ] 'he was'.

[7] The material in these eleven appendixes is substantially the same as that contained in the relevant sections of Derbyshire 1979.

A.1.3 Nasals

m labio-labial, n apico-alveolar, ny lamino-postalveolar [ɲ]. For voiced plosive alternants see A.1.1. Following the vowel e [ɲ] is realized as [jn] (not [jɲ], although this sequence does occur elsewhere, e.g., *oyoynye* [ɔjɔjɲi] 'one who rebukes you') when it precedes a postalveolar or velar: *wenytxano* [wejntʃænɔ] 'I heard it', *xenyxe* [ʃijnʃi] 'purposing to see it', *xenyko* [ʃijnkɔ] 'look at it'. Elsewhere nasals have their normal realization: *mawu* [mæ:wu] 'howler monkey', *omtari* [ɔmtærɯ] 'your mouth', *nuno* [nu:nɔ] 'moon', *anhi* [ænhɯ] 'evil', *nyamoro* [ɲæmɔ:rɔ] 'they', *honyko* [hɔɲkɔ] 'species of peccary'.

A.1.4 Liquids

r apico-alveolar flap [ɾ], ry apico-postalveolar flap with a distinct lateral release [ɽ]. Only [ɽ] occurs preceding the close front vowel e, but the two liquids contrast in other environments: *rakano* [ɾækæ:nɔ] 'he split it', *ryakoymo* [ɽækɔjmɔ] 'species of hornet', *Waraka* [wæɾæ:kæ] (man's name), *waryako* [wæɽæ:kɔ] 'I took it', *beryerye* [bɩɽi:ɽi] 'stool'.

A.1.5 Semivowels

w close back rounded, y close front unrounded [j]: *woto* [wɔ:tɔ] 'game animal', *kwakwaru* [kwækwæru] 'morning star', *yutu* [ju:tu] 'manioc squeezer', *iywaho* [ɯjwæhɔ] 'ahead of him'.

A.1.6 Vowels

e close to close-mid front, a open front [æ], i close back unrounded [ɯ], u close back rounded, o mid back [ɔ].

The close to close-mid front vowel e has allophones reflecting degree of closeness and tenseness. There is some free variation in the use of these allophones, but they are generally predictable according to the following rules:

(1) The vowel is closer and more tense [i] after a post-alveolar: *amnyerma* [æmɲiɾmæ] 'today', *yukryeka* [jukɽikæ] 'earth', *xeryko* [ʃiɽkɔ] 'star'.
(2) Before a syllable with a back vowel, a lengthened [i:] (see A.3.1 for length rule) has a following glide to central position [i:ᵊ]: *tiswanaturyemi* [tɯswænæ:tuɽi:ᵊmɯ] 'green thing', *xenyeno* [ʃiɲi:ᵊnɔ] 'new thing', *titxenotnye* [tɯtʃi:ᵊnɔtɲi] 'cold'.
(3) The vowel is closer and less tense [ɪ] in unstressed syllables (see A.3.3 for primary and secondary stress rules) where these are not followed by a syllable with stressed e: *ehni* [ɪhnɯ] 'river', *wekoko* [wɪkɔ:kɔ] 'hawk'.
(4) Elsewhere a less close tense [e] occurs: *meku* [me:ku] 'species of monkey', *weheto* [wehe:tɔ] 'fire', *imenhoniri* [ɯmenhɔnɯ:rɯ] 'the writing of it'.

The open front vowel a has the normal realization [æ] in all its occurrences: *akmatari* [ækmætæ:rɯ] 'branch'.

The close back unrounded vowel i is realized as a syllabic nasal [n̩] when it occurs word initial, unstressed, before [hV]: *ihahnohno* [n̩hæhnɔhnɔ] 'I approached him', *ihetxe* [n̩he:tʃi] 'his wife'. In word-final position following h, [ɯ] is nasalized: *ehi* [e:hɯ̃] 'its trunk, body'. Elsewhere it has its normal realization, although it is less tense in unstressed syllables: *kiri* [kɯ:rɯ] 'male', *ikano* [ɯkæ:nɔ] 'I said it'.

The close back rounded vowel u is nasalized in word-final position following h: *tohu* [tɔ:hũ] 'stone'. Elsewhere it is tense [u] in stressed syllables and lax [ʊ] in unstressed: *uhutxhuru* [ʊhut:ʃhuru] 'his skin' (see A.3.3).

Phonology

The mid back vowel o is closer [o] when it occurs in successive open syllables in the phrase-final sequence *komo: biryekomo* [buɾi:ᵊkomo] 'boy'. Elsewhere it is realized as [ɔ]: *okoye* [ɔkɔ:ji] 'snake'.

A.1.7 Other phonological units

There are a few additional contrastive units that occur in ideophones and baby talk. These are not listed or described since they have not been adequately studied. In certain response particles glottal plosive [ʔ] is used.

A.2 Phonotactics

In discussing phonotactics and suprasegmentals, I use the term *word* (unless it is specifically qualified in some way) to describe a phonological unit that may consist of one or more grammatical *words*, and whose defining feature is that it is bounded by pause. Thus, for example, syllable assignment (see A.2.8) and application of the vowel length rule (see A.3.1) apply across (grammatical) word—as well as morpheme—boundaries:

(1) wayamo txko yonyekoni ymo rma hati
    turtle DIMIN IIISIIIO-eat-DIST.PAST CONT. AUG same HSY

'He was still eating the poor old turtle.'

This is realized phonetically as

[wæ.jæ:.mɔtʃ.kɔ. / jɔ.ɲi:ᵊ.kɔ.nuɪj.mɔr.mæ.hæ:.tuɪ. /]

(Syllable division is marked by a period and pause by a solidus).

A.2.1 Word-final consonants

Word-final consonants do not occur except where there is apocope of the vowels i and e in certain suffixes and particles: *hati* 'HEARSAY' may be reduced to *hat*, *hami* 'DEDUCTION' to *ham*, *-yakoni* 'DISTANT PAST CONTINUATIVE' to *-yakon*, *-txowi* 'IMMEDIATE PAST COLLECTIVE' to *-txow*, and *-ye* 'DISTANT PAST COMPLETIVE' to *-y* when it follows a vowel.

A.2.2 Initial consonants

Initial consonants occur without any restrictions.

A.2.3 Word-initial consonant clusters

Only kr, kry, kh, kw, ky, th, tw, tk, sw, and xw occur.

A.2.4 Word-medial consonant clusters

(1) *Two-consonant clusters*. All the initial clusters occur and also many more. The only systematic restrictions are: p never occurs as the first member of a cluster, and only follows m and h within a grammatical word; f only precedes r, ry, and y, and only follows the same consonants and n within a grammatical word; b, d, and dy never occur in consonant clusters except as a noncontrastive variant of the corresponding nasals in some idiolects (see A.1.1); clusters in which each member is either alveolar or postalveolar are restricted within a grammatical word to a few which have y as the first of the cluster, or a nasal as either the first or second member of the cluster; k never precedes a voiceless nonsyllabic other than h in a grammatical word; and h never follows m, h, s, or x within a grammatical word (for rules relating to morpheme-initial

h in these environments, see A.4.1 and A.4.2). There is a general constraint against geminate clusters within a grammatical word.

(2) *Three-consonant clusters.* These are rare: either w, y, h, or tx occurs as the first segment of the cluster; only kry or kw can follow. Syllable division is always after the first segment (see A.2.8): *towkrye* 'sappy', *kwaykway* 'action of paddling', *nɨhkryemamno* 'he was in a convulsion', *kamotxkwɨwɨntano* 'I have an injured hand'.

A.2.5 Word-final vowels

These are obligatory, except where apocope occurs (see A.2.1), and there are no restrictions.

A.2.6 Word-initial vowels

These occur without any restrictions.

A.2.7 Sequences of (syllabic) vowels

These do not occur within a (grammatical) word, except in a few Portuguese loans, e.g., *paraesu* 'Paraiso', which is often realized with a glottal constriction between the vowels: [pæræesu] or [pæræʔesu].

A.2.8 Syllable assignment of medial units and clusters

There is a general rule which is independent of morphological structure or morpheme boundaries: syllable boundary falls in the environment V(C)⌣C. *hawana* 'visitor' is ha.wa.na; *oske* 'thus' is os.ke; *noknomtxowɨ* 'they stayed' is nok.nom.txo.wɨ; *towkrye* 'sappy' is tow.krye; *kratano* 'I wept' is kra.ta.no. (See A.2 for application of this rule across word boundaries also.)

A.2.9 The canonical syllable type

This is (C)CV(C). V and VC occur only word initial: *anaro* 'another' is a.na.ro; *omsamtxemo* 'young girl' is om.sam.txe.mo. Examples of the other possible expansions are found in A.2.4(2) and A.2.8.

A.2.10 Consonant-vowel sequences

The only restrictions are that e never follows r, and none of the vowels precedes b, d, or dy. I have no record of the sequences *up* and *txɨ*, but this may be accidental.

A.2.11 Restrictions between vowels of successive syllables

The vowels ɨ and u do not occur in successive syllables; across morpheme boundaries, ɨ changes to u (see A.4.1).

A.2.12 Modifications of phonotactic patterns in loan words

There are some idiolectal differences in the production of loan words from Portuguese. Some speakers adapt such words to normal Hixkaryana phonotactic patterns; others experiment with the Portuguese pronunciation and produce new patterns. Thus, Portuguese *soldado* 'soldier' is produced by some as *soknakdu* [sɔʔdæʔdu] (Hixkaryana phonotactics), and by others as *sordado* [sɔrdæ:du] (closer to the Portuguese), which has the nonnormal sequences rd and Vd, as well as different placement of vowel length; production by others is somewhere in between. It is not possible to identify any loanword subset of the lexicon that has its own systematic phonotactic patterns.

A.3 Suprasegmentals

A.3.1 Vowel length

There is no contrastive vowel length, but predictable length occurs under the following conditions: in a word that consists of only two syllables, both open, the vowel in the first syllable is lengthened; in longer words, in a sequence of open syllables, the vowel in every even-numbered syllable counting from the left is lengthened, except where the syllable is word final: *kwaya* [kwæ:jæ] 'red and green macaw', *torono* [tɔrɔ:nɔ] 'small bird', *akmatari* [ækmætæ:rɯ] 'branch', *atxowowo* [ætʃɔ:wɔwɔ] 'wind', *nemokotono* [nɪmɔ:kɔtɔ:nɔ] 'it fell', *naknyohyatxkenano* [nækɲɔhjætʃkɪnæ:nɔ] 'they were burning it'. This lengthening rule applies throughout the (phonological) word, ignoring morpheme and grammatical word boundaries. Thus, a morpheme may have different vowels lengthened depending on its cooccurrence with other morphemes:

(2) a. khananɨhno [khænæ:nɯhnɔ]
    (kɨ-   hananɨhɨ-no)
    (1SIIO-teach- IMM.PAST)
    'I taught you.'

 b. mɨhananɨhno [mɯhæ:nænɯhnɔ]
    (mɨ-   hananɨhɨ-no)
    (IISIIIO-teach- IMM.PAST)
    'You taught him.'

Similarly, where there is more than one grammatical word, different vowels in the same word may be lengthened, depending on the syllable patterning of the environment:

(3) a. owto hona [ɔwtɔhɔ:næ]
    village to
    'to the village'

 b. tohkurye hona [tɔhkuɾi:hɔnæ]
    Tohkurye to
    'to Tohkurye'

 c. tohkurye hona haxaha [tɔhkuɾi:hɔnæ:hæʃæ:hæ]
    Tohkurye to   finally
    'finally to Tohkurye'

A.3.2 Lengthening of stops

There is no contrast in length for stops, but see A.1.1 for a description of predictable lengthening.

A.3.3 Stress

Stress does not play any significant role in the language, except for the heavy stress associated with certain intonation patterns (see A.3.4). There is a primary stress on (phonological) word-final syllables and secondary stress on closed syllables and open syllables having lengthened vowels.

A.3.4 Intonation patterns

There are two intonation patterns for normal declarative sentences, **terminal** and **nonterminal**, and three patterns for other speech acts, **peremptory**, **interrogative**, and **response**.

Terminal intonation is a gradually rising pitch through the phrase or clause, reaching its peak on the penultimate syllable and falling on the last syllable, which is stressed:

(4) ito   naknyohyakon   ha
    there IIISIIIO-burn-DIST.PAST CONT INTENSFR.
    'He was burning it there.'

   [ɯtɔ:nækn̩ɔhjækɔnhá]

Nonterminal intonation is a gradually rising pitch that continues to rise, or levels off, on the last syllable, which is stressed. In (5) there are two intonation groups, the first being nonterminal and the second terminal:

(5) toy   hatɨ enatokoso
    IIIS-go-DIST.PAST COMPL HSY to-edge-of-village
    'He went to the edge of the village.'

   [tɔjhætɯ ɨnæ:tɔkɔ:sɔ́]

Nonterminal intonation occurs both in phrases which are not clause final, as in (5), and also in clauses which are not sentence final (see 1.6.4). Terminal intonation normally occurs sentence final, but it may also occur in nonfinal phrases as an optional variant of the nonterminal pattern. In the latter case, where each of a sequence of phrases in a sentence has the terminal pattern, the general level of pitch is usually slightly lower on each successive phrase.

Peremptory intonation is a rising pitch throughout the phrase, with the final syllable having high pitch and heavy stress. It occurs in imperative, interrogative, vocative, exclamative, and other utterances of a peremptory nature:

(6) ikahko   [ɯkæhkɔ́]
    'Make it!'

Interrogative intonation is a rising pitch throughout the phrase or clause, reaching high on the penultimate syllable, which is stressed, and then falling sharply on the final syllable. It occurs in interrogative utterances that are not of a peremptory nature:

(7) nomokno   [nɔmɔ́kno]
    'Has he come?'

Response intonation is relatively low pitch through the phrase or clause, with a very sharp rise to high on the last syllable. It occurs in responses to questions:

(8) omokhɨra   [ɔmɔk:hɯɾǽ]
    'Not coming'—could be a response to (7).

A.4 Morphophonology
A.4.1 Assimilatory processes

There are several assimilation processes and, in general, they occur only at morpheme boundaries within a (grammatical) word. They do not normally occur where clitic particles are involved (the rare exceptions are noted below), and this is one reason for treating particles as a separate word class (see 1.1.5).

Two processes of vowel harmony occur: (1) ɨ is replaced by u to harmonize with a preceding or following u, and this change takes place in both prefixes and suffixes: *muhutxuhkano* 'you took off the skin' (*mɨ-hutxuhka-no* IISIIIO-take off skin-IMM.

PAST); *ronuru* 'my eye' (*ro-onu-ri̵* I-eye-POSSN); and (2) o is replaced by a in prefixes and in the proclitic *mo-* 'out of sight' (see 1.1.5) to harmonize with a in a stem-initial syllable: *akamsukuru* 'your blood' (*o-kamsuku-ri̵* II-blood-POSSN); *amanhono* 'you danced' (*o-manho-no* IIS-dance-IMM.PAST).

Fusion occurs where morpheme-final n and r (after final vowel deletion—see A.4.3) combine with a following morpheme-initial y to become ny [ɲ] and ry [ɾ̥] respectively: *menyako* 'you drank it' (*mi̵-eni̵-yako* IISIIIO-drink-REC.PAST COMPL); *waryaha* 'I will take it' (*w-ari̵-yaha* ISIIIO-take-NONPAST). It is the application of the vowel-lengthening rule (see A.3.1) which helps determine the single-segmental status of ny and ry in the words [mɪɲæːkɔ] and [wæɾ̥æːhæ]; when n and y and r and y occur together across word boundaries, the length patterns in the sequences indicate that the ensuing segment sequences are [n.y] and [r.y]; that is, with syllable division between them (see A.2.8), as in *romi̵n yaka* [rɔmʊn.jækæ] 'to my house', *romur yakoro* [rɔmʊr.jækɔːrɔ] 'with my son', *en yawo* [en.jæwɔ] 'in the container'.

There are three palatalization processes:

(1) Morpheme-initial n changes to ny [ɲ] following e: *namomnyo* 'he rolled it up' (*ni̵-amome-no* IIISIIIO-roll up-IMM.PAST); *waknyohno* 'I burned it' (*w-ake-noh-no* ISIIIO-burn-CAUS-IMM.PAST); these examples reveal ordering of morphophonological rules, i.e., the change of n to ny precedes the deletion of e (see A.4.3 for deletion process).

(2) The segment r changes to ry preceding morpheme-initial e: *ryeryeni̵* 'my liver' (*r-erye-ni̵* 'I-liver-POSSN).

(3) Verb and derivational suffixes having initial s or t change to x or tx respectively when they follow a morpheme-final syllable containing the vowels e or a. With the suffix -*si̵* there is an accompanying change of vowel to e, forming -*xe:* *kemtakmaxe* 'let me take a meal' (*ki̵-emtakma-si̵* IS-take meal-IMP); *wenytxano* 'let me go see it' (*w-onye-tano* ISIIIO-see-MOT.IMP); *enkatxa* 'go take it out' (*∅-enka-ta* GEN.PREF-take out-MOT.IMP). The change from t to tx does not take place when the preceding morpheme-final syllable has initial t: *awanotata* 'go sing', not *awanotatxa (*a-wanota-ta* IIS-sing-MOT.IMP). This palatalization rule applies also to the derivational suffix -*tho* on verb stems (forming nominalizations—see Appendix F): *amatxho* 'thing for cutting it, axe' (*∅-ama-tho* III-cut-'thing' NOMLZN). But it does not apply to the homophonous morpheme *tho* 'DEVALUED' (see Appendix I): *xofrye tho* 'the poor old sloth' not **xofrye txho;* this is one of the grounds for considering particles like *tho* as a separate word class.

Two other replacement processes occur: (1) k is replaced by h when it occurs morpheme final preceding a morpheme-initial voiceless nonsyllabic other than h (this avoids nonpermitted clusters within the word—see A.2.4): *tohko* 'eat it' (*t-oki̵-ko* GEN.PREF-eat (nuts)-IMP); *wesnohsu* 'let me smell it' (*w-esnoku-si̵* ISIIIO-smell-IMP); (the latter example reveals more rule ordering, i.e., the assimilation of i̵ to u precedes deletion of u, and both these processes precede the change from k to h); (2) h is replaced by p when it occurs morpheme initial following a morpheme-final m or h (this also avoids nonpermitted clusters—see A.2.4): *ti̵mpi̵ra* 'not giving it' (*t-imi̵-hira* GEN. PREF.-give-NEG); *khanani̵hpono* 'I made (someone) teach you' (*ki̵-hanani̵hi-ho-no* ISIIO-teach-CAUS-IMM.PAST). These two replacement processes provide the few idiosyncratic exceptions there are to the general rule that assimilation does not occur across word boundaries, specifically where clitic particles are concerned (see first paragraph of this section). The k→h rule applies in two particle sequences (and not in any others): *xak(o)* 'MISFORTUNE' plus *tɨ* 'HEARSAY' becomes *xahtɨ*, and *mak(e)* 'ADVERSATIVE' plus *tɨ* 'HEARSAY' becomes *mahtɨ*. The h→p rule applies in a few cases involving the particle *heno* 'dead' or 'quantity, set of', e.g., *royɨmɨ* 'my father' plus *heno* becomes *royɨmpeno* 'my dead father'; *ekehɨ* 'dead body' plus *heno* becomes *ekehpeno* 'the dead one' (there are a few other examples, but in other cases involving a word-final m or h, the rule does not apply, e.g., *tamusnyem heno* 'the dead heavy thing'—referring to an anaconda; *sarah heno* 'the manioc plants'). It seems best to treat these exceptions as frozen, single-word forms (as written in the foregoing), and list them as such in the lexicon.

One other process occurs across morpheme boundaries within a word to avoid nonpermitted clusters involving a voiceless alveolar/postalveolar followed by y: the morpheme-initial y is deleted, and h is inserted immediately before the preceding morpheme-final alveolar/postalveolar. This results in the following rules: ty→ht, sy→hs, xy→hx (from my records tx and y do not seem to come together at morpheme boundaries): *nekahtaha* 'he flees' (*n-ekat-yaha* IIIS-flee-NONPAST); *wahohsako* 'I caught it' (*w-ahosɨ-yako* ISIIIO-catch-REC.PAST COMPL); *wehxaha* 'I am' (*w-exe-yaha* IS-be-NONPAST). Where ht results from this rule, there are two possible phonetic realizations: some idiolects have a palatalized t [htʲ]; others lack this palatalization [ht].

A.4.2 Metathesis processes

There is one general process that applies at any morpheme boundary within a word: morpheme-final s or x followed by morpheme-initial h changes to hs and hx respectively: *ahohsɨra* 'not catching it' (*∅-ahosɨ-hɨra* III-catch-NEG); *wamahxaka* 'let me cut it down' (*w-ama-xe-haka* ISIIIO-cut down-IMP-right now).

There are other more idiosyncratic changes, where certain CV sequences become VC when followed by certain suffixes or particles: *hu→uh* in *uhutxuhkano* 'I peeled it' (*ɨ-hutxhu-ka-no* ISIIIO-skin-REVERSATIVE-IMM.PAST); *hi→ih* in *tahotihke* 'having wings' (*tɨ-ahothɨ-ke* ADV-wing-having), and in *tehetihke* 'having value' (*tɨ-ehethɨ-ke* ADV-value-having); *tɨ→it* in *ewitheno* 'his brother, now dead' (*ewtɨ-heno* his brother-dead).

A.4.3 Deletion processes

The vowels i and u are deleted in any morpheme-final position other than before pause (for apocope at pause boundaries, see A.2.1), so long as the resulting sequence of segments is a permitted one. This occurs: (a) within the word, as in *kotmano* 'I gave you meat' (*kɨ-otɨ-ma-no* ISIIO-meat-BENEFACTIVE-IMM.PAST), and *namukno* 'he picked it up' (*nɨ-amuku-no* IIISIIIO-pick up-IMM.PAST); and (b) across word boundaries, as in *toh onɨ* 'this (is) a stone' (*tohu onɨ*), and *onok mokro* 'who (is) that one?' (*onokɨ mokro*) (cf. *onokɨ ryhe* 'who EMPHATIC', which cannot be reduced because it would result in a nonpermitted sequence).

The vowels e and o are deleted in more idiosyncratic ways. One class of e-final roots regularly has the e deleted, so long as the resulting sequence is a permitted one, e.g., *-ake-* 'burn': *naknyohno* 'he burned it' (*nɨ-ake-noh-no* IIISIIIO-burn-CAUS-IMM.PAST), *nataknyo* 'it got burnt' (*nɨ-at-ake-no* IIIS-DETRANS-burn-IMM.PAST), *katakyako* 'I got burnt' (*kɨ-at-ake-yako* IS-DETRANS-burn-REC.PAST COMPL), but cf. *ataketxhe* 'after it got burnt' (*∅-at-ake-txhe* III-DETRANS-burn-after), where deletion of e would result in a nonpermitted sequence. Another class of roots never has e deleted, e.g., *-ahe-* 'touch':

nahenohno 'he caused (someone) to touch it' (*ni̵-ahe-noh-no* IIISIIIO-touch-CAUS-IMM.PAST), *naheno* 'he touched it' (*ni̵-ahe-no* IIISIIO-touch-IMM.PAST); the two classes would need to be specified in the lexicon. Prefix-final o is regularly deleted in the case of *ro-* 'IIISIO' or 'I POSSR' when it precedes a vowel: *rarymano* 'he threw me' (*ro-aryma-no* IIISIO-throw-IMM.PAST); *rowani̵* 'my chest' (*ro-owa-ni̵* I-chest-POSSN). With regard to deletion of o and e at word boundaries, there are two classes of both o-final and e-final words, one class where o/e is deleted, and another where it is not. The final vowel is never deleted, for example, in *toto* 'human being' and *honye* 'piranha'; it is deleted in the other class of words when it occurs at word boundaries where no pause occurs and where the resulting sequence is a permitted one, e.g., *noro* 'third person' in *nor mehra nahko* 'it was not he'; *nemtakmaye* 'he took a meal' in *nemtakmay xarha* 'he also took a meal'. The two classes of words would need to be specified in the lexicon (in the case of *nemtakmaye* it would be the class of suffix that would be specified, i.e., *-ye* 'DISTANT PAST COMPLETIVE' belongs to the suffix class where final e is deleted, in contrast with *-ehe* 'NONPAST' (an allomorph of *-yaha*—see Appendix B), which belongs to the class where final e is never deleted, e.g., *nemtakmehe xarha* 'he also takes a meal'—never **nemtakmeh xarha*).

A.4.4 Insertion processes

Insertion of y takes place between the prefix o- (or its allomorph a-) 'IIS', 'IIISIIO', 'II POSSR' and a stem-initial vowel having the same quality: *oyonuru* 'your eye' (*o-onu-ri̵* II-eye-POSSN); *ayamryekyako* 'you went hunting' (*o-amryeki̵-yako* IIS-go hunting-REC.PAST COMPL).

There is insertion (epenthesis) of a brief vowel sound between syllables when certain sequences of consonants occur. The evidence that this is an epenthetic vowel comes from its failure to participate in the lengthening process (see A.3.1). Its quality is predictable in terms of the particular consonants in the sequence, according to the following rules:
(1) Where the first segment of the sequence is a postalveolar the vowel is the nontense close front [ɪ]: *atxketxko* [ætʃɪkɪtʃɪkɔ] 'small', *txororywa* [tʃɔrɔɲwæ] 'grey-breasted martin', *kwenywaha* [kweɲɪwæhæ] 'I am lazy'.
(2) Where the immediately preceding and following vowels are the same, it has a similar vowel quality, but always nontense: *marma* [mæræmæ] 'only', *ryehrye* [ɾihɪɾi] 'my weapon', *mokro* [mɔkɔrɔ] 'that person'.
(3) Elsewhere it approximates closely to the central mid [ə]: *arko* [ærəkɔ] 'take it', *itohra* [ɯtɔhəræ] 'not going', *hawxe* [hæwəʃi] 'curassow', *waywi̵* [wæjəwɯ].

The consonant sequences that condition the occurrence of these epenthetic vowels are: yf, yh, yw, txk, wx; all with ny as the first segment; all with r as the first or second segments (except wr when it is preceded by o, as in *owratano* [ɔwrætæːnɔ] 'you wept', and kr when it is followed by front vowels or the back unrounded vowel, as in *wakrakra* [wækrækræ] 'species of wild fruit' and *ikri̵ri̵* [ɯkrɯrɯ] 'flowing of river'); and all with ry as the first or second segment, other than the sequence *kry*, as in *akryeko* [ækɾikɔ] 'lift it up'.

APPENDIX B
INFLECTIONAL MORPHOLOGY: VERB

B.1 Coding of subject, direct object, and collective number

The persons of the subject and direct object are coded in the verb prefix. Although there is some overlap of individual forms, it is clearer to distinguish three sets of forms: transitive, intransitive, and copula. In the transitive set each prefix is a composite form that marks subject and object, although certain generalizations can be made concerning the particular category that has prominence. With the exception of the form **kɨ-**, which in one of its functions marks both subject (I) and direct object (II), only one category of person is marked in any verb, viz., (a) the first or second person object is marked if the subject is third person or contains third person (as in the I + III prefix), and (b) the person of the subject is marked in all other cases. (This is a modified form of the general statement proposed by Gudschinsky 1973.)

Collective number is coded in the verb suffix. The collective forms relate to the person of the subject and/or object, but never to the person categories I or I + III. The latter is always expressed by the free pronoun **amna** 'I + III', which takes the same form whether the referent is to a single third person or to a group of third persons. Subject to this constraint, collective refers to the person of the subject with intransitive stems and the copula, and to the person of either the subject or the object, or both, with transitive stems, so that in the latter case there can be ambiguity in the first person inclusive, second person, and third person forms. The collective marker on the verb is usually in agreement with the collective marker on the noun or pronoun subject or object; occasionally, however, the noun or pronoun may be collective when the verb is noncollective, especially in the case of a noun or pronoun direct object:

(1) a. **nomokyatxoko   hawana   komo**
     they-came-COLL visitor COLL
     'Visitors came.' (normal agreement)

b. **nomokyako   hawana komo**
   he-came-NONCOLL visitor COLL
   'Visitors came.' (rare nonagreement)
c. **hawana komo nyahmetxoko   Waraka**
   visitor COLL he-gave-them-food-COLL Waraka
   'Waraka gave food to the visitors.' (normal agreement)
d. **hawana komo nyahmeko   Waraka**
   visitor COLL he-gave-them-food-NONCOLL Waraka
   'Waraka gave food to the visitors.' (nonagreement, more
   frequent than (1b), and preferred by some speakers)

The human feature associated with the collective form of nouns and pronouns applies also to the collective marker in the verb (see 1.2.1).

B.2 Person-marking prefixes

B.2.1 The paradigm and the allomorphic conditioning factors

The complete paradigm of the person-marking prefixes in the verb is shown in the following matrix (it includes all the morphologically conditioned allomorphs):

	O I+II	II	I	III	Intrans. S only	Copula S only
S I+II				tɨ-	tɨ-	t-
I		kɨ-		ɨ-	kɨ-	w-
I+III		o-		nɨ-	nɨ-	n-
III	kɨ-	o-	ro-	(-O) nɨ- (+O) y-	nɨ-	n-
II			mɨ-	mɨ-	mɨ-, o-, ow-	man-, m-

The conditioning factors for the allomorphs are as follows:

IIISIIIO:

    y- occurs following a direct object NP
    nɨ- occurs elsewhere

Intransitive IIS:

    mɨ- occurs with two subclasses of stems:

        (i) those which have been derived from transitive or neutral stems by adding the prefix **e-** (or its allomorphs) 'DETRANSITIVIZER' (see Appendix E)

        (ii) the stems of certain verbs of motion, e.g., **-to-** 'go', **-omokɨ-** 'come', **-ahataka-** 'come out', 'arrive'

Inflectional Morphology: Verb

   ow- occurs with two stems, **-nɨkɨ-** 'sleep' and
   -rata- 'weep'
   o- occurs elsewhere

Copula IIS:

   man- occurs only in the words **manaha** 'you are' and
   manaye 'are you?'
   m- occurs elsewhere

There are also phonologically conditioned allomorphs. Some undergo the normal processes of vowel deletion and assimilation (see Appendix A.4). Others, specifically related to these prefixes, are:

ɨ- 'ISIIIO' has an allomorph **w-** which occurs before vowels (it is thus the same form as the copula IS)

kɨ- 'IS' has an allomorph **ɨ-** which occurs only before the consonants **t, tx,** and **x,** with **kɨ-** occurring before other consonants and all vowels

nɨ- 'IIIS' has an allomorph **Ø** that occurs in (phonological) phrase-initial position before stem-initial consonants other than **n, ny,** and **r,** with **nɨ-** occurring before those three consonants, and (in its reduced form **n-**) before all vowels and also before other consonants when these are not in phrase-initial position

nɨ- 'IIISIIIO' has an allomorph **Ø** before a stem-initial consonant in (phonological) phrase-initial position

y- 'IIISIIIO' has an allomorph **Ø** before a stem-initial consonant.

The effect of the last two is to neutralize the distinction between (-O) and (+O) in the IIISIIIO forms when they occur in (phonological) phrase-initial position--this is rare but it can lead to ambiguity as to whether a preceding NP is subject or object (see 3.3).

There is one other more general type of phonologically conditioned allomorph, which applies where the stem initial is a nasal (**m, n, ny**). The **kɨ-** prefixes are reduced to zero, and the initial nasal changes to a homorganic voiced plosive (**b, d, dy**), e.g., **bomokno** 'I was waiting for you' (**kɨ-momokɨ-no** ISIIO-wait for-IMM. PAST) or 'he was waiting for us' (**kɨ-momokɨ-no** IIISI+IIO-wait for-IMM.PAST); **dyakyatxhe** 'he will send us' (**kɨ-nyake-yatxhe** IIISI+IIO-send-NONPAST COLL); **dɨkno** 'I slept' (**kɨ-nɨkɨ-no** IS-sleep-IMM.PAST). A restricted form of the same rule applies in the case of the **tɨ** prefixes when these precede an initial **m** (but not **n, ny**). This results in ambiguity for forms like **bomokno**, which, in addition to the meanings above, can also mean 'we were waiting for him' (**tɨ-momokɨ-no** I+IIISIIIO-wait for-IMM.PAST); compare also **banhono** 'I danced' or 'we danced' (**kɨ-manho-no** or **tɨ-manho-no**).

Before **n** and **ny**, the prefix remains **tɨ-**: **tɨnyakyatxhe** 'we will send them' and **tɨnɨkno** 'we sleep'. This reflects the fact that the prefix vowel **ɨ-** is not deleted because historically, and still today in some people's speech, **tn** and **tny** are not permitted sequences (see Appendix A.1.1 for a fuller description of the segmental units **b, d,** and **dy,** and the allophone of **t** before **n** and **ny**).

Stem-initial **o** changes to **e** when it follows the prefix **nɨ-** in both transitive and intransitive verbs, and when it follows the prefixes **tɨ-**, **mɨ-** and **w-** (allomorph of **ɨ-** --see above) in transitive verbs:

  netahano 'he hit him' (**nɨ-otaha-no** IIISIIIO-hit-IMM.PAST)
  nekahtɨmno 'he fled' (**nɨ-okaht-ɨmɨ-no** IIIS-flee-STEM FORM-
      IMM.PAST)
  tenyo 'we saw him' (**tɨ-onye-no** I+IISIIIO-see-IMM.PAST),
      also **wenyo** 'I saw him' and **menyo** 'you saw him'.

This change applies to most stems having initial **o**, but there are a few exceptions, e.g., **wonono** 'I ate it (meat)', **nonono** 'he ate it', where the stem -ono- 'eat (meat)' never changes its form. The stems to which the rule applies also change to initial **e** where the 'GENERAL PREFIX' occurs (see B.2.3), as in imperatives (e.g., **etahako** 'hit him', **xenyko** 'look at it') and some derived forms (e.g., **etahaxaho** 'the one that was hit', **xenyhera** 'not seeing it').

The paradigm does not show I+III in the O(bject) columns because the only way in which I+III is signalled as an object is by the free form pronoun **amna**. The pronoun is also obligatory when it is the subject, but in this case it cooccurs with the prefixes which also signal third person.

The other gaps in the paradigm are where there is sameness of referent in both subject and object. These are accounted for either by the special reflexive forms or through the universal "inclusion constraint" (Postal 1966) (see 1.2.2).

The first person pronoun **uro** is obligatory to express first person object where the subject is second person.

For the close correspondence between the transitive prefixes that mark the direct object (when the subject is third person) and the noun person-marking prefixes, see Appendix C.

B.2.2 The prefixes exemplified

The following are examples of the prefixes, including the principal allomorphs not already illustrated:

  (i) transitive: **taknyohno** 'we (INCL) burned it' (**tɨ-ake-noh-no** I+IISIIIO-burn-CAUS-IMM.PAST); **tɨnyahmetxhe** 'we (INCL) will supply

Inflectional Morphology: Verb

them with food' (**tɨ-nyahma-yatxhe** I+IISIIIO-supply with food-NONPAST COLL); **kɨtaymano** 'I pushed you' (**kɨ-tayma-no** ISIIO-push-IMM.PAST); **kotahehe** 'I will hit you' (**kɨ-otaha-yaha** ISIIO-hit-NONPAST); **ɨkorokano** 'I washed him' (**ɨ-koroka-no** ISIIO-wash-IMM.PAST); **wehekatno** 'I bought it' (**w-ehekatɨ-no** ISIIIO-buy-IMM.PAST); **amna ohorohkehe** 'we (EXCL) will make you stop' (**amna-o-horohɨ-ka-yaha** I+III-I+IIISIIO-stop-CAUS-NONPAST); **amna oyonyo** 'we (EXCL) saw you' (**amna-oy-onye-no** I+III-I+IIISIIO-see-IMM.PAST); **amna nɨrakano** 'we (EXCL) split it' (**amna-nɨ-raka-no** I+III-I+IIISIIIO-split-IMM.PAST); **amna netahano** 'we (EXCL) hit him' (**amna-nɨ-otaha-no** I+III-I+IIISIIIO-hit-IMM.PAST); **kukukmetxhe** 'he will try us (INCL) out' (**kɨ-kukma-yatxhe** IIISI+IIO-try out-NONPAST COLL); **khananɨhyatxkonɨ** 'he used to teach us (INCL)' (**kɨ-hananɨhɨ-yatxkonɨ** IIISI+IIO-teach-DIST.PAST CONT.COLL; **omomokyaha** 'he is waiting for you' (**o-momokɨ-yaha** IIISIIO-wait for-NONPAST); **oyonkukmehe** 'it baffles you' (**oy-onkukma-yaha** IIISIIO-baffle-NONPAST); **ronyahmetxkonɨ** 'they used to feed me' (**ro-nyahma-yatxkonɨ** IIISIO-feed-DIST.PAST CONT.COLL); **rakoronomehe** 'he helps me' (**ro-akoronoma-yaha** IIISIO-help-NONPAST); **nɨyweronɨhyametxhe** 'he teaches them the traditions' or 'they teach him the traditions' or 'they teach them the traditions' (**nɨ-yweronɨhyama-yatxhe** IIIS-IIIO-teach traditions-NONPAST COLL); **hananɨhno** 'he taught him' (**Ø-hananɨhɨ-no** IIISIIIO-teach-IMM.PAST); (**woto**) **yonono** 'he ate (the meat)' (**y-ono-no** IIISIIIO-eat-IMM.PAST); **uro menytxano** 'you heard me' (**uro-mɨ-onytxa-no** I-IISIO-hear-IMM.PAST); **mɨkano** 'you said it' (**mɨ-ka-no** IISIIIO-say-IMM.PAST); **menkuhtotxowɨ** 'you deceived them' or 'you all deceived him' (**mɨ-onkuhto-txowɨ** IISIIIO-deceive-IMM.PAST COLL).

(ii) intransitive: **tɨtehe** 'we (INCL) are going' (**tɨ-to-yaha** I+IIS-go-NONPAST); **tamryekyaha** 'we (INCL) will go hunting' (**tɨ-amryekɨ-yaha** I+IIS-go hunting-NONPAST); **kratano** 'I wept' (**kɨ-rata-no** IS-weep-IMM.PAST); **kɨkɨtano** 'I rushed' (**kɨ-kɨta-no** IS-rush-IMM.PAST); **amna nɨnɨkno** 'we (EXCL) slept' (**amna-nɨ-nɨkɨ-no** I+III-I+IIIS-sleep-IMM.PAST); **nɨnono** 'it sank' (**nɨ-no-no** IIIS-sink-IMM.PAST); **nahyehyaha** 'he is hungry' (**nɨ-ahyehɨ-yaha** IIIS-be hungry-NONPAST); **wayehno** 'he has died' (**Ø-wayehɨ-no** IIIS-die-IMM.PAST); **mɨtehe** 'you will go' (**mɨ-to-yaha** IIS-go-NONPAST); **momokno** 'you have come' (**mɨ-omokɨ-no** IIS-come-IMM.PAST); **ohorohno** 'you stopped' (**o-horohɨ-no** IIS-stop-IMM.PAST); **oyontano** 'you woke up' (**oy-onta-no** IIS-wake up-IMM.PAST); **ayamryekyano** 'are you going hunting?' (**ay-amryekɨ-yano** IIS-go hunting-NONPAST UNCERT); **owratehe** 'you are weeping' (**ow-rata-yaha** IIS-weep-NONPAST).

(iii) copula: (**ɨtohra**) **tehtxe** 'let us be (not going)' (**t-exe-txe** I+IIS-be-IMP.COLL); (**ɨtohra**) **wahko** 'I was (not going)' (**w-ah-ko** IS-be-IMM.PAST); (**ɨtohra**) **amna naha** 'we (EXCL) are (not going)' (**amna-n-a-yaha** I+III-I+IIIS-be-NONPAST); (**ɨtohra**) **nehxatxkonɨ** 'they were (not going)' (**n-exe-yatxkonɨ** IIIS-be-DIST.PAST CONT.COLL); (**ɨtohra**) **mahko** 'you were (not going)' (**m-ah-ko** IIS-be-IMM.PAST).

B.2.3 The general prefix

There is a "general prefix" that occurs with verb stems in second person imperative forms and in certain derived nominals and adverbials. It sometimes functions as third person and sometimes as absence of person, depending on the type of stem and the particular derivation, in accordance with the following rules:

(a) Third person object is marked in transitive imperatives and transitive derivations which have the form of possessed nouns or adverbs.

(b) Absence of person is marked in derivations (both transitive and intransitive) which are nonpossessed forms.

(c) Third person subject is marked in intransitive derivations which have the form of possessed nouns or adverbs.

(d) Absence of person is marked in intransitive imperatives, but this applies only to the subclass of intransitive stems which elsewhere cooccur with the allomorph mɨ- of the second person subject-prefix (see B.2.1). Other intransitive stems, which cooccur with the other second person subject allomorphs (o-, ow-, and a- by vowel harmony process), retain these prefixal forms in the imperative.

The general prefix takes the following forms (examples correspond to the (a) to (d) rule assignment given above):

(i) **s-** occurs only with the transitive stem -okɨ- 'bring': (a) **soko** 'bring it' (**s-okɨ-ko** GEN-bring-IMP); **soknɨrɨ** 'the bringing of it' (**s-okɨ-nɨ-rɨ** GEN-bring-ACTION NOMLZN-POSSN); (b) **sokhɨnɨ** 'thing that is not brought' (**s-okɨ-hɨnɨ** GEN-bring-NEG.NOMLZN). (The stem -okɨ- 'bring' is one where the initial **o** normally changes to **e** under certain conditions (see B.2.1), but it does not do so when the general prefix occurs.)

(ii) **x-** occurs only with the transitive stem -onye- 'see': (a) **xenytxa** 'go see it' (**x-onye-txa** GEN-see-MOT.IMP); **xenyhera** 'not seeing it' (**x-onye-hɨra** GEN-see-NEG); (b) **xenyxaho** 'one that was seen' (**x-onye-xaho** GEN-see-OBJ. OF PAST ACTION).

(iii) **tx-** occurs only with the transitive stem -e(rye)- 'do, fix, put down': (a) **txeryko** 'put it down' (**tx-e-rye-ko** GEN-put down-STEM FORM-IMP); **txenye** 'one who fixes it' (**tx-e-nye** GEN-fix-DOER NOMLZN); (b) **txexenyeno** 'thing that has just been put down' (**tx-e-xenyeno** GEN-put down-OBJ. OF RECENT ACTION).

(iv) **t-** occurs with seven stems, all transitive:

-ɨhɨ- 'bathe': (a) **tɨhta** 'go bathe him' (**t-ɨhɨ-ta** GEN-bathe-MOT.IMP); **tɨhnye** 'one who bathes him' (**t-ɨhɨ-nye** GEN-bathe-DOER NOMLZN); (b) **tɨhxenyeno** 'one who has just been bathed' (**t-ɨhɨ-xenyeno** GEN-bathe-OBJ. OF RECENT ACTION).

Inflectional Morphology: Verb 193

-ɨmɨ- 'give': (a) **tɨmko** 'give it' (**t-ɨmɨ-ko** GEN-give-IMP); **tɨmnɨrɨ** 'the giving of it' (**t-ɨmɨ-nɨ-rɨ** GEN-give-ACTION NOMLZN-POSSN); (b) **tɨmpɨnɨ** 'thing that is not to be given' (**t-ɨmɨ-hɨnɨ** GEN-give-NEG.NOMLZN).

-okɨ- 'eat (bread)': (a) **tohko** 'eat it' (**t-okɨ-ko** GEN-eat-IMP); **tokhɨra** 'not eating it' (**t-okɨ-hɨra** GEN-eat-NEG); (b) **tohsaho** 'thing that was eaten' (**t-okɨ-saho** GEN-eat-OBJ. OF PAST ACTION).

-ono- 'eat (meat)': (a) **tonotatxko** '(all of you) go eat it' (**t-ono-tatxko** GEN-eat-MOT.IMP.COLL); **tonohtorɨ** 'the not eating of it' (**t-ono-hɨto-rɨ** GEN-eat-NEG.ACTION NOMLZN-POSSN); (b) **tonosaho** 'thing that has been eaten' (**t-ono-saho** GEN-eat-OBJ. OF PAST ACTION).

-owɨ- 'take away': (a) **towko** 'take it away' (**t-owɨ-ko** GEN-take away-IMP); **towhɨra** 'not taking it away' (**t-owɨ-hɨra** GEN-take away-NEG); (b) **towhɨnɨ** 'thing that is not to be taken away' (**t-owɨ-hɨnɨ** GEN-take away-NEG.NOMLZN).

-wo- 'shoot': (a) **twota ha** 'go shoot it' (**t-wo-ta-ha** GEN-shoot-MOT.IMP-INTENSFR); **twohra** 'not shooting it' (**t-wo-hɨra** GEN-shoot-NEG); (b) **twosaho** 'thing that was shot' (**t-wo-saho** GEN-shoot-OBJ. OF PAST ACTION).

-yo- 'boil' (in this case the prefix is realized as **tɨ**- to avoid a nonpermitted consonant cluster): (a) **tɨyoko** 'boil it' (**tɨ-yo-ko** GEN-boil-IMP); **tɨyonɨrɨ** 'the boiling of it' (**tɨ-yo-nɨ-rɨ** GEN-boil-ACTION NOMLZN-POSSN); (b) **tɨyosaho** 'thing that has been boiled' (**tɨ-yo-saho** GEN-boil-OBJ. OF PAST ACTION).

(v) **Ø**- occurs with all other stems that begin with a vowel. This applies to both transitive and intransitive stems. It is also the normal marker (zero allomorph) for third person possessor in nouns when there is no preceding noun phrase possessor (see Appendix C).

Transitive -ahe- 'touch': (a) **aheko** 'touch it' (**Ø-ahe-ko** GEN-touch-IMP); **ahenɨrɨ** 'the touching of it' (**Ø-ahe-nɨ-rɨ** GEN-touch-ACTION NOMLZN-POSSN); (b) **ahehnɨ** 'thing that is not to be touched' (**Ø-ahe-hɨnɨ** GEN-touch-NEG.NOMLZN).

Intransitive -eryewta- 'sit down': (b) **eryewtaxaho** 'one who sat down' (**Ø-eryewta-xaho** GEN-sit down-SUBJ. OF PAST ACTION); (c) **eryewtanɨrɨ** 'his sitting down' (**Ø-eryewta-nɨ-rɨ** GEN-sit down-ACTION NOMLZN-POSSN) in the set which includes **ryeryewtanɨrɨ** 'my sitting down' (with prefix **ro-** 'first person' subject to vowel loss and palatalization processes); (d) **eryewtako** 'sit down' (**Ø-eryewta-ko** GEN-sit down-IMP).

Copula -exe- 'be' is included in the rule at this point, since it begins with a vowel: (b) **ehxera** 'not being' (**Ø-exe-hɨra** GEN-be-NEG); (c) **ehtoko** 'when his being' i.e. 'when he is' (**Ø-exe-toko** GEN-be-SIMULT) in the set that includes **ryehtoko** 'when my being', 'when I am' (with prefix **ro-** 'first person'--see above); (d) **exko** 'be' (**Ø-exe-ko** GEN-be-IMP).

(vi) ɨ- occurs with all other stems that begin with a consonant, both transitive and intransitive. It is also the normal marker for third person possessor in nouns when there is no preceding noun phrase possessor (see Appendix C).

Transitive **-koroka-** 'wash': (a) **ɨkorokatxa** 'go wash it' (**ɨ-koroka-txa** GEN-wash-MOT.IMP); **ɨkorokahra** 'not washing it' (**ɨ-koroka-hɨra** GEN-wash-NEG); (b) **ɨkorokaxaho** 'thing that was washed' (**ɨ-koroka-xaho** GEN-wash-OBJ. OF PAST ACTION).

Intransitive **-to-** 'go': (b) **ɨtosaho** 'one who has gone' (**ɨ-to-saho** GEN-go-SUBJ. OF PAST ACTION); **ɨtohra** 'not going' (**ɨ-to-hɨra** GEN-go-NEG); (c) **ɨtonɨrɨ** 'his going' (**ɨ-to-nɨ-rɨ** GEN-go-ACTION NOMLZN-POSSN); (d) **ɨtoko** 'go' (**ɨ-to-ko** GEN-go-IMP).

B.3 Tense-aspect-number-mood suffixes

B.3.1 Imperative mood

There are two parameters in the imperative suffix paradigm: individual vs. collective number; and nonmotion vs. motion, i.e., whether motion is, or is not, involved in the performance of the intended action. The forms differ according to the person of the subject: in the nonmotion paradigm there are distinct forms for four categories of person; and in the motion paradigm two categories of person are distinguished. (See 6.3 for use of motion proclitics with I+II nonmotion forms, for I+III imperatives, and for other syntactic factors involved in the use of imperative forms.)

The nonmotion imperative paradigm is:

	Individual	Collective
II	-ko	-txoko
I	-sɨ/-xe	-sɨnye/-xenye
I+II	-nye	-txe
III	-no haka	-txow(ɨ) haka

The III suffixes **-no** and **-txowɨ** have as their primary meaning 'IMMEDIATE PAST' (see B.3.2.1); it is cooccurrence with the particle **haka** 'right now', IMPERATIVE' that gives the specifically imperative meaning. (In the case of the copula, the irregular forms of 'IMMEDIATE PAST' cooccur with **haka** to express III imperative: **nahko haka** 'let him be'; **nahtxok(o) haka** 'let them be'; cf. B.3.2.2.)

The usual person-marking prefixes cooccur with the above suffixes (see B.2.1), except for the second person imperative, where the general prefix cooccurs with all transitive stems and one subset of intransitive stems, and allomorphs of the 'IIS' prefix cooccur with the other set of intransitive stems (see B.2.3).

Inflectional Morphology: Verb   195

Examples: **awanotako** 'sing' (**a-wanota-ko** IIS-sing-IMP); **awanotatxoko** 'all of you sing' (**a-wanota-txoko** IIS-sing-IMP.COLL); **kwanotaxe** 'let me sing' (**kɨ-wanota-xe** IS-sing-IMP); **twanotanye** 'let us (two) sing' (**tɨ-wanota-nye** I+IIS-sing-IMP); **twanotatxe** 'let us (all) sing' (**tɨ-wanota-txe** I+IIS-sing-IMP.COLL); **wanotan(o) haka** 'let him sing' (**Ø-wanota-no-haka** IIIS-sing-IMM.PAST-IMP); **wanotatxow haka** 'let them sing' (**Ø-wanota-txowɨ-haka** IIIS-sing-IMM.PAST COLL-IMP); **ɨhanaɨɨhko** 'teach him' (**ɨ-hanaɨɨhɨ-ko** GEN.PREF-teach-IMP); **ɨhanaɨɨhtxoko** 'teach them' or 'all of you teach him/them' (**ɨ-hanaɨɨhɨ-txoko** GEN.PREF-teach-IMP.COLL); **ɨhanaɨɨhsɨ** 'let me teach him' (**ɨ-hanaɨɨhɨ-sɨ** ISIIIO-teach-IMP); **ɨhanaɨɨhsɨnye** 'let me teach them' (**ɨ-hanaɨɨhɨ-sɨnye** ISIIIO-teach-IMP.COLL); **thanaɨɨhnye** 'let us (two) teach him' (**tɨ-hanaɨɨhɨ-nye** I+IISIIIO-teach-IMP); **thanaɨɨhtxe** 'let us (two) teach them' or 'let us (all) teach him/them' (**tɨ-hanaɨɨhɨ-txe** I+IISIIIO-teach-IMP. COLL); **hanaɨɨhno haka** 'let him teach him' (**Ø-hanaɨɨhɨ-no-haka** IIISIIIO-teach-IMM.PAST-IMP); **hanaɨɨhtxow haka** 'let him teach them' or 'let them teach him/them' (**Ø-hanaɨɨhɨ-txowɨ-haka** IIISIIIO-teach-IMM.PAST COLL-IMP).

The motion imperative paradigm is:

	Individual	Collective
II	-ta	-tatxko
I	-tano	-tanyeno

Examples: **ewehta** 'go take a bath' (**Ø-ewehɨ-ta** GEN.PREF-take a bath-IMP.MOT); **ewehtatxko** 'all of you go take a bath' (**Ø-ewehɨ-tatxko** GEN.PREF-take a bath-IMP.MOT.COLL); **kewehtano** 'let me go take a bath' or 'I must go take a bath' (**kɨ-ewehɨ-tano** IS-take a bath-IMP.MOT); **xenytxa** 'go see it' (**x-onye-ta** GEN.PREF-see-IMP.MOT); **xenytxatxko** 'go see them' or 'all of you go see it/them' (**x-onye-tatxko** GEN.PREF-see-IMP.MOT); **wenytxano** 'let me go see it' (**w-onye-tano** ISIIIO-see-IMP.MOT); **wenytxanyeno** 'let me go see them' (**w-onye-tanyeno** ISIIIO-see-IMP.MOT.COLL).

B.3.2 Nonimperative mood

All finite verb forms other than the imperative have one set of suffixes that mark tense, aspect, and number (only 'COLLECTIVE' is marked). Transitive and intransitive verbs take the same set of suffixes (B.3.2.1 below). The copula has some different suffixal forms, and there are also stem variants, so that it is clearer to give the full set of forms for the copula (B.3.2.2 below).

B.3.2.1 Transitive and intransitive suffixes. The complete paradigm is:

	Individual	Collective
nonpast	**-yaha**	**-yatxhe**
nonpast uncertain	**-yano**	**-yatxowɨ**
immediate past	**-no**	**-txowɨ**
recent past completive	**-yako**	**-yatxoko**
recent past continuative	**-yaknano**	**-yatxkenano**
distant past completive	**-ye**	**-txownɨ**
distant past continuative	**-yakonɨ**	**-yatxkonɨ**

"Completive" forms express semelfactive or punctual aspects; "continuative" forms express habitual, continuous, or progressive aspects. "Uncertain" is included here, rather than treated as a separate mood, since it relates only to nonpast and its form fits the general pattern found in this set.

The "nonpast" forms are used with reference to present, future, and universal, without any formal distinction between the three types of tense: **namryekyaha** 'he is going hunting (now)', or 'he will go hunting (sometime soon)', or 'he hunts' (i.e., he is a man who hunts).

The "nonpast uncertainty" forms have a modal value: they are used to express interrogatives, and also noninterrogatives, in which case they usually cooccur with certain verification particles (see Appendix K). In all these uses they can refer to present, future, or universal: **amanheno** 'do you dance?' or 'are you dancing (now)?' or 'are you going to dance?' (**a-manho-yano** IIS-dance-NONPAST UNCERT); **wanoten hana** 'maybe he sings', or 'maybe he is singing now', or 'maybe he will sing (if you ask him)' (**∅-wanota-yano-hana** IIIS-sing-NONPAST UNCERT-UNCERT).

The past forms show three degrees of remoteness:

'Immediate past' refers to actions done the same day or the previous night, e.g., **kahatakano** 'I came out' (**kɨ-ahataka-no** IS-come out-IMM.PAST); **oyotahatxowɨ** 'they hit you' (**oy-otaha-txowɨ** IIISIIO-hit-IMM.PAST COLL).

'Recent past' refers to actions done on the previous day or any time earlier up to a period of a few months (this is the norm, but it is relative to the total situation, and sometimes an event of only a few weeks ago will be expressed with the distant past suffix), e.g., **nɨnɨkyako** 'he went to sleep' (**nɨ-nɨkɨ-yako** IIIS-go to sleep-REC.PAST COMPL); **ronyatxoko** 'they saw me' (**r-onye-yatxoko** IIISIO-see-REC.PAST COMPL.COLL), with a reduction of stem-final **nye** and suffix-initial **ya** to form **nya**, that applies throughout the paradigm of this verb); **omomokyaknano** 'he was waiting for you' (**o-momokɨ-yaknano** IIISIIO-wait for-REC.PAST CONT);

Inflectional Morphology: Verb   197

menyhoryetxkenano 'you all were making them' (**mɨ-onyhorye-yatxke-nano** IISIIIO-make-REC.PAST CONT.COLL, with the normal reduction of stem-final **e** and suffix-initial **ya**--see below).

'Distant past' refers to actions done any time earlier, e.g., **wamaye** 'I felled it' (**w-ama-ye** ISIIIO-fell-DIST.PAST COMPL); **tekonɨ** 'he used to go' (**Ø-to-yakonɨ** IIIS-go-DIST.PAST CONT).

There are two morphophonological rules that affect the suffixes beginning with **-ya-**:

(i) **-ya-** changes to **-e-** and replaces stem-final **a**, **e**, and **o**: **rotaheko** 'he hit me' (**r-otaha-yako** IIISIO-hit-REC.PAST COMPL); **oyowakryetxkonɨ** 'they made you happy' (**oy-owakrye-yatxkonɨ** IIISIIO-make happy-DIST.PAST CONT.COLL); **ɨhomeno** 'I may plant (the field)' (**ɨ-homo-yano** ISIIIO-plant-NONPAST UNCERT). That change results in another affecting only the nonpast (individual): the final **-ha** changes to **-he** following **e-**: **rotahehe** 'he will hit me' (**r-otaha-yaha** IIISIO-hit-NONPAST NONCOLL).

(ii) The **y** of the suffix-initial **-ya-** is deleted following stem-final **n**, **t**, and **w**: **nemenakonɨ** 'he used to steal' (**nɨ-emen-yakonɨ** IIIS-steal-DIST.PAST CONT); **kokahtako** 'I fled' (**kɨ-okaht-yako** IS-flee-REC.PAST COMPL); **neryewaha** 'he has pain' (**nɨ-eryew-yaha** IIIS-have pain-NONPAST).

B.3.2.2 The copula. The copula has basic stem forms: **-exe-** (with phonologically conditioned variants), **-ah-** (cooccurring with immediate past suffixes), and **-a-** (cooccurring with second and third person subject prefixes and the nonpast suffixes). The complete set of finite (nonimperative) forms for the copula is:

	I+II	I	III	II
nonpast:				
individ	tehxaha	wehxaha	naha	manaha
coll	tehxatxhe		natxhe	manatxhe
nonpast uncert:				
individ	tehxano	wehxano	naye	manaye
coll	tehxatxowɨ		natxowɨ	manatxowɨ
imm.past:				
individ	tahko	wahko	nahko	mahko
coll	tahtxoko		nahtxoko	mahtxoko
rec.past compl:				
individ	tehxako	wehxako	nehxako	mehxako
coll	tehxatxoko		nehxatxoko	mehxatxoko

rec.past cont:

individ	tehxaknano	wehxaknano	nehxaknano	mehxaknano
coll	tehxatxkenano		nehxatxkenano	mehxatxkenano

dist.past compl:

individ	texeye	wexeye	nexeye	mexeye
coll	tehtxownɨ		nehtxownɨ	mehtxownɨ

dist.past cont:

individ	tehxakonɨ	wehxakonɨ	nehxakonɨ	mehxakonɨ
coll	tehxatxkonɨ		nehxatxkonɨ	mehxatxkonɨ

I+III forms are identical with the individual forms of III and always cooccur with the free pronoun **amna** 'I+III'.

B.3.3 Stem formative suffixes occurring with subsets of verb roots

There is a stem formative -rɨ-, which is added to a small subset of transitive and intransitive stems, when the stem precedes a suffix-initial **y** (and also when it precedes suffix-initial **k** in the imperative suffix paradigm): **warɨye** 'I took it' (w-a-rɨ-ye ISIIIO-take-STEM FORM-DIST.PAST COMPL); **waryaha** 'I will take it' (w-a-rɨ-yaha ISIIIO-take-STEM FORM-NONPAST). Cf. **wano** 'I took it' (w-a-no ISIIIO-take-IMM.PAST), where the suffix does not begin with **y**. Other stems to which **rɨ-** is added in this way include -ahu- 'shut in' (the vowel harmony rule results in -ahuru-), -amo- 'put on (clothing)', -ano- 'be dry', -eho- 'look for', -e- 'make, fix, put down' (the vowel harmony rule results in -ery(e)- as in **weryeye** 'I put it down' and **weryaha** 'I will put it down'), -onu- 'be born'.

There is another stem formative, -ɨmɨ-, which is added to stems (all intransitive) ending with **n**, **t**, and **w**. It is obligatory preceding suffixes which do not have initial -ya, and optional in other cases: **ɨtxokonɨmno** 'I hiccoughed' (ɨ-txokon-ɨmɨ-no IS-hiccough-STEM FORM-IMM.PAST) (the form *ɨtxokon(n)o does not occur); **ɨtxokonɨmyako** (ɨ-txokon-ɨmɨ-yako) or **ɨtxokonako** (ɨ-txokon-yako) to which is applied the **y** reduction rule described in B.3.2.1) 'I hiccoughed (recent past)'. Other stems to which -ɨmɨ- is added in this way include -amen- 'refuse to give', -arurun- 'grow profusely', -ehɨn- 'be precious', -emen- 'steal', -kokon- 'crow', -komsɨn- 'be cold', -otaken- 'whistle', -rwon- 'talk', -haraht- 'throw', -ɨht- 'crow', -okaht- 'flee', -eryew- 'have pain'.

APPENDIX C
INFLECTIONAL MORPHOLOGY: NOUN

Inflectional affixes in N function primarily as markers of possession (in the case of some classes of derived N other underlying relations are expressed--see 1.2.1): prefixes mark person of the possessor; and suffixes mark possession, tense, and number.

C.1 Person-marking prefixes

The person-marking prefixes (the forms cited are nonpast and noncollective) are as follows:

I: **ro-, r-**

    e.g. **rokanawarɨ** 'my canoe' (**ro-kanawa-rɨ**)

        rowanɨ 'my chest' (**r-owa-nɨ**)

I+II: **kɨ-, ku-, k-**

    kɨkanawarɨ 'our (INCL) canoe'

    kukukuru 'our (INCL) relative' (**ku-kuku-ru**)

    kowanɨ 'our (INCL) chests'

II: **o-, oy-, ow-, a-, ay-**

    ohunu 'your flesh' (**o-hun-nu**)

    oyowanɨ 'your chest'

    owotɨ 'your meat' (**ow-ot-tɨ**)

    akanawarɨ 'your canoe'

    ayamorɨ 'your hand' (**ay-amo-rɨ**)

III reflexive: **tɨ-, tu-, t-**

    tɨhrorɨ 'his own foot' (**tɨ-hro-rɨ**)

    tunyuru 'his own tongue' (**tu-nyu-ru**)

    tkanawarɨ 'his own canoe'

    towanɨ 'his own chest'

III with a preceding NP: **y-, ∅-**
    Waraka yowanɨ 'Waraka's chest'
    Waraka kanawarɨ 'Waraka's canoe'
III without a preceding NP: **ɨ-, u-,** (stem-initial change:
o   e), **∅-**
    ɨkanawarɨ 'his canoe'
    uhunu 'his flesh'
    ewanɨ 'his chest'
    amorɨ 'his hand'
I+III: **(amna) y-, (amna) ∅-**
    amna yowanɨ 'our (EXCL) chests'
    amna kanawarɨ 'our (EXCL) canoes'

Many of the allomorphs, included above for the sake of a complete description, are phonologically conditioned (see Appendix A.4 for the processes involved). I+III is included in the paradigm, although, as the forms indicate, the prefixes are identical with III with a preceding NP, that NP in this case being the pronoun **amna** 'we/our (EXCL)'.

    The modifying particle **komo** 'COLLECTIVE' (see Appendix I) is used with possessed nouns and relates to (i) the possessor, when this is a human referent and refers to a group, e.g., **kɨkanawar komo** (**kɨ-kanawa-rɨ-komo** I+II-canoe-POSSN-COLL) 'our (INCL.COLL) canoes'; **ohun komo** (**o-hun-nu-komo** II-flesh-POSSN-COLL) 'your (COLL) bodies', or (ii) the possessed item, when this is a human referent and refers to a group, e.g., **rowtɨ komo** (**r-ow-tɨ-komo** I-brother-POSSN-COLL) 'my brothers'; **ɨhar komo** (**ɨ-ha-rɨ-komo** III-grandchild-POSSN-COLL) 'his grandchildren'. It may refer to both possessor and possessed item, where both are human and a group: **kukukur komo** (**ku-kuku-ru-komo** I+II-relative-POSSN-COLL) 'our (INCL.COLL) relatives'. In this case there is always ambiguity, since the same form can also mean 'our (two only) relatives' or 'our (COLL) relative'. The particle **komo** is not used to mark plurality or group in nonhuman referents, so **rokanawarɨ** (**ro-kanawa-rɨ** I-canoe-POSSN) can mean 'my canoe' or 'my canoes' (not *****rokanawar komo**). There is another collective marker, the suffix **-yamo**, which occurs with certain nominals (mostly derived) where **komo** does not occur, but with some speakers and with a few nouns the two forms are optional variants (see C.2).

    Comparing the list of noun prefixes with the paradigm for person-marking prefixes in the verb (see Appendix B.2.1), it can be seen that there is exact correspondence between the possessives

Inflectional Morphology: Noun   201

and the group of verb prefixes which mark the direct object
occurring when the subject is third person, except for III, where
the basic allomorph in the noun prefix is ɨ- and that in the verb
is nɨ-. In addition, of course, 'III reflexive' does not occur in
the verb paradigm (although the form it takes in the noun,
i.e., tɨ-, does occur in the verb paradigm, signalling something
quite different, i.e., 'I+IIS').

C.2 Possession-tense-number suffixes

The following suffixes occur:

-rɨ, -nɨ, -tɨ, -txe, -Ø 'POSSESSED ITEM'

-thɨrɨ (-txhɨrɨ), -tho (-txho), -nhɨrɨ, -nho 'POSSESSED ITEM,
SIMPLE PAST' (-nhɨrɨ can also cooccur with -thɨrɨ (-txhɨrɨ),
always following that form, with the meaning 'remote past')

-nano 'DEPOSSSESSION'

-yamo 'COLLECTIVE'

The allomorphs shown in parentheses are phonologically conditioned (see Appendix A.4). The forms -nɨ, -tɨ, -txe, and -Ø occur
with relatively small sets of stems, -rɨ being the form used with
most stems. The -tho and -nho forms occur with the prefixes
marking I, III with a preceding NP, and I+III; -thɨrɨ and -nhɨrɨ
occur elsewhere (but where these two forms occur in sequence it is
always -thɨrɨnhɨrɨ (-txhɨrɨnhɨrɨ), never *-thonho, *-thɨrɨnho, or
*-thonhɨrɨ). The allomorph -tho is homophonous with both an allo-
morph of the derivational suffix -toho 'THING, TIME, OR PLACE AS-
SOCIATED WITH THE ACTION' (see Appendix F), and the modifying
particle tho 'DEVALUED' (see Appendix I). The latter is closely
related in meaning with the past tense suffix allomorph being
described here. One part of the evidence that there are two distinct morphemes is that the modifier meaning 'DEVALUED' occasionally occurs in the middle of the -thɨrɨnhɨrɨ sequence to form
-thɨrɨthonhɨrɨ, with a literal meaning of 'PAST, DEVALUED, RE-
MOTE', e.g., ɨnekarymatxhɨrɨthonhɨrɨ (ɨ-n-okaryma-txhɨrɨ-tho-
nhɨrɨ III-NOMLZN-tell-PAST NOMLZN-DEVALUED-REMOTE) 'the things he
used to tell long ago, but no longer tells (because he is dead)'
(for the forms of nominalization involved in this example see
Appendix F).

Examples of the allomorphs of 'POSSESSED ITEM' are **rokanawarɨ**
(ro-kanawa-rɨ) 'my canoe', **ewanɨ** ((o   e)wa-nɨ) 'his chest',
owotɨ (ow-ot-tɨ) 'your meat', **ɨhetxe** (ɨ-he-txe) 'his wife',
rokatxho (ro-katxho-Ø) 'my things'.

The corresponding forms of these for 'SIMPLE PAST' are **rokan-
awatho** 'my former canoe' (cf. **ɨkanawathɨrɨ** 'his former canoe'),
ewanɨthɨrɨ 'his (sick) chest (i.e., when there is something wrong

with it)' (cf. **Waraka yowanɨtho** 'Waraka's (sick) chest'), **owotɨthɨrɨ** 'that which was your meat' (cf. **rotɨtho** 'that which was my meat'), **ɨhetxenhɨrɨ** 'his former wife', **amna katxhotho** 'our (EXCL) old things' (cf. **kɨkatxhothɨrɨ** 'our (INCL) old things' or **ɨkatxhothɨrɨ** 'his old things'). It will be noted that the 'SIMPLE PAST' suffix replaces the allomorph -**rɨ** 'NONPAST', but cooccurs with, and follows, the other allomorphs of that suffix (cf. **ɨkanawathɨrɨ**, not *i**kanawarɨthɨrɨ** and **ewanɨthɨrɨ**, not *e**wathɨrɨ**). The forms -**nhɨrɨ** and -**nho**, when they carry the meaning 'SIMPLE PAST', occur with only a small set of stems, including -**he**- 'wife of' (see above) and -**nyo** 'husband of', as in **ronyo** 'my husband', **ronyonho** 'my former husband', **ɨnyonhɨrɨ** 'her former husband'. These forms, -**nhɨrɨ** and -**nho** (but not -**thɨrɨ**), also occur with nonpossessed words: **wahanho** 'one who had been a killer', **totothonhɨrɨ** (**toto-tho-nhɨrɨ** human-DEVALUED-REMOTE PAST) 'one who had been a human being'.

The suffix -**nhɨrɨ** has the meaning 'REMOTE PAST' in the sequence -**thɨrɨnhɨrɨ**. The suffix -**thɨrɨ** corresponds to and replaces the nonpast -**nɨrɨ** in two types of nominals derived from verb stems: -**nɨ**- 'ACTION NOMINALIZATION' and -**nɨ**-...-**nɨ**- 'OBJECT RESULTING FROM ACTION' (see Appendix F). Examples of these derived nominals are **rotothɨrɨnhɨrɨ** (**ro-to-thɨrɨ-nhɨrɨ** I-go-PAST-REMOTE) 'my going long ago', **ekarymatxhɨrɨnhɨrɨ** ((o e) **karyma-txhɨrɨ-nhɨrɨ** (III) tell-PAST-REMOTE) 'the telling of it long ago', **onmenhothɨrɨnhɨrɨ** (**o-n-menho-thɨrɨ-nhɨrɨ** II-OBJECT NOMLZN-write-PAST-REMOTE) 'the thing you wrote long ago', **Waraka nmenhothɨrɨnhɨrɨ** (not *W**araka nmenhothonho**) 'the thing written by Waraka long ago'. The 'REMOTE' meaning of -**nhɨrɨ**/-**nho** need not be in any absolute sense of 'a long time ago', but can refer to an action that is earlier than another action, however recent the two actions may have been. Thus, **rotothɨrɨnhɨrɨ** (see above) may mean 'my earlier going' when two goings have been referred to or implied; the more recent one would be **rototho** 'my going (past)'; both these forms contrast in tense with **rotonɨrɨ** 'my going (present or future)'.

The form -**nhɨrɨ** also occurs with other derived nominals:

- **nye** 'DOER OF THE ACTION' (see Appendix F) with the meaning 'PAST', e.g., **oyokarymanyenhɨrɨ** (**oy-okaryma-nye-nhɨrɨ** II-tell-DOER NOMLZN-PAST) 'the one who told about you' (here there is no distinction between 'simple' and 'remote' past)

- **saho** 'SUBJECT (INTRANS) or OBJECT (TRANS) OF PAST ACTION' (see Appendix F), when the meaning is 'REMOTE PAST', e.g., **ekarymaxahonhɨrɨ** ((o e)**karyma-xaho-nhɨrɨ** (III) tell-OBJ. OF PAST ACTION-REMOTE) 'thing that was told long ago'

Inflectional Morphology: Noun

-hɨnɨ 'NEGATION NOMINALIZATION' (see Appendix F), but only (so far as I am aware) when this follows the **-nye** derivation referred to above: **rokarymanyehnɨnhɨrɨ** (r-okaryma-nye-hnɨ-nhɨrɨ I-tell-DOER NOMLZN-NEGATION-PAST) 'not the one who told about me'

The suffix **-nano** 'DEPOSSESSION' substitutes for the 'POSSESSED ITEM' suffix (and also the possessor prefix), when these occur in what are normally obligatorily possessed nouns, and it has the effect of removing the possession element: cf. **rahonɨ** 'my stool (seat)' and **ahonano** 'stool(s)'. These depossessed forms are rarely used except for a few frozen forms like **katxhonano** 'things, goods' (cf. **rokatxho** 'my things') and **atunano** 'fever' (cf. **atunu** 'his fever' or 'its heat'). The preferred form for things in general is the generic use of I+II forms: **kownarɨ komo** 'our noses', i.e., 'people's noses'.

The suffix **-yamo** 'COLLECTIVE' occurs with two sets of forms. In its fully productive usage it follows only **-thɨ-** 'PAST' and **-nhɨ-** 'REMOTE' and substitutes for the final **-rɨ** that normally occurs with these two suffixes: **ɨtothɨyamo** (ɨ-to-thɨ-yamo III-go-PAST-COLL) 'their going (past)', **ekarymatxhɨyamo** ((o e) karyma-txhɨ-yamo (III) tell-PAST-COLL) 'the telling about them (past)', **ɨtothɨrɨnhɨyamo** (ɨ-to-thɨrɨ-nhɨ-yamo III-go-PAST-REMOTE-COLL) 'their earlier going (past)', i.e., when two past events of going have been referred to, the earlier of the two, **rokarymanyenhɨyamo** (r-okaryma-nye-nhɨ-yamo I-tell-DOER NOMLZN-PAST-COLL) 'the ones who told about me'. With just a few nouns **-yamo** replaces the modifying particle **komo** 'COLLECTIVE' (see Appendix I), which is the form that usually occurs with nonpast possessed nouns (as well as nonpossessed nouns). In this case also **-yamo** substitutes for the suffix **-rɨ** 'POSSESSED ITEM', **rohokyamo** (ro-hoku-yamo I-child-COLL) 'my children'; cf. the noncollective form, **rohokru** 'my child', and the past forms, **rohokutho** 'my child (past)' and **rohokuthuyamo** 'my children (past)'. With these nouns **komo** is also used by some speakers as an optional variant of **-yamo**: **rohokru komo** or **rohokyamo** 'my children'.

APPENDIX D
INFLECTIONAL MORPHOLOGY: LOCATIVE

Locative words belong to the A class. They consist of a small set of deictic and nondeictic forms (see 1.3). In addition there is a much larger set of R locatives, and these are listed in this Appendix (for the general properties of R, see 1.4).

R locatives fall into two main groups:

(i) Semantically simple forms that carry no meaning other than the simple local 'at', 'to', 'past', etc. These local meanings are expressed in most cases by the same set of suffixes that occur with many of the group (ii) forms, i.e., **-wo** 'at', **-ka** 'to', **-ye** 'from', **-ha** 'past', and **-rye** 'through'. But in the group (i) forms they are preceded by a monosyllabic morpheme (**ya-**, **wa-**, **kwa-**, **hya-**, **na-**, or **Ø-**; see D.3) that carries no meaning other than that of signalling the (semantic) subclass of noun that it follows; the other cases of simple forms have a different set of suffixes following the morpheme **ho-**, which signals another subclass of noun (see D.1).

(ii) Semantically complex forms in which the suffixes follow stems that carry a more specific local meaning. These stems can also occur with the suffix **-rɨ** 'possessed item' to form a possessed noun, e.g., **ahetarɨ** 'its edge', where the stem with the specific meaning is **aheta-** 'edge'. One of the local suffixes replaces **-rɨ** to give the additional local meaning: **ahetawo** 'at its edge', **ahetaka** 'to its edge', **asama yahetawo** 'at the edge of the trail', **asama yahetaka** 'to the edge of the trail' (see D.5, 10ff.). The suffixes in most cases are the same set that occurs with the group (i) forms (the **-wo** 'at' set listed above), but there are idiosyncratic forms that have different suffixes: **-ye** 'at', **-koso** 'to', and **-koko** 'past' (see D.6, 7, 8, 9).

There are a few other special forms that express the local function: those which occur with the question word **henta** 'where?' (**henta ya** 'to where?', **henta nyero** 'from where?'); forms derived from **anaro** 'other, another' (**anana** 'to another place', 'to another direction', **anato** 'in another place'); and **txomo na** 'down to the ground'. There are also special forms in relation to river directions: **huhona** 'to the direction of upriver', **huhoye** 'from the direction of upriver', **huhyaka** 'to the direction of downriver', **huhyaye** 'from the direction of downriver'; the suffixes in these river directions have the same forms as some of the local relators (**hona, hoye**--see D.1--and **(h)yaka, (h)yaye**--see D. 3), but they are used irregularly in these expressions. The root **hu-** does not occur as an independent form, the word normally used for river being **tuna** 'water'. There is a more specific word, **ehnɨ** 'river', but it is not much used. (Historically, this may be related to **hu-**, since final **u** is a weak vowel, and the final **-nɨ** of **ehnɨ** may originally have been the suffix **-nɨ-** 'POSSESSED ITEM'.)

D.1 General location

There are several "general" types of location, each type having a different subclass of noun and a different set of relators. Most of these are given in D.3, since they can have an "interior" meaning as well as a more general one, and all the relators for these types have the same set of suffixes. This leaves only one type to be dealt with here. The forms of the relators are **ho** 'at', **hona** 'to', **hoye** 'from', and **horye** 'along' or 'through'. The nouns with which they primarily occur are those which refer to geographical locations, such as village, field, sky: **owto hona** 'to the village', **Manawsɨ hoye** 'from Manaus', **mararɨ ho** 'at the field (i.e., planation)', **kahe hona** 'to the sky', **wewe horye** 'along (the trunk of) the tree'. Some of the forms have extended meanings beyond the local one: **ho** can be used to express location in time: **domenku ho** 'on Sunday'; **hona** is used as a relator with the objects of the verbs **-oseryehɨ-** 'be afraid of' and **-onye-** 'see', the latter when it has the special meaning of 'beware of'; **hona** also has the meaning of 'negative purpose' (see 4.2):

(1) a. **koseryehyaha kamara hona**
   I-am-afraid jaguar towards
   'I am afraid of the jaguar.'

   b. **okoye hona   mpɨnɨ   xenyko**
   snake towards warning see-IMP
   'Beware of the snake!'

   c. **kanawa yarketxkonɨ,   towomrɨ**
   canoe they-were-emptying-it their-going-under

   kom hona
   COLL towards
   'They were baling out the canoe so they wouldn't sink.'

There is another form that should probably belong to the **ho** series: **hoko** 'concerning, occupied with, attached to'. It has a lo-

Inflectional Morphology: Locative

cal function in some peripheral usages, e.g., **ɨhyosɨr hoko** 'on his leg', i.e., 'attached to his leg', but usually it has the more general meaning 'concerning, occupied with':

(2) a. **ewakhɨra natxhe toto   komo Waraka hoko**
       angry   they-are person COLL Waraka concerning
       'The people are angry with Waraka.'

   b. **kuraha hoko   wehxaha**
       bow   occupied-with I-am
       'I am working at making a bow.'

D.2 Proximate location

Proximate location is expressed by the forms: **mɨhto** 'near', **mɨtkoso** '(approaching) near', **mɨthoye** '(departing from) near', **mɨtkoko** '(passing) near'. The root of these forms is a separate word **mɨtɨ** 'circumference, horizon', and the forms themselves have the circumferential (see D.16), as well as the proximate, function. The form **mɨhto** seems to be an idiosyncratic case of metathesis (from **mɨt(ɨ) ho**, cf. **mɨthoye** where metathesis does not take place). The forms occur postposed to nonhuman nouns (with human nouns, the proximate function is expressed by the **hyawo** series-- see D.3(2)):

(3) a. **owto   mɨhto nehxako honyko heno**
       village near it-was peccary herd
       'The herd of peccary was near the village.'

   b. **honyko heno mɨtkoso nteko   Waraka**
       peccary herd near-to he-went Waraka
       'Waraka went near to the peccary herd.'

3. Interior (general) location

Interior location is expressed in the same way as general location, so that there is ambiguity in some forms, i.e., those which can have the interior meaning as well as the more general one. These are group (i) semantically simple forms, consisting of a stem that varies according to the subclass of noun it follows, and one of a series of suffixes that remains the same for all stems. There are six series of forms, corresponding to the six subclasses of nouns with which they occur. Two of these subclasses are easily definable semantically as (1) liquid and (2) animate; the others are more idiosyncratic and need to be listed (some would be long lists, and only examples are given here).

(1) Liquid nouns: **kwawo** 'in', **kwaka** 'to, into', **kwaye** 'from, out of', **kwaha** 'through'. (In the other series, where an 'interior' meaning is possible, there are two suffixes that distinguish

'past, along' (**-ha**) and 'through the interior of' (**-rye**), but in the **kwa-** series only **-ha** is used, and this with the nonnormal meaning of 'through the interior of'.) There are only a few nouns with which the **kwa-** set is used: **tuna** 'water, river' (but not when it refers to 'rain', when the **wa-** set is used--see (4) below), **ehnɨ** 'river', **ukuthonɨ** 'pool, lake, large expanse of water', **-kamsukuru** 'blood', proper names relating to these items, e.g., **Wemana** 'Nhamundá (name of river)', and words for various types of drink food:

(4) a. **ekeyu yameno yuhso kwaka**
　　　　bread he-dipped-it manioc-drink into
　　　　'He dipped the bread into the manioc drink.'

　　b. **tuna kwaha nteko**
　　　　water through he-went
　　　　'He went through the water' (i.e., 'he swam underwater') or 'He swam along the surface.'

(2) Animate nouns: **hyawo** 'with', **hyaka** 'to', **hyaye** 'from', **hyaha** 'past', **hyarye** 'through'. These are used with all nouns that refer to humans and animals, and they occur frequently with noun person-marking prefixes instead of a preceding noun. I have not specifically checked the form **hyarye**, and do not have any record of its actual usage, but I included it in the set on the assumption that it could be used in an utterance like (5c):

(5) a. **Waraka hyaye komokno** (cf. **ɨhyaye komokno**)
　　　　Waraka from I-came (III-from I-came)
　　　　'I have come from Waraka.' ('I came from him.')

　　b. **apaytara hyawo naha bɨryekomo**
　　　　chicken with he-is boy
　　　　'The boy is with the chickens.'

　　c. (?) **koso hyarye nteko waywɨ**
　　　　deer through it-went arrow
　　　　'The arrow went right through the deer.'

(3) A relatively large subclass of nouns is followed by **yawo** 'in, at', **yaka** 'to, into', **yaye** 'from', **yaha** 'past', **yarye** 'through, along'. The interior meaning is often in focus when this set is used (but not necessarily so); it probably accounts for the difference in meaning between **kahe yaka** 'into the sky' and **kahe hona** 'to the sky' (see D.1):

(6) a. **nɨmno ymo yaye nahatakano**
　　　　house AUG from he-came-out
　　　　'He came out of the big house.'

Inflectional Morphology: Locative   209

   b. **oyosamar   yarye ɨtono**
      your-trail along I-went
      'I went along your trail.'

   c. **kanawa ymo yaha amna   nomokno**
      canoe AUG past we-EXCL came
      'We came past the big boat.'

(4) A smaller subclass of nouns is followed by **wawo** 'in, with', **waka** 'to', **waye** 'from', **waha** 'past, through', **warye** 'through'. The two latter are both used with the meaning 'through' but only **waha** has the meaning 'past'. This set is also used with animate nouns, when it normally has the medial location meaning (see D.15), but can also have the same meanings as the **hyawo** set (see (2) above). This set is used with **tuna** 'water, river, rain', but only when it specifically refers to rain (see (1) above):

(7) a. **txetxa waha   ntetxhe onokna   komo**
     forest through they-go creature COLL
     'Creatures go through the forest.'

   b. **wɨrɨmno waka harye   weryako**
      ashes   onto potatoes I-put-them
      'I put the potatoes on the ashes (to roast).'

   c. **Waraka kom wawo wahko**
      Waraka COLL with I-was
      'I was with Waraka's group.'

   d. **tuna waha   komokno**
      rain through I-came
      'I came in the rain.'

The form **wawo** is also used with a temporal meaning 'during', 'at the time of', 'in the season of', e.g., **asahxemton wawo** 'during the feasting', and as a derivational suffix (see Appendix G) in **ahawawo** 'in the dry season'.

(5) There is only one noun I know of, **kamɨmɨ** 'sun', that is followed by **nawo** 'in', **naka** 'in(to)', **naye** 'out of', **naha** 'through':

(8) a. **neryeye   kamɨm naka**
     he-put-it sun   in
     'He put it in the sun.'

   b. **nowye   kamɨm naye**
      he-took-it-away sun   out-of
      'He took it out of the sun.'

While this is the only known occurrence of the postpositions of this set, the same forms occur as a sequence of stem final and suffix in the pattern described in (6) below, e.g., **awasnawo** 'in daylight' from the possessed form **awasnarɨ** 'light of, day of'.

(6) With a large number (but not all) of obligatorily possessed nouns, the **-wo** set of suffixes, which occur as part of the postpositions described in (1) to (5) above, replaces the noun suffix **-rɨ** 'POSSESSED ITEM' to give a general location meaning. This includes all (semantically appropriate) body parts, but they may sometimes have special extended meanings:

(9) a. **ɨmtaka   txeryko   (from ɨ- mta- rɨ)**
       into-his-mouth put-it (III-mouth-POSSN)
       'Put it into his mouth.' ('his mouth')

   b. **wewe txeryko osomtaka   (oso- mta- ka)**
      wood put-it end-to-end (RECIP-mouth-to)
      'Put the pieces of wood together, end to end.'

Other examples are: **romotarɨ** 'my shoulder', **romotawo** 'on my shoulder'; **akrotnarɨ** 'its shade', **akrotnaye omoko** 'come out of the shade'. It is the same process that occurs with the semantically complex relators which occur with the specific local functions described in the following subsections, although not all of these take the basic **-wo** set of suffixes.

D.4 Exterior location

Exterior location is expressed by the forms **mɨmyaye** 'outside' and 'away from', **mɨmyaka** 'up to', **mɨmyaha** 'past'. They have the stem of the possessed noun **-mɨnɨ** 'house of', and there is also a possessed noun form to complete the set, as in **romɨmyarɨ** (ro-mɨmya-rɨ I-outside-POSSN) 'the outside area of my house':

(10) a. **mɨmyaye exko**
        outside be
        'Stay outside.'

   b. **mɨmyaye ɨtoko**
      outside go
      'Go outside' or 'Go away from the outside area.'

   c. **kohsamnohtoho   kom mɨmyaka   ɨtoko**
      our-meeting-place COLL to-outside go
      'Go to the area outside of our meeting house.'

D.5 Anterior location

Anterior location relating to a nonmoving object is expressed by the set **akratawo** 'in front of', **akrataka** 'to the front of',

Inflectional Morphology: Locative   211

akrataye 'from in front of', **akrataha** 'past the front of'. There is also a possessed noun form to complete the set: **akratarɨ** (∅-akrata-rɨ III-front of-POSSN) 'the front of him':

(11) a. **Waraka yakratawo   manhotxowɨ**
       Waraka in-front-of   they-danced
       'They danced in front of Waraka.'

   (cf. **akratawo   manhotxowɨ**)
   (in-front-of-him they-danced)
   ('They danced in front of him.')

   b. **romɨn   yakrataha   nataryeknohtxowɨ**
      my-house past-the-front-of   they-walked
      'They were walking around in front of my house.'

Anterior location relating to a moving object is expressed by one of two forms, both of which are derived from the root **-waho-** 'first'. One is the nonpossessed form **wahoro** 'first, leading, going in front of'; the other is the obligatorily possessed form **-ywaho**, with the same meanings. Both forms can have a temporal meaning as well as the local one.

(12) a. **wahoro ntehe   Waraka, asama yarye**
       first   he-goes Waraka   trail along
       'Waraka goes first along the trail.'

   b. **Waraka ywaho   komokyaha**
      Waraka ahead-of I-come
      'I will come ahead of Waraka.'

   c. **ɨywahonye   ntono   (ɨ- ywaho-   nye**
      in-front-of-them he-went   (III-in front of-COLL)
      'He was leading them.'

   d. **sekunta ywaho   komokyako**
      Monday   before   I-came
      'I came before Monday.'

See also D.18 for anterior position that is relative to medial and posterior positions.

D.6 Posterior location

Posterior location relating to a nonmoving object is expressed by the set **mahyaye** 'behind' and 'from behind', **mahyaka** 'to the back of', **mahyaha** 'past the back of'. There is also a possessed noun form to complete the set: **romahyarɨ** (ro-mahya-rɨ I-behind-POSSN) 'the area behind me':

(13) a. **wewe mahyaye nay   hamɨ**
       tree behind   he-is DEDUCT
       'He must be behind the tree.'

b. **wewe mahyaye   omoko**
      tree from-behind come
      'Come from behind the tree.'

   c. **amahyaka   ntono   mokro**
      behind-you he-went that-one
      'He has gone behind you.'

See also D.9 for the **-mkawo** set, which sometimes has this meaning.

Posterior location relating to a moving object is expressed by one of two forms, both of which are obligatorily possessed: **mahtukme** 'behind, following', which is derived from the same root as the **mahyaye** set above, but more specifically from the possessed noun **-mahtumuru** 'buttocks'; and **wenarye** 'behind, following':

(14) a. **amahtukme   komokyaha**
        behind-you I-come
        'I will come behind you.'

   b. **Waraka wenarye ntotxowɨ omeroro**
      Waraka behind   they-went all
      'They all went behind Waraka.'

There is not much difference between the meanings of the two forms, but there is a preference to use **-wenarye** when following in close proximity is involved.

See also D.18 for posterior position that is relative to anterior and medial positions.

D.7 Superior location

Superior location is expressed by the set **-ohoye** 'above, over' and 'from above', **-ohokoso** 'to above', **-ohokoko** 'passing above'. The root is the comparative postposition **-oho** 'greater than', and in this case there is not a corresponding possessed noun form, only the more general nominalized form **-ohono** 'one who is greater than' or 'one who is above'. The reason for the hyphen preceding these forms is that there is not any free form of the same phonological shape, in contrast with most other sets in which the neutral form is the same as the third person possessed form, e.g., **mimyaye** 'outside of it' (see D.4), **akratawo** 'in front of him' (see D.5). The third person form of **-ohoye** is **ehoye** 'above it' when there is no preceding noun phrase, and **yohoye** 'above it' when there is a preceding noun phrase.

(15) a. **xeka   yohoye nahko   tukusu**
        fish-trap above it-was hummingbird
        'The hummingbird was above the fish-trap.'

Inflectional Morphology: Locative

b. **xeka   yohokoko   ntono   tukusu**
   fish-trap passing-above it-went hummingbird
   'The hummingbird flew over the fish-trap.'

c. **rohokoso nomokno mawu**
   above-me it-came howler-monkey
   'The howler monkey came right above me.'

D.8 Superior-contact location

Superior-contact location is expressed by the set **ryetwo** 'on top of', **ryetkoso** 'on to the top of', **ryehtye** 'from the top of', **ryetkoko** 'along the top of'. The corresponding possessed noun is **ryetɨrɨ** 'top of', 'crown of head', and **ryetɨr hoye** is, in fact, a preferred form to **ryehtye** 'from the top of'.

(16) a. **nɨmno ryetkoso   ntono   kunoro**
       house to-the-top-of it-went red-macaw
       'The red macaw flew on to the top of the house.'

   b. **waywɨ ryetwono   ɨro ha,   kyakwe mamtunu**
       arrow top-of-NOMLZN that INTENSFR toucan feather-of
       'The toucan feather, that thing at the end of the arrow.'

In (16b) **ryetwono** is the nominalized form of the relator. All relators can be nominalized by the addition of the suffix **-no** (see Appendix F). The **ryetwo** set relates to the top or end of rounded or pointed objects, as distinct from objects with a longer or wider surface, which have different relators (see below).

D.9 Surface-contact location

Surface-contact location is expressed by two sets. The first occurs with only a few nouns of unusual surface properties like liquids, e.g., **tuna** 'water' and **kahe** 'sky', and I have only heard two forms used, **ratokoso** 'on to the surface' and **ratokoko** 'along the surface', apart from the possessed noun form **ratorɨ** 'surface of': **kahe ratorɨ** 'expanse of the sky'; **tuna ratokoso** 'on to the surface of the water'. The two missing forms seem likely to be **rator ho** 'on the surface' and **rator hoye** 'from off the surface'. The root is closely related to **-rarɨ** 'front part of body of', e.g., **rorarɨ** 'my body front', and sometimes **roratorɨ** is used with the same meaning.

The other set expressing surface-contact location is **-mkawo** 'on the exterior surface of', **-mkakoso** 'on to the exterior surface of', **-mkaye** 'from off the exterior surface of', **-mkaha** 'along the exterior surface of'. The root is that of the possessed noun **-mkarɨ** 'back of', e.g., **romkarɨ** 'my back'. While the primary meaning is surface-contact, the forms are sometimes used without the 'contact' component of meaning, i.e., in the sense of 'the back of, behind', being then equivalent to the **mahyaye** set (D.6), and with this meaning **-mkaye** is also used in time expressions.

(17) a. **yamata   mkakoso   mukawa yeryeye**
       box   on-top-of gun   he-put-it
       'He laid the gun on the box.'

   b. **eknu   mkaha nehxako asotɨ**
      his-waist along it-was his-belt
      'His belt was around his waist.'

   c. **sekunta mkaye komokyaha**
      Monday after I-come
      'I will come after Monday.'

D.10 Inferior location

Inferior location is expressed by the set **ahomyawo** 'under', **ahomyaka** '(to) under', **ahomyaye** 'from under', **ahomyaha** or **ahomyarye** 'passing under'; there is also a possessed noun form **ahomyarɨ** (∅-ahomya-rɨ III-under-POSSN) 'place under it':

(18) a. **maw   yahomyawo wahko**
       howler-monkey under   I-was
       'I was under the howler monkey.'

   b. **wewe horye rokayɨmɨtxhe,   rahomyarye**
      tree along after-my-climbing passing-under-me

      ntetxoko honyko
      they-went peccary
      'After I climbed the tree, the peccary passed underneath me.'

The set that expresses inferior-contact, **-osnawo** (see D.11), is also sometimes used without the 'contact' component of meaning (see (19c)); conversely, the **ahomyawo** set described above is occasionally used with a 'contact' meaning, as in:

(18) c. **tahomyaka   menu   hnɨnkaye**
       on-to-her-own-underparts black-dye she-put-it
       'She applied the black dye to the front part
          of her body.'

D.11 Inferior-contact location

Inferior-contact location is normally expressed by the set **-osnawo** 'under', **-osnaka** '(to) under', **-osnaye** 'from under', **-osnaha** 'along under'; there is also a possessed noun form **-osnarɨ** 'underneath place':

(19) a. **toh yosnaka txeryko**
       stone under   put-it
       'Put it under the stone.'

Inflectional Morphology: Locative   215

    b. **wato   yosnaye   nahatakano   okoye**
       house from-under it-came-out snake
       'The snake came out from under the roof of the house.'

    c. **wenyxe   haka, warata yosnarɨ**
       let-me-see-it IMP   bed   under-part
       'Let me see the underneath surface of the bed' or
       'Let me see the area underneath the bed.'

See D.10 for use of the **ahomyawo** set with the 'contact' meaning.

D.12 Lateral location

Lateral (and lateral-contact) location is expressed by the set **hanawo** 'at the side of', **hanaka** 'to the side of', **hanaye** 'from the side of'. I have no record of a form corresponding to 'passing the side of', and assume that the **hyaha** form (see D.3) would always be used to express this sense. The **hanawo** set is derived from the possessed noun **-hanarɨ** 'ear of'. There is a set of recip rocal forms: **ehanawo** 'side by side'.

(20) a. **eryewtako rohanaka**
       sit-down to-my-side
       'Sit at my side.'

    b. **xuhxu   mkano,   kanawa hanaye**
       swimming-action (ideophone) he-did-it canoe from-side-of
       'He swam from the side of the boat.'

There is another set which expresses the lateral function, more specifically with the meaning of 'edge of': **ahetawo** 'side of, edge of', **ahetaka** 'to the edge of', **ahetaye** 'from the edge of', **ahetaha** or **ahetarye** 'along the edge of'. There is also a possessed noun form: **ahetarɨ** (Ø-aheta-rɨ III-edge of-POSSN) 'edge of it'.

(21) a. **asama yahetawo nehxakonɨ hawxe**
       trail edge-of it-was   wild-turkey
       'The wild turkey was at the edge of the trail.'

    b. **natxownɨ,   ehnɨ yahetaka**
       they-took-it river to-the-side-of
       'They took it to the bank of the river.'

D.13 Citerior and ulterior location

Citerior and ulterior local functions are expressed by the **ho** set of relators (D.1) following the demonstrative pronouns **onɨ** 'this' and **monɨ** 'that' respectively. The use of these expressions presupposes that the object referred to by 'this' or 'that' is understood by the hearer, and when nothing else is specified the river is understood to be that object, i.e., **on ho** 'this side of the river', **mon hona** 'to that side of the river'. When the speaker needs to specify the object in relation to the local function, he uses the anterior and posterior forms (see D.5-6).

D.14 Medial location (two entities)

Medial location, when two entities are involved, is expressed by the set **amrakatawo** 'between', **amrakataka** 'to a position between', **amrakataye** 'from between', **amrakataha** 'passing between'. There is also a possessed form: **amrakatarɨ** (∅-amrakata-rɨ III-between-POSSN) 'position between (the two)'.

(22) a. **nɨmno yamrakataye nomokno okoye**
 house from-between it-came snake
 'The snake came from between the (two) houses.'

 b. **ɨto nehxatxkonɨ Waraka homo, Kaywerye xarha;**
 there they-were Waraka COLL Kaywerye also

 amrakatawonye nehxakonɨ kamara
 between-them it-was jaguar
 'There they were, Waraka and Kaywerye, and
 between them was the jaguar.'

Since there is no way of saying 'between A and B' in one phrase, the objects represented by A and B must be first introduced and then the medial local function expressed in a separate clause, as in (22b). It is only possible to avoid this, and make the complete statement in one clause when the two objects are of the same kind, as in (22a).

D.15 Medial location (three or more entities or large expanses)

Medial location, when more than two entities are involved, is expressed by the **wawo** 'in, with, among' set, which is described in D.3 (4), and which has the primary meaning of 'among' when occurring with animate nouns: **totokom wawo** 'among the people', **honyko heno kom waka** 'into the herd of peccary'. Another set refers to large expanses and occurs with nonanimate nouns: **rakatawo** 'in the middle of', **rakataka** 'into the middle of', **rakataye** 'from the middle of', **rakataha** 'through the middle of'. There is also a possessed noun form **rakatarɨ** 'the middle of'.

(23) a. **kanawa amna naryako ehnɨ rakataka**
 canoe we-EXCL took-it river to-the-middle-of
 'We took the boat into midstream.'

 b. **marar rakataha ɨtoko**
 field through go
 'Go through the middle of the field.'

Inflectional Morphology: Locative   217

The **rakatawo** set is also used in temporal expressions: **kohsa rakatawo** 'in the middle of the night'. See also D.18 for the set **awrutawo** 'midposition'.

D.16 Circumferential location

Circumferential location is usually expressed by the **mɨhto** 'near, around' set (see D.2).

Another set is used to refer to the environs of the village. It is not strictly circumferential, and the **mɨhto** set can also be used in relation to the village. The set is **-onatowo** 'in the area around the village', **-onatokoso** 'to the area around the village', **-onatoye** 'from the area around the village', **-onatokoko** 'along the area around the village'. There is a possessed noun form **-onatorɨ** 'area around village'.

(24) a. **owto   yonatokoso   nahatakano**
       village to-the-area-around he-came-out
       'He arrived at the area around the village.'

   b. **nataryeknohno, enatokoko**
      he-walked   around-its-environs
      'He walked around the village environs.'

D.17 Citerior-anterior location

There are only two forms I know of that express the citerior-anterior local function: **-ompataye** 'opposite, facing, from the face of', and **-ompataka** 'opposite, towards the face of'. The first is used in a static situation and when movement is involved away from, and the second when movement is involved towards, but in both cases the focus is on a point opposite. The forms are derived from the possessed noun **-ompatarɨ** 'face of'.

(25) a. **rompataye nahko kamara**
       facing-me it-was jaguar
       'A jaguar was facing me.'

   b. **Waraka yompataka komokye**
      Waraka to-face-of I-came
      'I came to a point facing Waraka.'

D.18 Related anterior, medial, and posterior locations

There are special sets expressing anterior, medial, and posterior local functions, which are closely related to each other, and which have more specific meanings than those described in D.5, 6, 15 for the more general types of these particular functions. They express a position relative to the other two positions in the triad. The anterior set is **hotwo** 'in front position', **hotkoso** 'to the front position', **hohtye** 'from the front position', **hotkoko** 'past the front position'; there is a possessed noun form: **hoturu** 'front position of' or 'pointed end of'. The medial set is **awrutawo** 'in midposition', **awrutaka** 'to midposition', **awrutaye** 'from midposition', **awrutaha** 'past midposition'; there is a possessed noun form: **awrutarɨ** 'midposition'. The posterior set is **mahtawo** 'in back position', **mahtakoso** 'to back position', **mahtaye** 'from back position', **mahtakoko** 'past back position'; there is a possessed noun form: **mahtarɨ** 'back position'. They are used in relation to many different objects and situations, but they most often refer to positions in a canoe, and this is the referent when they are used in an absolute sense, i.e., without specifying any other referent for the possessor prefix.

(26) a. **ɨhotkoso   ɨtoko**
to-its-front-position go
'Go to the front of the boat.'

b. **mahtawono   mokro**
one-at-its-rear-position that-one
'That is the man who is at the back of the boat.'

c. **ɨh   yawrutaka   horohtxownɨ**
hill to-its-mid-point they-stopped
'They stopped half way up the hill.'

d. **omam hotkoso   neryeye**
reed to-its-front-end he-fixed-it
'He fixed it to the tip of the rod.'

D.19 Perpendicular-lateral location

There is a perpendicular-lateral set of forms: **etxehtawo** 'at the side of', **etxehtaka** 'to the side of', **etxehtaye** 'from the side of', **etxehtaha** 'along or past the side of'. The forms are derived from the possessed noun **etxehɨ** 'upright support, central pole of house', and there is another possessed noun form in the set: **etxehtarɨ** 'the side of'.

(27) a. **ehnɨ yetxehtawo   nehxakonɨ**
river at-the-bank-of he-was
'He was at the bank of the river.'

b. **etxehtaha   mpɨnɨ mɨtehe ha**
along-its-side OBLIG you-go ITENSFR
'You must go along the side of (the waterfall).'

D.20 Sloping surface location

There is a sloping surface set of forms: **awxawo** 'on the slope', **awxaka** 'on to the slope', **awxaye** 'from off the slope', **awxaha** 'along the slope'; there is also a possessed noun form **awxarɨ** 'slope of'.

Inflectional Morphology: Locative   219

(28) a. ɨh   yawxawo   nehxakonɨ honyko
         hill on-the-slope-of   it-was   peccary
         'The peccary was on the hillside.'

   b. nɨmno yawxaye   nothahno   apaytara
       house from-the-slope-of   it-dropped   chicken
       'The chicken dropped down from the roof of the house.'

D.21 Negative local function

There is one set of relator forms that expresses a negative local function: **hnawo** 'not with, in the absence of', **hnaka** 'to ...', **hnaye** 'from ...', **hnaha** 'through ...', and the possessed noun form **hnarɨ** 'the absence of', 'the not being'. The forms involving motion are difficult to gloss in isolation, and '...' has been used to indicate this. The semantic function of these relators is as much temporal as it is local. They seem in many ways to be the negative counterpart of the **hyawo** 'with' set of forms (see D.3), except that they are not restricted to use with animate nouns. They are used in two ways: (i) as relators that either follow a noun or occur with a possessor prefix, as in the following:

(29) a. rohnaka   nomohtxownɨ   hawana   komo
         to-my-not-being   they-came   visitor COLL
         'The visitors came in my absence.'

   b. ɨto   wehxakonɨ, Waraka hnawo
       there I-was   Waraka at-his-not-being
       'I was there when Waraka was away.'

and (ii) as suffixes with verb stems. This is much rarer, and seems to be a further derivation linked to the negative nominalization suffix -**hnɨ** (see Appendix F). Thus, from the verb stem -**ahe**- 'touch' is first derived the nominal **ahehnɨ** 'person or thing that is not to be touched' and from this the locative forms **ahehnawo** 'in the place that is not touched' (i.e., 'deserted place') and **ahehnaka** 'to the lonely place', etc.

(29) c. ahehnaha   ntotxownɨ
         through-the-untouched-place   they-went
         'They went through the lonely, deserted area.'

There is a set derived from the possessed noun -**yarɨrɨ** 'contents of', which is used with animate (possibly only human, these being the only data I have) nouns, with the same meaning as the simple relator set **hnawo**: **yarɨhnawo, yarɨhnaka, yarɨhnaye** (I have no record of (?*)**yarɨhnaha**). In (29a), **rohnaka** could be replaced by **royarɨhnaka**, and in (29b) **Waraka hnawo** could be replaced by **Waraka yarɨhnawo**, without any change of meaning in either case. The two sets of forms seem to be freely interchangeable with animate nouns.

APPENDIX E
DERIVATIONAL MORPHOLOGY: VERB STEM FORMATION

E.1 Verb stems derived from nouns

There are two main types of process by which verb stems are derived from nouns:

(i) Intransitive stems are formed by adding one of the following suffixes to possessed noun stems:

-ta is added to stems other than those that occur with the allomorph **-nɨ** of the inflectional suffix 'POSSESSED ITEM': **-onta-** 'be awake' is derived from **-onu-** 'eye of' as in **ronuru** 'my eye', thus **kontano** 'I am awake' (**kɨ-onta-no** IS-be awake-IMM.PAST); **-eherkotuhta-** 'flower, be in flower' is derived from **-eherkotku-** 'flower of' as in **eherkotkuru** 'its flower' (i.e., the flower of a particular plant), thus **neherkotuhtano** 'it was in flower'.

-nta or **-na** is added to noun stems that occur with the allomorph **-nɨ** of the 'POSSESSED ITEM' suffix (see Appendix F.4 for other properties of these noun stems): **-xmanta-** 'blow tobacco smoke (in a healing rite)' is derived from **xuma** 'tobacco', which has the possessed form **-xmanɨ** as in **roxmanɨ** 'my tobacco', thus **nɨxmantekonɨ** 'he was blowing tobacco smoke' (**nɨ-xma-nta-yakonɨ** IIIS-tobacco-INTRANSITIVZR-DIST.PAST CONT); **-amusna-** 'be heavy' is derived from **-amusunu** 'weight of' as in **koso yamusunu** 'the weight of the deer', thus **namusnano** 'it was heavy' (**nɨ-amusna-no** IIIS-be heavy-IMM.PAST). See (ii) below for the transitivizing counterparts (**-rye**, **-mrye**, **-ka**, and **-nka**) of **-ta** and **-nta**.

(ii) Transitive stems are formed by adding one of the following suffixes to noun stems; they are all in the semantic range of benefactive or malefactive:

-ma and **-ha** 'BENEFACTIVE'. The form **-ha** occurs with only a few stems: **-wokha-** 'give a drink to' is derived from **woku** 'drink', thus **kwokhatxowɨ** 'he gave us (INCL) a drink' (**kɨ-wokha-txowɨ** IIISI+IIO-give drink to-IMM.PAST COLL). The form **-ma** occurs with other noun stems that are semantically compatible with the benefactive function: **-ohtxema-** 'give medicine to, heal' is derived from **-ohtxe** 'medicine', as in **rohtxe** 'my medicine', thus **rohtxemano** 'she gave me medicine' (**r-ohtxema-no** IIISIO-give medicine to-IMM.PAST).

-to, **-hto**, and **-mto** 'BENEFACTIVE INVOLVING LABOR'. These occur with different sets of stems: **-yhoto-** 'make a plantation for' is derived from **-yho-** 'plantation', i.e., 'field for planting', which is a possessed stem, as in **ɨyhorɨ** 'his plantation', thus **royhototxowɨ** 'they made a plantation for me' (**ro-yhoto-txowɨ** IIISIO-make a plantation for-IMM.PAST COLL); **-osamahto-** 'make a trail for' is derived from **asama** 'trail' and its possessed form **-osamarɨ** 'trail of' as in **oyosamarɨ** 'your trail', thus **uro esamahtoko** 'make a trail for me' (**uro-Ø-osamahto-ko** I-GEN.PREF-make a trail for-IMP); **-ahomto-** 'make a stool for' is derived from the possessed stem **-ahonɨ** 'stool of' as in **rahonɨ** 'my stool', thus **kahomtono** 'I have made a stool for you' (**kɨ-ahomto-no** ISIIO-make a stool for-IMM.PAST).

-rye and **-mrye** 'PRODUCTIVE'. The semantic range is close to that of causatives and benefactives, but differs from the first in that these apply to noun stems and there is no intermediate agent, and from the second in that what is produced is not necessarily for the benefit of anyone. The form **-mrye** occurs with the same set of stems as the intransitive derivation form **-nta** (see (i) in this section) and the transitive derivation form **-nka** (see next paragraph): **-onyxemrye-** 'make aware or conscious', 'produce awareness or knowledge' is derived from the possessed stem **-onyxenɨ** 'awareness, consciousness, knowledge' as in **ronyxenɨ** 'my awareness', thus **wenyxemryeno** 'I made him aware' (**w-onyxemrye-no** ISIIIO-make aware-IMM.PAST). Cf. the **-nta** form **konyxentano** 'I was conscious, I was aware' (**kɨ-onyxenta-no** IS-be aware-IMM.PAST). The form **-rye** occurs with the same set of stems as the intransitive derivation form **-ta** (see (i) in this section) and the transitive derivation form **-ka** (next paragraph): **-kamsukrye** 'make bloody', 'smear blood on' is derived from the possessed stem **-kamsukuru** 'blood of' as in **rokamsukuru** 'my blood', thus **ɨkamsukryeno** 'I smeared him with blood' (**ɨ-kamsukrye-no** ISIIIO-smear with blood-IMM.PAST). Cf. the **-ta** form **kamsuhtehe** 'he is bleeding' (**Ø-kamsuhta-yaha** IIIS-be bloody-NONPAST).

-ka and **-nka** 'MALEFACTIVE, REVERSATIVE'. The form **-nka** occurs with the same set of stems as **-nta** and **-mrye** (see above paragraph): **-onyxenka-** 'make (someone) lose consciousness or awareness', thus **wenyxenkano** 'I made him lose consciousness'. The form **-ka** occurs with the same set of stems as **-ta** and **-rye** (see above paragraph): **-kamsuhka-** 'make (someone) lose blood', thus **kamsuhkano** 'he made him bleed' (**Ø-kamsuhka-no** IIISIIIO-make bleed-IMM.PAST). There is another form, **-hoka**, which occurs with a few stems

Derivational Morphology: Verb Stem Formation

and has the same meaning as **-ka**: **-eryehoka-** 'upset (someone)', lit., 'make (someone) lose the liver', is derived from the possessed stem **-eryenɨ** 'liver of' as in **eryenɨ** 'his liver', thus **ryeryehokano** 'he upset me' (**r-eryehoka-no** IIISIO-upset-IMM.PAST).

Stems resulting from the above transitivizing processes can themselves be made intransitive by the addition of one of the detransitivizing prefixes, **e-**, **os-**, etc. (see E.2): **-osohtxema-** 'give oneself medicine' as in **kosohtxemano** 'I gave myself medicine' (**kɨ-osohtxema-no** IS-give oneself medicine-IMM.PAST); **-oseryehoka-** 'be upset, upset oneself' as in **koseryehokano** 'I got upset' (**kɨ-oseryehoka-no** IS-get upset-IMM.PAST).

E.2 Verb stems derived from verb stems

There are four main types of process by which verb stems are derived from verb stems:

(i) Intransitive stems are formed by adding one of the following prefixes to transitive stems: **e-**, **os-**, **ot-**, **as-**, **at-** (the last two resulting from the vowel assimilation process--see Appendix A.4.1). These prefixes are glossed as 'DETRANSITIVIZER' and can have the reflexive, reciprocal, and pseudopassive functions (see 8.1 and 9.4). The form **os-** normally occurs before a vowel: **noseryehno** 'he was afraid' (**nɨ-os-eryehɨ-no** IIIS-DETRANS-scare-IMM.PAST). It also substitutes for a stem-initial vowel when the resulting consonant cluster is a permitted one: **koskarymano** 'I told about myself', 'I confessed' (**kɨ-os-okaryma-no** IS-DETRANS-tell about-IMM.PAST), and the metathesis process applies if the ensuing consonant is **h** (see Appendix A.4.2): **nohsekahtako** 'it was bought' (**nɨ-os-ehekatɨ-yako** IIIS-DETRANS-buy-REC.PAST COMPL). The form **ot-** occurs mainly before consonants of certain stems: **nothahno** 'it dropped' (**nɨ-ot-hahɨ-no** IIIS-DETRANS-drop(TRANS)-IMM.PAST), and if the resulting cluster would not be permitted, the vowel **ɨ** is inserted: **notɨ-hnɨnkatxownɨ** 'they left each other' (**nɨ-ot-ɨ-hnɨnka-txownɨ** IIIS-DETRANS-(epenthesis)-leave-DIST.PAST COMPL.COLL). With some stems having initial vowels, **os-** and **ot-** are optional variants: **nosonkano** or **notonkano** 'it was taken out' (**nɨ-os/ot-onka-no** IIIS-DETRANS-take out-IMM.PAST). The form **e-** occurs only preceding a consonant, sometimes optionally with **ot-** as in **nehenyeknyo** or **nothenyeknyo** 'it was kept' (**nɨ-e/ot-henyeke-no** IIIS-DETRANS-keep-IMM.PAST), but exclusively with some stems as in **nehutwaye** 'he thought to himself' (**nɨ-e-hutwa-ye** IIIS-DETRANS-think(TRANS)-DIST.PAST COMPL)--never ***nothutwaye**. The form **as-** occurs with a few stems having initial **a**. The only ones I have a record of are: **-anɨmɨ-** 'lift up', **-awnuku-** 'climb', **-awoto-** 'tear', as in **kasanɨm-no** 'I got up', **nasawnukyaha** 'it (fish) goes up(stream)', **nasawotono** 'it got torn'. The form **at-** occurs with most stems having initial **a**: **natamano** 'it (tree) was felled' (**nɨ-at-ama-no** IIIS-DETRANS-fell-IMM.PAST). The **os-** and **ot-** forms occur with a few relator stems with a reflexive or reciprocal meaning (see 8.1).

(ii) Transitive stems are formed from intransitive stems by adding one of a set of causative suffixes. Most stems take one of three suffixes:

-nɨh occurs with stems that have already undergone the derivational process -ta 'INTRANSITIVIZER' (see E.1): **rontanɨhyako** 'he woke me up' (**r-onu-ta-nɨh-yako** IIISIO-eye-INTRANS-CAUS-REC.PAST COMPL).

-noh occurs with some stems: **horymamnohyaha** 'she is raising him' (**Ø-horymamɨ-noh-yaha** IIISIIIO-grow-CAUS-NONPAST).

-ka occurs with some other stems: **awayehkehe** 'he will kill you' (**a-wayehɨ-ka-yaha** IIISIIO-die-CAUS-NONPAST).

Other suffixes apply idiosyncratically to a few stems:

-nohka: **ononohkehe** 'it will cause you to sink' (**o-no-nohka-yaha** IIISIIO-sink-CAUS-NONPAST)

-nɨhka: **katɨknanɨhkatxowɨ** 'they made us stop' (**k-atɨkna-nɨhka-txowɨ** IIISI+IIO-stop-CAUS-IMM.PAST COLL)

-nɨhyama: **nɨrwonɨhyamano** 'he read it' or 'he caused him to speak' (**nɨ-rwon-nɨhyama-no** IIISIIIO-talk-CAUS-IMM.PAST)

-yehka: **nahayehkaye** 'he caused it (river level) to drop' (**n-aha-yehka-ye** IIISIIIO-drop-CAUS-DIST.PAST COMPL)

-mohso: **khokamohsono** 'I made you rest' (**k-hoka-mohso-no** ISIIO-rest-CAUS-IMM.PAST) (-**mohso** also occurs with two transitive stems--see (iii) below.)

(iii) Transitive stems undergo a causative process by the addition of the suffix -ho 'CAUSATIVE': **wenyhono** 'I showed it (**w-onye-ho-no** ISIIIO-see-CAUS-IMM.PAST); **ayhoko** 'order (somebody) to bake it' (**Ø-aye-ho-ko** GEN.PREF-bake-CAUS-IMP). The suffix -**mohso** 'CAUSATIVE', which occurs with a few intransitive stems (see (ii) in this section), also occurs with two transitive stems as an optional variant of -ho: **nenytxamohsono** or **nenytxahono** 'he caused (someone) to hear it' (**nɨ-onytxa-mohso/ho-no** IIISIIIO-hear-CAUS-IMM.PAST); **thutwamohsotxowɨ** or **thutwahotxowɨ** 'we (INCL) caused (someone) to understand it' (**tɨ-hutwa-mohso/ho-txowɨ** I+IISIIIO-understand-CAUS-IMM.PAST COLL).

(iv) There are three derivational suffixes that can occur with any type of verb stem to form stems of the same class:

-htxe 'INGRESSIVE': **kana yanɨmɨhtxetxkonɨ** 'they began catching fish' (**kana-y-anɨmɨ-htxe-yatxkonɨ** fish-IIISIIIO-lift-INGR-DIST.

Derivational Morphology: Verb Stem Formation

PAST CONT.COLL). It can focus either on the beginning of an action, as in the foregoing example, or on the primacy of a participant (subject or object) in relation to other participants, as in **ɨtohtxexe** 'let me go first' (**ɨ-to-htxe-xe** IS-go-INGR-IMP); **honye yanɨmɨhtxetxownɨ** 'they caught a piranha first' (**honye-y-anɨmɨ-htxe-txownɨ** piranha-IIISIIIO-lift-INGR-DIST.PAST COMPL.COLL). The form -htxe 'begin' also occurs as a transitive stem.

-tɨhka/-txehka 'COMPLETIVE, TERMINATIVE': **ɨhananɨhtɨkatxowni** 'I finished teaching them' or 'I taught all of them' (**ɨ-hananɨhtɨ-tɨhka-txownɨ** ISIIIO-teach-COMPL-DIST.PAST COMPL.COLL) (there is **h** reduction when the preceding syllable ends with **h**); **nahatakatxeh-katxownɨ** 'they finished coming out' or 'they all came out' (**nɨ-ahataka-tɨhka-txownɨ** IIIS-come out-COMPL-DIST.PAST COMPL.COLL). The form -tɨhka- 'finish, complete' occurs also as a transitive stem.

-hkah 'CESSATIVE': **nahatakahkahtxownɨ** 'they stopped coming out' (**nɨ-ahataka-hkah-txownɨ** IIIS-come out-CESS-DIST.PAST COMPL.COLL).

Complex verb stems can be formed by a sequence of derivations from any of the four types of process described in this section. The ordering is predictable from the type of stem and the function of each affix. Thus, from the most basic intransitive stem -ohamɨ- 'be many' can be formed:

nehamtxowɨ 'they were many' (**nɨ-ohamɨ-txowɨ** IIIS-be many-IMM. PAST COLL)

wehamnohtxowɨ 'I caused them to be many' (**w-ohamɨ-noh-txowɨ** ISIIIO-be many-CAUS-IMM.PAST COLL)

tohsamnohtxowɨ 'we (INCL) have gathered ourselves together' (**tɨ-os-ohamɨ-noh-txowɨ** I+IIS-DETRANS-be many-CAUS-IMM.PAST COLL)

wehamnohpotxowɨ 'I caused (someone) to gather them together' (**w-ohamɨ-noh-ho-txowɨ** ISIIIO-be many-CAUS-CAUS-IMM.PAST COLL)

nohsamnohpotxowɨ 'they let themselves be gathered together' (**nɨ-os-ohamɨ-noh-ho-txowɨ** IIIS-DETRANS-be many-CAUS-CAUS-IMM.PAST COLL)

nohsamnohpotɨhktaxowɨ 'they all let themselves be gathered together' (**nɨ-os-ohamɨ-noh-ho-tɨhka-txowɨ** IIIS-DETRANS-be many-CAUS-CAUS-COMPL-IMM.PAST COLL).

The -tɨhka set of suffixes, i.e., the three described in (iv) above, could be added at any stage of the complex derivation, but the others are ordered in the way shown.

There are a few verb stems that have affixes added idiosyncratically to form new verb stems. It is sometimes difficult to attach any specific meaning to the affix:

om- 'CAUSATIVE(?)' is added to the stem **-haka-** 'wake up (INTRANS)' to form **-ompaka-** 'wake (someone) up' (TRANS) as in **rompakano** 'he woke me up' (**r-ompaka-no** IIISIO-wake up-IMM.PAST).

on- 'NEGATIVE RESULT(?)' is added to the transitive stem **-kukma-** 'try, test, prove' to form another transitive stem **-onkukma-** 'baffle, perplex' as in **ronkukmano** 'it baffles me' (**r-onkukmano** IIISIO-baffle-IMM.PAST).

otx- 'IMITATIVE(?)' is added to the transitive stem **-kukma-** 'try, etc.' to form another transitive stem **-otxkukma-** 'imitate, try the call of' as in **horoto yotxkukmekonɨ** 'he was making the call of the spider monkey' (**horoto-y-otxkukma-yakonɨ** spider monkey-IIISIIIO-imitate-DIST.PAST CONT).

a- 'inside of' is added to transitive stems to form other transitive stems, as in **wakorokano** 'I washed the inside of it (a pan, etc.)' (**w-a-koroka-no** ISIIIO-inside-wash-IMM.PAST), and in **watxemnyo** 'I applied the fish poison inside it (a hole)' (**w-a-txeme-no** ISIIIO-inside-apply fish poison to-IMM.PAST).

E.3 Verb stems derived by compounding noun stem and verb stem

The stems of nouns that refer to body parts can be placed immediately before a (semantically compatible) verb stem to form a compound verb stem. This is the only productive compounding process in the language.

When the verb stem is transitive, the noun stem functions as its direct object: **kahowosɨ** 'let me inject you' (**kɨ-aho-wo-sɨ** ISIIO-arm-shoot/pierce-FIRST PERS.IMP), in which **-wo-** 'shoot' is a transitive stem, and **-aho-** 'arm' functions as direct object; **ryexemnukyaha** 'he is choking me' (**ro-exe-munuku-yaha** IIISIO-throat-press-NONPAST), where **-munuku-** is a transitive stem. The construction also occurs, however, with intransitive stems: **nexeyanorɨye** 'he had a parched throat' (**nɨ-exe-y-ano-rɨ-ye** IIIS-throat-(?)-be dry-STEM FORM-DIST.PAST COMPL), where there is a problem in determining the function of the **y** which occurs between the noun stem **-exe-** and the verb stem **-ano-**. It fits the pattern of the IIISIIIO prefix that occurs with transitive stems when there is a preceding object NP, but **-ano-** is an intransitive stem. It also fits the pattern of the nominal prefix **y-** 'third person when there is a preceding possessor NP', and this could occur with an intransitive stem that has been nominalized: **txuf yanonɨrɨ** 'the grass's being dry' (**txufu-y-ano-nɨ-rɨ** grass-III-be dry-ACTION NOMLZN-POSSN). The compound stem **-exeyano-** would seem to be functioning in this latter way, but without the nominalization, and it is inflected as an intransitive stem, as can be seen most clearly in the first person: **kexeyanono** 'I have a dry throat' (**kɨ-exe-yano-no** IS-throat-dryness of-IMM.PAST). The type of verb stem with which the body-part noun stem occurs thus determines the

Derivational Morphology: Verb Stem Formation

type of compound stem that results. Body-part nouns are obligatorily possessed, but when compound stems are formed, the noun suffix 'POSSESSED ITEM' is deleted, as is also sometimes a stem formative. Thus only the stem of **ayahorɨ** 'your arm' (**ay-aho-rɨ** II-arm-POSSN) occurs in the compound **-ahowo-** 'inject', and in the case of **exenarɨ** 'his throat' (**Ø-exe-na-rɨ** III-throat-STEM FORM-POSSN) both the stem formative and the suffix are deleted in forming the compound **-exeyano-** 'to have a dry throat'. In addition, of course, there is a change in the person-marking prefixes from the nominal to the verbal set, resulting in **kahowosɨ** 'let me inject you' the prefix being **kɨ-** 'ISIIO' in place of **ay-** 'II', and **nexeyanorɨye** 'he had a parched throat', where the prefix is **nɨ-** 'IIISIIIO' in place of **Ø-** 'III' in the noun. The detransitivizer prefix can be added to a transitive compound stem: **kosexemnukyaha** 'I am choking myself' (**kɨ-os-exe-munuku-yaha** IS-DETRANS-throat-press-NONPAST).

Body-part stems also occur in compounds with:

(i) the derivational suffix **-ka** 'REVERSATIVE', which occurs with many other noun stems (see E.1): **ramokano** 'he cut my hand' (**ro-amo-ka-no** IIISIO-hand-REVERS-IMM.PAST), and **natamokano** 'he cut his own hand' (**nɨ-at-amo-ka-no** IIIS-DETRANS-hand-REVERS-IMM.PAST).

(ii) a few other suffixes that do not occur with any other stems or as separate verb stems: **katamokryaxnyo** 'I splintered my finger' (**kɨ-at-amo-kryaxe-no** IS-DETRANS-hand-splinter-IMM.PAST); **rahryeskahano** 'it cracked me on the elbow' (**ro-ahryesɨ-kaha-no** IIISIO-elbow-crack-IMM.PAST); and **ayahohorono** 'did you have cramp in the arm?' (**ay-aho-horo-no** IIS-arm-cramp-IMM.PAST).

E.4 Verb stems derived from nominalized relators

There are three relators which, when nominalized, can have derivational suffixes added to form verb stems. Two of these undergo exactly the same process: **(y)akoro** 'with, accompanying' and **hoko** 'occupied with'. The nominalizing suffix **-no** 'GENERAL NOMLZN' (see Appendix F.4) is first added, and this is followed by the suffix **-ma** 'BENEFACTIVE' (see E.1), resulting in the transitive verb stems: **-akoronoma-** 'help, accompany' and **-hokonoma-** 'work on behalf of', as in the forms **rakoronomano** 'he helped me' (**ro-akoronoma-no** IIISIO-help-IMM.PAST) and **ɨhokonomano** 'I worked for him' (**ɨ-hokonoma-no** ISIIIO-work on behalf of-IMM.PAST). The other relator is **xe** 'DESIROUS OF'. It also first undergoes the nominalizing process, which results in the form **-xano** 'one who desires'; there are then two verbalizing processes, first the suffix **-mkah**, which is an idiosyncratic variant of **-hkah** 'CESSATIVE' (see E.2), and then the suffix **-noh** 'CAUSATIVE', resulting in the form **-xanomkahnoh-** 'reject, regard as of no value' as in **roxanomkahnohyaha** 'he looks down on me' (**ro-**

xanomkahnoh-yaha IIISIO-look down on-NONPAST) and **wayw+ xanomkahnohno** 'he rejected the arrows as no good' (**wayw+-Ø-xanomkahnoh-no** arrow-IIISIIIO-reject-IMM.PAST). Both verbal suffixes are needed to form a stem (*-**xanomkah**- and *-**xanonoh** are not well-formed), but the nominal suffix alone can be added: **roxano** 'one who likes me'; **wayw+ xano** 'one who wants arrows'.

APPENDIX F
DERIVATIONAL MORPHOLOGY: NOUN FORMATION

F.1 Nouns derived from nouns

There is only one process by which a noun is derived from a noun: the addition of the suffix **-hɨnɨ** 'NEGATION' (there are alternate forms **-hnɨ** and **-pɨnɨ** resulting from normal phonological processes (see Appendix A.4)). There is one set of stems with which **-hɨnɨ** never occurs: the set that takes the suffix **-mnɨ** 'NEGATION' (see F.4). There are three types of noun stem with which **-hɨnɨ** occurs:

(i) simple nouns and pronouns, nonderived and nonpossessed, when the more specific meaning of the suffix is 'negation of identity of the item': **totohnɨ** 'one who is not a human being' (**toto-hnɨ** human being-NEG); **kanawahnɨ** 'thing that is not a canoe' (**kanawa-hnɨ** canoe-NEG); **urohnɨ** 'not I' (**uro-hnɨ** I-NEG).

(ii) simple possessed nouns, when the more specific meaning of the suffix is 'negation of possession of the item'. It replaces the possession suffix **-rɨ**, and the person-marking prefixes are replaced by the general prefix (see Appendix B.2.3), which in this case takes the form of **ɨ-** before a stem-initial consonant, and **∅** before a vowel: **ɨkanawahnɨ** 'one who is without a canoe' (**ɨ-kanawa-hnɨ** GEN.PREF-canoe-NEG) (cf. **rokanawarɨ** 'my canoe', **ɨkanawarɨ** 'his canoe', and also the negation of the nonpossessed form above, viz., **kanawahnɨ** 'thing that is not a canoe'); **enhunu** 'one without an eye' (**∅-onu-hɨnɨ** GEN.PREF-eye-NEG). In this latter example there is a stem-initial vowel change identical with the change that takes place for the prefix 'III without a preceding NP' (see Appendix C.1), and there is an assimilation process that changes the vowels in the suffix (see Appendix A.4); normal possessed forms are **ronuru** 'my eye', **enuru** 'his eye'.

(iii) derived nouns, when the meaning is simply the negative counterpart of the particular positive derivation. In all cases the negative suffix **-hɨnɨ** is added to the full derived form, and does not replace any other suffix, either derivational or inflectional. There are only two derivations with which **-hɨnɨ** regularly cooccurs in this way: (1) with **-nye** 'DOER OF THE ACTION', which is restricted to transitive stems (see F.2), e.g., **rohananɨhnyehnɨ** 'one who does not teach me' (**ro-hananɨhɨ-nye-hnɨ** I-teach-DOER-NEG); and (2) with **-no** 'GENERAL NOMINALIZATION', which can occur with different types of stem (see F.2, 3, 4), e.g., **ɨtonohnɨ** 'one who is not there' (**ɨto-no-hnɨ** there-GEN.NOMLZN-NEG) and **ohxanhɨnɨ** 'one who is not good' (**ohxe-no-hɨnɨ** good-GEN.NOMLZN-NEG) where the stem-final change from **e** to **a** is idiosyncratic. The sequence of the two suffixes **-no** and **-hɨnɨ** results in vowel reduction, and normally it is the first **ɨ** that is dropped (as in **ɨtonohnɨ** above), but in a few cases it is the **o** of **-no** that is dropped, as in **ohxanhɨnɨ** and also in **roxanhɨnɨ** 'one who does not like me' (**ro-xe-no-hɨnɨ** I-desirous of-GEN.NOMLZN-NEG), which also undergoes the stem-final vowel change from **e** to **a**, this time in a relator stem, **xe** 'desirous-of'. I have occasionally heard the suffix **-hɨnɨ** used with other derived nouns, specifically **-saho** 'SUBJECT (INTRANS) OR OBJECT (TRANS) OF PAST ACTION' (F.2) and **-mɨ** 'ADVERB NOMINALIZATION' (F.3), but I think these are generally regarded by native speakers as deviant, and there are other ways of expressing the negative counterparts to these derived forms (see under the description of **-saho** and **-mɨ**): (?*) **ɨtosahohnɨ** 'one who did not go' (**ɨ-to-saho-hnɨ** GEN.PREF-go-SUBJ. OF PAST ACT-NEG); (?*) **tonosomɨhnɨ** 'thing that is not to be eaten' (**t-ono-so-mɨ-hnɨ** ADVBLZR-eat-ACT.ADV-NOMLZN-NEG).

The suffix **-hɨnɨ** 'NEGATION' also occurs directly with verb stems (see F.2). In form and function it is related to the adverb derivation **-hɨra** (see Appendix G).

There is one other idiosyncratic form of negative nominalization. It occurs with only one stem, so far as I know: **-xano** 'one who desires', which is illustrated above as a stem that cooccurs with **-hɨnɨ** to form, e.g., **roxanhɨnɨ** 'one who does not like me'. The stem occurs with another suffix, **-mtorɨ** 'NEGATION', with a different meaning: **roxanomtorɨ** 'my not being liked'. Its uniqueness is probably explained by the fact that **xe** 'desirous of' is the only relator that is semantically more like a verb, i.e., it expresses an event notion, and this unusual form compensates for its inability, as a relator, to undergo the range of nominalizations available to verb stems.

F.2 Nouns derived from verb stems

There are a number of processes by which nouns are derived from verb stems:

(i) **-nɨ-** 'ACTION NOMINALIZATION'. It is followed by the inflectional suffix **-rɨ** 'POSSESSED ITEM', or the time derivation **-toko** 'SIMULTANEOUS ACTION' (see Appendix G.2), and it cooccurs with the person-marking possessor prefixes: **rowanotanɨrɨ** 'my singing'

Derivational Morphology: Noun Formation 231

(**ro-wanotanɨ-rɨ** I-sing-ACT.NOMLZN-POSSD); **oyotahanɨrɨ** 'your being hit' (**oyotaha-nɨ-rɨ** II-hit-ACT.NOMLZN-POSSD); **ryesnɨrɨ** 'my being' (**r-exenɨ-rɨ** I-be-ACT.NOMLZN-POSSD). The suffix -**nɨ**- is optionally-omitted by some speakers, and regularly by others, after stem final **m(ɨ)** or **h(ɨ)**: **tɨmrɨ** or **tɨmnɨrɨ** 'its being given' (**tɨ-ɨmɨ-(nɨ)-rɨ** GEN.PREF-give-(ACT.NOMLZN)-POSSD); for use of the general prefix **t-** to function as 'third person object' see Appendix B.2.3); **ayatanɨhnohrɨ** or **ayatanɨhnohnɨrɨ** 'your being made bad' (**ay-at-anɨhnohɨ-(nɨ)-rɨ** II-DETRANS-make bad-(ACT.NOMLZN)-POSSD). For past action the sequence -**nɨrɨ** is replaced by the inflectional suffix -**thɨrɨ** 'PAST TENSE' (see Appendix C.2, where the allomorphs are listed and the conditions described): **amna yomokɨthɨrɨ** 'our (EXCL) coming (in the past)' (**amna-y-omokɨ-thɨrɨ** I+III-III-come-PAST ACT.NOMLZN); **ekarymatxhɨrɨ** 'its being told' ((o→e) **karyma-txhɨrɨ** (III) tell-PAST ACT.NOMLZN); **ryexetxhɨrɨ** 'my being (in the past)' (**r-exe-txhɨrɨ** I-be-PAST ACT.NOMLZN). There is one irregular 'ACTION NOMINALIZATION' form, that for the verb **ka** 'say, do', viz., **tawro** 'saying, doing it'; the corresponding 'PAST ACTION' form is regular: **ɨkatxhɨrɨ** 'saying, doing it (in the past)'.

(ii) -**hɨto**- 'NEGATIVE NOMINALIZATION OF ACTION'. It is also followed by the possession suffix -**rɨ** or the time derivation -**toko** (see (i) above), and cooccurs with the person-marking possessor prefixes: **ɨnɨkɨhtor komo** 'their not going to sleep' (**ɨ-nɨkɨ-hto-rɨ-komo** III-sleep-NEG.NOMLZN-POSSD-COLL); **ayanɨmpɨtorɨ** 'your not being lifted up' (**ay-anɨmɨ-pɨto-rɨ** II-lift up-NEG. NOMLZN-POSSD). Negation of past action is expressed by adding the particle **tho** 'DEVALUED' (see Appendix I): **ryexehtorɨ tho** 'my not being (in the past)' (**r-exe-hto-rɨ-tho** I-be-NEG.NOMLZN-POSSD- DEVLD). For the rules governing the occurrence of the collective forms **komo** and -**yamo** in relation to derived nouns, see Appendix C.1 and C.2.

(iii) -**toho** 'THING, TIME, OR PLACE ASSOCIATED WITH THE ACTION'. This cooccurs with the person-marking possessor prefixes. The allomorph -**tho** occurs after vowels. It is homophonous with the allomorph of the past tense suffix -**thɨrɨ** and with the particle **tho** 'DEVALUED' (see Appendixes C.2 and I). An assimilation process results in the further allomorphs -**txoho** and -**txho** (see Appendix A.4.1): **omohtoho** 'the time of his coming' (**Ø-omokɨ-toho** III-come-'THING' NOMLZN); **ɨhkototho** 'saw, thing for cutting it in two' (**ɨ-hkoto-tho** III-cut in two-'THING' NOMLZN); **rotahatxho** 'club, thing for hitting me' (**r-otaha-txho** I-hit-'THING' NOMLZN); **ryeh-txoho** 'time or place of my being' (**r-exe-txoho** I-be-'THING' NOMLZN).

(iv) -**hɨyemɨ** 'person associated with the action as companion'. This cooccurs with the person-marking prefixes: **rorwonɨmpɨyemɨ** 'the one I talk with' (**ro-rwonɨmɨ-hɨyemɨ** I-talk-COMPANION NOMLZN); **oyompamnohpɨyemɨ** 'one who is your companion in being taught' (**oy-ompamnohɨ-hɨyemɨ** II-teach-COMPANION NOMLZN).

(v) **-txhetɨ** 'payment for the action'. This also cooccurs with the person-marking prefixes: **ramryekɨtxhetɨ** 'payment for my going hunting' (**r-amryekɨ-txhetɨ** I-go hunting-PAYMENT NOMLZN); **wewe yamatxhetɨ** 'payment for felling the tree' (**wewe-y-ama-txhetɨ** tree-III-fell-PAYMENT NOMLZN).

(vi) **-saho** 'SUBJECT (INTRANS) OR OBJECT (TRANS) OF PAST ACTION'. There are no possessor markings with this form, but the general prefix occurs under the conditions described in Appendix B.2.3: **ɨmanhosaho** 'the one who danced' (**ɨ-manho-saho** GEN.PREF-dance-SUBJ. OF PAST ACT); **ekarymaxaho** 'thing that was told' (**Ø-okarymaxaho** GEN.PREF-tell-OBJ. OF PAST ACT). There is a special collective form for this suffix: **-xemo**, as in **axemo** 'the ones who were taken' (**Ø-a-xemo** GEN.PREF-take-OBJ. OF PAST ACT.COLL), but the collective particle **komo** is optionally added, as in **axemo komo**, with the same meaning as **axemo**. The nonpast equivalent of this derivation is the process involving **-mɨ** 'ADVERB (tɨ-) NOMINALIZATION', more specifically when this process is applied to the **tɨ-...-so** derived adverb (see Appendix G.2) to yield the form **tɨ-...-somɨ** (see F. 3). The negative counterpart to the **-saho** derivation consists of the sequence of the suffix **-hɨnɨ** 'NEGATION', added to the verb stem (see below, (xi) of this section), and followed by the particle **tho** 'DEVALUED' (see Appendix I), to form **-hɨnɨ tho** 'SUBJECT (INTRANS) OR OBJECT (TRANS) OF THE NEGATION OF PAST ACTION': **ɨmanhohnɨ tho** 'one who did not dance' (**ɨ-manho-hnɨ-tho** GEN.PREF-dance-NEG-DEVLD); **ekarymahnɨ tho** 'thing that was not told' (**Ø- okaryma-hnɨ-tho** GEN.PREF-tell-NEG-DEVLD). See also F.1 for another possible negative counterpart to **-saho**.

(vii) **-xenyeno** 'SUBJECT (INTRANS) OR OBJECT (TRANS) OF A RECENTLY PERFORMED ACTION': **enuxenyeno** 'one that has just been born' (**Ø-onu-xenyeno** GEN.PREF-be born-SUBJ. OF REC.ACT); **tɨmxenyeno** 'thing that has just been given' (**t-ɨmɨ-xenyeno** GEN.PREFgive-OBJ. OF REC.ACT). This form is not used very much, but the same constraints apply to it as to **-saho** (see above).

(viii) **-nye** 'DOER OF THE ACTION'. This occurs only with transitive stems and with person-marking possessor prefixes that refer to the underlying object: **rompamnohnye** 'the one who teaches me' (**r-ompamnohɨ-nye** I-teach-DOER NOMLZN); **kohtxemany komo** 'the one who gives us (INCL) medicine' (**k-ohtxema-nye-komo** I+II-give medicine to-DOER NOMLZN-COLL).

(ix) **-nɨ-...-nɨ-** 'OBJECT RESULTING FROM THE ACTION'. This also occurs only with transitive stems. The initial **-nɨ-** is preceded by the person-marking possessor prefixes, but in this case, which is unique in this respect for transitive derivations, the prefix refers to the underlying subject. The second **-nɨ-** is a suffix immediately following the stem, and it is followed by the inflectional suffix **-rɨ** 'POSSESSED ITEM' (cf. the derivation **-nɨ-** 'ACTION NOMINALIZATION' in (i) of this section). The suffix **-nɨ-** can be replaced by **-hɨto-** 'NEGATIVE NOMINALIZATION' (see (ii) of

Derivational Morphology: Noun Formation

this section): **ronɨnyaknyɨrɨ** 'the one being sent by me' (**ro-nɨ-nyake-nɨ-rɨ** I-OBJ.NOMLZN-send-ACT.NOMLZN-POSSD); **ronɨnyakehtorɨ** 'the one who will not be sent by me' (**ro-nɨ-nyake-hto-rɨ** I-OBJ. NOMLZN-send-NEG.ACT.NOMLZN-POSSD). Past action can be expressed by replacing the suffix sequence -**nɨrɨ** by -**thɨrɨ** as described in (i) of this section, e.g., **ronɨnyaketxhɨrɨ** 'the one sent by me' (**ro-nɨ-nyake-txhɨrɨ**), and the negative past form is derived by adding the particle **tho** as described in (ii) above, e.g., **ronɨnyakehtorɨ tho** 'the one who was not sent by me'.

(x) -**no** 'GENERAL NOMINALIZATION'. There are no possessor markings with this form, nor does the general prefix occur with it. It is the most general type of nominalization and can occur with adverb (F.3) and relator (F.4) stems, as well as intransitive and transitive stems. The derived form consists only of the stem and -**no**, without any inflectional affixes. In the case of intransitive stems it relates the action to a nonspecific subject: **omokno komo** 'the coming of people' (**omokɨ-no-komo** come-GEN.NOMLZN-COLL); **asanɨmno** 'something that lifts itself up' (e.g., 'river bank') (**as-anɨmɨ-no** DETRANS-lift up-GEN.NOMLZN). In the case of transitive stems it relates the action to a nonspecific object: **otahano** 'the killing of people' (**otaha-no** kill-GEN.NOMLZN). With both types of stem these derived forms are frequently the object of the verb -**e(rye)**- 'do, fix': **ahyehno yeryaha** 'he will make people hungry' (**ahyehɨ-no** be hungry-GEN.NOMLZN); **onono yeryakonɨ** 'he used to eat people' (**ono-no** eat-GEN.NOMLZN).

(xi) -**hɨnɨ** 'NEGATION' (see F.1, where the same suffix is described in its occurrence with noun stems). With intransitive stems the meaning of -**hɨnɨ** is 'one that does not do the action', and with transitive stems it is 'one on which the action is not done'. There are no possessor markings with this form, but the general prefix occurs under the conditions described in Appendix B.2.3: **ɨmanhohnɨ** 'one who does not dance' (**ɨ-manho-hnɨ** GEN.PREF-dance-NEG.NOMLZN); **ekarymahnɨ** 'thing that is not told' or 'person who is not told about' (**Ø-okaryma-hnɨ** GEN.PREF-tell-NEG. NOMLZN); **ehxenɨ** 'one that is not' (**Ø-exe-hɨnɨ** GEN.PREF-be-NEG. NOMLZN), in which three phonological processes takes place, vowel harmony, vowel reduction, and metathesis--see Appendix A.4. It functions as the nominalized equivalent of the derived adverb -**hɨra** 'NEGATIVE' (see Appendix G.2), but there is an important morphological difference with regard to transitive stems: the adverb derived by -**hɨra** has the person-marking possessor prefix that refers to the direct object of the action: **rokarymahra nahko** 'he was not telling about me' (**r-okaryma-hra** I-tell-NEG.ADV); the nominal derived by -**hɨnɨ**, on the other hand, has only the general prefix: **ekarymahnɨ uro** 'I (am) one who is not told about' (**Ø-okaryma-hnɨ**--see above). There is no such distinction with intransitive stems, where the general prefix is used with both -**hɨra** and -**hɨnɨ**: **ɨmanhohra** 'not dancing' and **ɨmanhohnɨ** 'one who does not dance'. (See above and also 9.4 for more on this does not dance'. (See above and also 9.4 for more on this contrast, and on the pseudopassive status of transitive **-hɨnɨ** forms).

F.3 Nouns derived from adverbs

There are two processes by which nouns are derived from adverbs:

(i) **-mɨ** 'ADVERB (**tɨ-**) NOMINALIZATION'. This suffix occurs only with classes of derived adverbs that are marked by the prefix **tɨ-** (see Appendix G.1 and G.2): **teryewryemɨ** 'one who is in pain' (**teryewrye-mɨ** in pain-ADV.NOMLZN); **totkemɨ** 'one who has meat food' (**totke-mɨ** having meat-ADV.NOMLZN); **tɨmporyemɨ** 'thing that ought to be given' (**tɨmporye-mɨ** ought to be given-ADV.NOMLZN); **tkanawahoryemɨ** 'one who has a good canoe' (**tkanawahorye-mɨ** having a good canoe-ADV.NOMLZN); **tonusomɨ** 'the one being born' or 'the one to be born' (**tonuso-mɨ** being born-ADV.NOMLZN); **takaxemɨ** 'the thing to be hollowed out' (**takaxe-mɨ** to be hollowed out-ADV. NOMLZN); **tehxemɨ** 'one that is' (**tehxe-mɨ** being-ADV.NOMLZN); **tɨnɨhtxahkemɨ** 'one trying to sleep' (**tɨnɨhtxahke-mɨ** trying to sleep-ADV.NOMLZN).

The negative counterpart of **-mɨ** forms involves the **-hɨnɨ** process (see F.1 and F.2), either:

(a) to the underlying stem before any adverbial form is derived (this applies to the following adverbial derivations: **-rye**, e.g., **eryewhunu** 'one who is not in pain'; **-ke**, e.g., **ethɨnɨ** 'one without meat food'; **-so**, e.g., **enurhunu** 'one not being born' (∅-**onu-ru-hunu** GEN.PREF-be born-STEM FORM-NEG); **akahnɨ** 'one that is not to be hollowed out'; **ehxenɨ** 'one that is not' (∅-**exe-hɨnɨ** GEN. PREF-be-NEG)); or

(b) to the derived adverb stem, i.e., before **-mɨ** is added (this applies only to the adverbial derivation: **-horye**, e.g., **tɨmporyehnɨ** 'thing that ought not to be given').

The **-txahke** adverb derivation is irregular, the negative being formed by changing the form of the suffix to **-txako-** and adding the suffix **-mnɨ** (see F.4), and by substituting the **tɨ-** adverbial prefix with the general prefix, e.g., **tɨnɨhtxahke** 'trying to sleep' has the negative nominalized form **ɨnɨhtxakomnɨ** 'one who is not trying to sleep' (**ɨ-nɨkɨ-txako-mnɨ** GEN.PREF-sleep-try-NEG).

(ii) **-no** 'GENERAL NOMINALIZATION' (see F.2 where the same suffix is described in its occurrence with verb stems). It occurs with all simple (nonderived) adverbs, and with certain classes of derived adverb other than the **tɨ-** classes.

The following are examples with simple adverbs: **ohxano** 'one that is good' (**ohxe-no** good-GEN.NOMLZN) (the vowel change being idiosyncratic); **karyheno** 'one who is strong' (**karyhe-no**); **tanono** 'one that is here' (**tano-no**); **amnyeno** 'one that is in the future'

Derivational Morphology: Noun Formation

(**amnye-no**); **asakon komo** 'a group of two' (**asako-no-komo** two-GEN. NOMLZN-COLL); **oskeno** 'one that is thus' (**oske-no**). The form **thenyehra** 'much, many' is a basic negative form, and is nominalized by inserting **-no** and changing the negative suffix to the nominal negation form **-hɨnɨ**: **thenyenohnɨ** 'one that is much' or 'ones that are many'.

The following are the classes of derived adverbs with which **-no** occurs (see Appendix G.1 and G.2):

-henye 'big', as in **ɨkanawahenyeno** 'one that is a big canoe' (**ɨkanawahenye-no**); for the negative counterpart the suffix **-hɨnɨ** is added (see F.1), **ɨkanawahenyenohnɨ** 'one that is a small canoe' (**ɨkanawahenyeno-hnɨ**)

-kenyehra 'in a bad state', which is a basic negative form without a positive counterpart, like **thenyehra** (see preceding paragraph), and is nominalized in the same way, as in **ɨmɨnkenyenohnɨ** 'one that is a leaky old house' (**ɨmɨnkenye-no-hnɨ**)

-toko 'at the same time as', as in **romoknɨtokono** 'one that is at the time of my coming' (**romoknɨtoko-no** when I come-GEN.NOMLZN)--this is a rarely used form and I do not know its precise semantico-syntactic function

-wawo 'during the time of', as in **atakɨhtowawono** 'one (who lived) during the time of creation' (**at-akɨhto-wawo-no** DETRANS-create-during-GEN.NOMLZN); this derivation seems more common than **-tokono** (see above)

It is possible that the time adverb derived by **-txhe** 'after' could also be nominalized by adding **-no**, but I have no record of this.

The negative derived adverb **-hɨra** (see Appendix G.1, G.2 and G.3) is not usually subject to the **-no** suffixal process, but it occurs idiosyncratically, as in **amnyehrano** 'one in the past' (**amnyehra-no** past-GEN.NOMLZN). The usual way of nominalizing **-hɨra** forms, when the stem with which it occurs is a verb stem, is to replace that suffix with **-hɨnɨ**, 'NEGATION NOMINALIZATION' (see Appendix F.2). Where the stem with which **-hɨra** occurs is an adverb or relator, however, the nominalizing suffix **-no** is first added to the stem, and then **-hɨnɨ** is added (see F.1).

Some **-no** forms derived from adverbs have a property that is unique among nominalizations normally nonpossessed (as **-no** forms are): they can be optionally possessed by adding the **-nɨ** form of the 'POSSESSED ITEM' suffix (see Appendix C.2) and the appropriate personmarking prefix. This applies to adverbs relating to quantification and measurement: **ɨmoxenonɨ** 'its distance' (**ɨ-moxe-no-nɨ** IIIdistant-NOMLZN-POSSD); **kanawa kawononɨ** 'the length of the canoe' (**kanawa-Ø-kawo-no-nɨ** canoe-III-long-NOMLZN-POSSD); **bɨryekomo yakenon komo** 'the number of the children' (**bɨryekomo-Ø-yake-no- nɨ-komo** child-III-many-NOMLZN-POSSD-COLL).

F.4 Nouns derived from other stems

Nouns can be derived from relators by adding the suffix -no 'GENERAL NOMINALIZATION' (see F.2 and F.3, where the same suffix is described in the derivation of nouns from verb stems and adverbs). The process involving relators results in, e.g., **nɨmno yawono** 'the one in the house' (**nɨmno-yawo-no** house-in-GEN.NOMLZN); **roxano** 'one who likes me' (**ro-xe-no** I-desirous of-GEN.NOMLZN; the change of vowel in the relator is idiosyncratic). Such nominalized forms can undergo the further process of negative nominalization by the addition of the suffix -**hɨnɨ** (see F.1): **nɨmno yawonohnɨ** 'not the one in the house' or 'one who is not in the house'; **roxanhɨnɨ** 'one who does not like me'.

There is one other nominalizing process that applies primarily to a subclass of stems that are either verbal or nominal or both: -**mnɨ** 'NEGATION' (cf. -**hɨnɨ** 'NEGATION' in F.1 and F.2, which does not apply to this subclass of stems). The stems with which -**mnɨ** occurs are (i) verb stems that end with **n**, and to which the stem formative -**ɨmɨ**- is obligatorily added with certain inflectional tense-aspect suffixes and optionally added with others (see Appendix B.3.3 for a list of these stems, all of which are intransitive), and (ii) stems of obligatorily possessed nouns that occur with the -**nɨ** allomorph of the 'POSSESSED ITEM' suffix (see Appendix C.2). The verb stems in (i) above all have nominal counterparts with the suffix -**nɨ** 'POSSESSED ITEM', e.g., -**rwon**- 'talk' and -**rwonɨ** 'talk of' as in the forms **nɨrwonaha** 'he talks' and **ɨrwonɨ** 'his talk' or 'his language'. The forms that are derived by adding -**mnɨ** are not marked for possession, but they have the general prefix (see Appendix B.2.3): **ɨrwomnɨ** 'one who does not talk' (**ɨ-rwo(n)-mnɨ** GEN.PREF-talk-NEG); **ememnɨ** 'one who does not steal' (**Ø-eme(n)-mnɨ** GEN.PREF-steal-NEG); **amusumnu** 'thing without weight' (**Ø-amusu(nu)-mnu** GEN.PREF-weight-NEG).

There are two other derivations which apply to this set of stems: -**mra** 'NEGATIVE ADVERBIAL' (Appendix G.1, G.2, and G.3); and **tɨ-...-nye** 'STATE ADVERBIAL' (Appendix G.1).

The -**mnɨ** (and -**mra**) negation derivations also apply to adverbs derived by the suffix -**txahke** 'desire involving effort' (see Appendix G.2, and F.3 for one example relating to an intransitive stem). When -**txahke** is applied to a transitive stem, the resulting form is marked with the person possessor prefixes, not the general prefix, and these possessor prefixes are retained when the negation process is applied: **oyonytxakomnɨ** 'one who is not wanting to see you' (**oy-onye-txako-mnɨ** II-see-wanting-NEG); cf. **oyonytxahke** 'wanting to see you' (for the change of form from -**txahke** to -**txako**-, see F.3).

There is one stem to which the -**mnɨ** (and -**mra** and **tɨ-...-nye**) derivations apply which does not fit any of the above categories: -**nyo** 'husband of' as in **ronyo** 'my husband', **ɨnyo** 'her husband'; the negative nominalization takes the form **ɨnyomnɨ** 'one without a husband'.

APPENDIX G
DERIVATIONAL MORPHOLOGY: ADVERB FORMATION

G.1 Adverbs derived from nouns

There are eight processes by which adverbs are derived from nouns:

(i) **tɨ-...-rye** 'STATE' is derived from possessed noun stems and functions to signify an attribute or state of being. The suffix is -ye with a few stems: **tɨhye** 'wifed', 'having a wife', 'being with a wife' from the stem -he- 'wife' as in **ɨhetxe** 'his wife'; **tɨhroye** 'by foot' from the stem -hro- 'foot' as in **rohrorɨ** 'my foot'. The form of the suffix is -rye with most stems: **tahoxerye** 'strong' from -ahoxe- 'strength' as in **ayahoxetɨ** 'your strength'; **tkamsukrye** 'bloody' from -kamsuku- 'blood' as in **ɨkamsukuru** 'his blood'.

(ii) **tɨ-...-nye** 'STATE'. This is complementary to the **tɨ-...-rye** form described above. It has the same meaning and function, but applies to the subclass of noun and verb stems which are also the subject of the -mnɨ and -mra derivations (see Appendix F.4): **tɨrwonye** 'talking, having speech' from -rwon- 'talk' as in **nɨrwonaha** 'he talks' and **ɨrwonɨ** 'his talk'; **temenye** 'stealing, whispering' from -emen- 'steal, furtive', as in **nemenaha** 'he steals' and **emenɨ** 'his furtiveness, his stealing propensity'; **tamusnye** 'heavy' from -amusu(n)- as in **namusnano** 'it weighs heavy' and **amusunu** 'its weight'.

(iii) **tɨ-...-ke** 'having, in possession of' is derived from possessed stems: **tahotɨhke** 'having wings' from -ahotɨ- 'wing' as in **torono yahothɨrɨ** 'the bird's wing'; **totke** 'having meat' from -otɨ- 'meat of' as in **owotɨ** 'your meat'; **tɨhpoke** 'hairy, having hair' from -hpo- 'hair of' as in **rohpotxe** 'my hair'.

(iv) **tɨ-...-horye** 'state of fitness, good'. This derivation process also applies to verb stems, when it has more specific meanings (see G.2). So far as I know this also applies only to possessed (noun) stems, or at least to nouns that are capable of being possessed, thus: **tkanawahorye** 'having a good canoe' from **kanawa** 'canoe', which has an optional possessed form **-kanawarɨ** 'canoe of'; **tokatohorye** 'having a good spirit' from the obligatorily possessed stem **-okato** 'spirit of'. This is not a much used form with noun stems, but it is probably generally productive with respect to stems that can be possessed.

(v) **-hɨra** 'NEGATIVE'. This is a much used process which also applies to verb stems (see G.2), adverb stems (see G.3), and relator stems (see Appendix H). Applied to nouns, it occurs only with possessed stems and results in nonpossessed forms that have the general prefix. It is the negative antonym of the derived adverbial **tɨ-** forms that occur with the suffixes **-rye** (see (i) above) and **-ke** (see (iii) above): **ɨhehra** 'without a wife' (**ɨ-he-hɨra** GEN.PREF-wife-NEG); **ɨkamsukhura** 'without blood' (**ɨ-kamsuku-hɨra** GEN.PREF-blood-NEG); **ethɨra** 'without meat food' (**Ø-otɨ-hɨra** GEN.PREF-meat-NEG). The stem **-ahoxe-** 'strength of' (cf. **tahoxerye** 'strong' in (i) above) is irregular in that it undergoes the **-mra** process (see (vi) below): **ahoxemra** 'not strong, weak' (never *ahohxera). It also undergoes the **-mnɨ** 'negative nominalization' process (see Appendix F.4) and not the **-hɨnɨ** process (see F.1).

(vi) **-mra** 'NEGATIVE' applies to the same set of stems as the **-mnɨ** process (see Appendix F.4), and also the **tɨ-...-nye** process (see (ii) above), and is mutually exclusive with **-hɨra** (see (v) above). It also results in forms that are nonpossessed and that have the general prefix: **ɨrwomra** 'not talking' (**ɨ-rwo(n)-mra** GEN.PREF-talk-NEG); **ememra** 'not stealing' (**Ø-eme(n)-mra** GEN.PREF-steal-NEG); **amusumra** 'not heavy, light' (**Ø-amusu(n)-mra** GEN.PREF-heaviness-NEG). The irregular form **ahoxemra** 'not strong' is described in (v) above.

(vii) **-henye** 'big, associated with possession' is derived from possessed noun stems (or, at least, stems that can optionally be possessed), but the resulting adverb form is nonpossessed and marked with the general prefix: **ɨhokhenye** 'having a big child' (**ɨ-hoku-henye** GEN.PREF-child-big); **ɨkanawahenye** 'having a big canoe' (**ɨ-kanawa-henye** GEN.PREF-canoe-big). It functions syntactically as the complement of the copula: **ɨhokhenye wehxaha** (having-a-big-child I-am) 'I have a big child' or 'my child is big'. The negative is formed by adding the suffix **-hɨra** (see (v) above) to the whole form: **ɨkanawahenyehra wehxaha** (having-a-small-canoe I-am) 'my canoe is small'.

(viii) **-kenyehra** 'in a bad state, associated with possession' is also derived from possessed stems (i.e., obligatorily or optionally possessed), and the resulting form is nonpossessed and marked with the general prefix. It is a negative form (marked by the suffix **-hra**) that does not have a positive counterpart of the same basic form. The equivalent positive form is **tɨ-...-horye** (see (iv) above): **ɨminkenyehra wehxaha** 'my house is in a bad state' (**ɨ-mɨn-kenyehra-wehxaha** GEN.PREF-house-bad state-I am); cf. the positive form **bɨnhorye** 'having a good house' (**tɨ-mɨn-horye** ADVBLZR-house-good).

Derivational Morphology: Adverb Formation

G.2 Adverbs derived from verb stems

There are nine processes by which adverbs are derived from verb stems:

(i) **tɨ-...-so** 'ACTION ADVERBIAL' is derived from any verb stem. There is a phonologically conditioned suffix allomorph **-xe** (see Appendix A.4.1). For the pseudopassive function with transitive stems see 9.4. Examples are as follows: **tomohso** 'coming' (**tɨ-omokɨ-so** ADVBLZR-come-ACT.ADV); **tahatakaxe** 'coming out' (**tɨ-ahataka-xe** ADVBLZR-come out-ACT.ADV); **tonoso** 'to be eaten, can be eaten, edible' (**tɨ-ono-so** ADVBLZR-eat-ACT.ADV); **tamaxe** 'to be cut down, can be cut down' (**tɨ-ama-xe** ADVBLZR-cut down-ACT.ADV); **tehxe** 'being' (**tɨ-exe-xe** ADVBLZR-be-ACT.ADV).

(ii) **tɨ-...-horye** 'state of fitness, good, proper, ought to be'. This process applies also to noun stems (see G.1). Examples are as follows: **tɨtohorye** 'right to go' (**tɨ-to-horye** ADVBLZR-go-good) as in **tɨtohorye naha** 'it is right for him to go', 'he ought to go' (**naha** 'he is'); **tɨmporye** 'ought to be given', 'good to be given' (**tɨ-ɨmɨ-horye** ADVBLZR-give-good); **tehxorye** 'good to be, ought to be' (**tɨ-exe-horye** ADVBLZR-be-good).

(iii) **-txahke** 'desire involving effort', 'trying', 'seeking'. With intransitive stems the prefix **tɨ-** 'ADVERBIAL' cooccurs (also with the copula stem), but with transitive stems the possessor prefixes cooccur to signal the object of the action. This is the only derivational process in which the intransitive and transitive stems differ in this way. Another irregular feature of the **-txahke** suffix is that the negative counterpart is formed by adding the suffix **-mra** 'NEGATIVE' (see Appendix F.4 with reference to **-mnɨ**, the nominal equivalent of **-mra**). Examples of the positive forms are: **tɨnɨhtxahke** 'wanting to sleep', 'trying to sleep' (**tɨ-nɨkɨ-txahke** ADVBLZR-sleep-desire); **rotahatxahke** 'seeking to hit me' (**r-otaha-txahke** I-hit-desire); **tehtxahke** 'trying to be' (**tɨ-exe-txahke** ADVBLZR-be-desire).

(iv) **-hɨra** 'NEGATIVE'. This process applies also to noun stems (see G.1), adverb stems (see G.3), and relator stems (see Appendix H). With intransitive stems it results in either (a) a non-possessed form having the general prefix, which is the normal form of intransitive negative, e.g., **ɨwanotahra** 'not singing' (**ɨ-wanota-hra** GEN.PREF-sing-NEG) and **omokhɨra** 'not coming' (**ø-omokɨ-hɨra** GEN.PREF-come-NEG) (also the copula **ehxera** 'not being' (**ø-exe-hɨra** GEN.PREF-be-NEG)), or (b) a possessed form, where the possessor prefix refers to the subject of the action--this occurs only in the single context where it is followed by the particle **ro** 'TIME', either alone or in the particle sequence **ro rma haka** (TIME-CONT-yet) 'while still yet', in a special kind of temporal expression meaning 'before' or 'until': **rowanotahra ro** 'before I sing' or 'until I sing', more literally 'while my not singing' (**ro-wanota-hra-ro** I-sing-NEG-TIME); **oyomokhɨra ro rma haka** 'before you come' or 'until you come', more literally 'while you are still not yet coming' (**oy-omokɨ-hɨra-ro-rma-haka** II-come-NEG-TIME-CONT-yet). With transitive stems it results in a possessed form where the prefix refers to the object of the action: **rohorhɨra** 'not looking for me' (**ro-oho-rɨ-hɨra** I-look for-STEM FORM-NEG). The -**hɨra** suffix is mutually exclusive with -**mra**, which occurs with a small subclass of verb and noun stems (see G.1).

(v) -**so** 'PURPOSE OF MOTION'. With intransitive stems and the copula it results in a nonpossessed form with the general prefix, and with transitive stems a possessed form where the prefix refers to the underlying object of the action; there is a phonologically conditioned allomorph -**xe** (see Appendix A.4.1): **ewehso** 'purposing to take a bath' (**Ø-ewehɨ-so** GEN.PREF-take a bath-MOT.PURP); **oyonyxe** 'purposing to see you' (**oy-onye-xe** II-see-MOT.PURP); **ehxe** 'purposing to be' (**Ø-exe-xe** GEN.PREF-be-MOT.PURP)). This derived adverb form does not occur as the complement of the copula, but only as an adjunct in a sentence where the superordinate verb is a verb of motion.

(vi) -**haya** 'almost', 'about to be'. This also results in non-possessed forms with intransitive stems and the copula, and in possessed forms with transitive stems: **enurhaya** 'about to be born' (**Ø-onu-ru-haya** GEN.PREF-be born-STEM FORM-almost); **ayahohsaya** 'almost catching hold of you' (**ay-ahosɨ-haya** II-catch hold of-almost); **ehxaya** 'almost being' (**Ø-exe-haya** GEN.PREF-be-almost).

(vii) -**toko** 'SIMULTANEOUS ACTION', 'same time as', 'when', 'if'. This derivation normally functions in subordinate clauses and expresses an action that occurs simultaneously with another action expressed by the verb in the main clause. I regard it as basically a derivation from a verb stem, although it normally follows one of the nominalizing suffixes, either -**nɨ**- or -**hɨto**- (see Appendix F.2), which has already been added to the verb stem. With all types of verb stems the resulting form is possessed, with the prefixes referring to the subject of the action in the case of intransitive stems and the copula, and to the object of the action in the case of transitive stems: **ohorohnɨtoko** 'when you stop' (**o-horohɨ-nɨ-toko** II-stop-ACT.NOMLZN-SIMULT); **rarymantoko** 'when (someone) throws me', 'when my being thrown' (**r-aryma-nɨ-toko** I-throw-ACT.NOMLZN-SIMULT); **ryehtoko** 'when my being', 'when I am' (**r-exe-toko** I-be-SIMULT); this copula form is irregular in that the -**nɨ**- suffix is not first added to the verb stem. The co-occurrence of -**hɨto** and -**toko** to produce a negative time expression results in **omokɨhtotoko** 'when his not coming' (**Ø-omokɨ-hɨto-toko** III-come-NEG.NOMLZN-SIMULT). The suffix -**toko** occurs idiosyncratically with a few nonverbal stems: the question word **ɨsokentoko** 'when?', derived from another question word **ɨsoke** 'how?', to which has been added the nominalizing suffix -**n(o)**; **oskentoko** 'when (it is) thus' (**oske-n(o)-toko** thus-NOMLZN-SIMULT); **anatoko** 'another time', 'perhaps' (**ana-toko** other-SIMULT); **onɨ wyarontoko** 'when it is like this' (**onɨ-wyaro-n(o)-toko** this-like-NOMLZN-

Derivational Morphology: Adverb Formation   241

SIMULT). The suffix also occurs with the general prefix alone, without any stem: **ɨtoko** 'at that time', when it functions as a sentence connective linking the sentence in which it occurs with the preceding discourse.

(viii) **-txhe** 'after'. This derivation also functions in subordinate clauses. It expresses an action that is prior to the action expressed by the verb in the main clause. It occurs immediately following the verb stem (unlike **-toko**). The resulting form is possessed under the same conditions as for **-toko**: **rototxhe** 'after my going', 'after I go' (**ro-to-txhe** I-go-after); **ryeryewhamnohɨtxhe** 'after my being persecuted', 'after (someone's) persecuting me' (**r-eryewhamnohɨ-txhe** I-persecute-after); **ryexetxhe** 'after my being' (**r-exe-txhe** I-be-after).

(ix) **-wawo** 'during the time of' (cf. the relator of the same form expressing location (see Appendix D.3 (4)). Occurring as a suffix of verb stems it expresses an action that is contemporaneous with the main verb of the sentence. The process results in forms that are possessed under the same conditions as for **-toko**: **ohohtawawo** 'during the time you carry a child (in the womb)' (**o-hohta-wawo** II-have child-during); **kakɨhtowawonye** 'during the time of our being created', 'when people (were) created', (**kɨ-akɨhto-wawo-nye** I+II-create-during-COLL); **waha me ryexwawo** 'during the time of my being a soldier' (**waha-me-r-exe-wawo** fighting man-DENOMLZR-I-be-during).

G.3 Adverbs derived from adverbs

The only processes by which adverbs can be derived from adverbs relate to the negative derivations **-hɨra** (see G.1 and G.2) and **-mra** (see Appendixes F.4 and G.1). There is only one type of adverb with which **-mra** occurs, the derived adverb **-txahke**, and the negative is formed by changing that suffix to **-txakomra** (see Appendixes F.4 and G.2). The occurrence of **-hɨra** in the derived adverb forms **-henyehra** and **-kenyehra** is described in G.1. It also occurs with simple adverb stems: **ohxehra** 'not good, bad' (**ohxe-hra** good-NEG); **tanohra** 'not here' (**tano-hra** here-NEG); **amnyehra** 'PAST' (**amnye-hra** future-NEG); **yakehra** 'not many, few' (**yake-hra** many-NEG). It is not much used with numerals, the double nominalization being preferred: **towenyxanohnɨ** 'not one' (**towenyxa-no-hnɨ** one-NOMLZN-NEG.NOMLZN). For other stems with which the double nominalization **-nohnɨ** occurs, see Appendix F.1 and F.3. The suffix **-hɨra** also occurs with one other derived adverbial, the **tɨ-...-horye** form (see G.2), and the resulting form is unique in that the prefix **tɨ-** 'ADVERBIALIZER' is retained with the negative suffix: **tɨtohoryehra** 'not right to go', 'ought not to go' (**tɨtohorye-hra** right to go-NEG); **tɨmporyehra** 'ought not to be given', 'not good to be given' (**tɨmporye-hra** ought to be given-NEG); **tehxoryehra** 'not good to be', 'ought not to be' (**tehxorye-hra** good to be-NEG).

APPENDIX H
DERIVATIONAL MORPHOLOGY: RELATOR FORMATION

Relators are derived only from relators. There are two processes, both of which occur in the derivation of other forms:

(i) **-hɨra** 'NEGATIVE' (see Appendix G.1, G.2 and G.3): **roxehra** 'not liking me' (**ro-xe-hra** I-desirous of-NEG); **romɨn yawohra** 'not in my house' (**romɨn-yawo-hra** my house-in-NEG); **kanawa mehra** 'not (being) a canoe' (**kanawa-me-hra** canoe-DENOMLZR-NEG).

(ii) One of the set of prefixes: **e-, os-, ot-, as-, at-** 'DE-TRANSITIVIZER' (see Appendix E.2 (i)). With relators these prefixes function as either reflexive or reciprocal, or both (see 8.1). They replace the inflectional person-marking prefixes and the derived relators are free forms: **ehanaye** 'side by side with each other' (**e-hanaye** RECIP-from the side of, cf. Appendix D.12); **osoxe** 'liking oneself' or 'liking each other' (**os-o-xe** REFL/RECIP-(epenthesis)-desirous of); **othoko** 'occupied with each other' (**ot-hoko** RECIP-occupied with); **asaworo** 'towards each other' (**as-(y)aworo** RECIP-directly towards); **atakratawo** 'in front of each other' (**at-akratawo** RECIP-in front of). The forms of these reflexive/reciprocal relators do not change except for the normal phonological processes, as in **osox** in (1); the collective suffix **-nye** does not occur with them, as it does with relators generally (see 1.4); and they do not change for person:

(1) a. **osox(e)**   **wehxaha**
    REFL-desirous-of I-am
    'I love myself.'

  b. **osox**   **tehtxe**
    RECIP-desirous-of let-us(INCL)-be
    'Let us love one another.'

  c. **osox**   **ehtxoko**
    RECIP-desirous-of be-COLL
    'Love each other.'

  d. **osoxe**   **rmahaxa**   **nehxatxkon hatɨ**
    REFL/RECIP-desirous-of very-much they-were HSY
    'It is said they used to love themselves very much' or
    'It is said they used to love each other very much.'

APPENDIX I
MODIFYING PARTICLES

There are five forms which clearly belong to the set of modifying particles:

heno, which has two meanings, depending on the semantic class of the word it modifies: (i) 'dead' with regard to persons--it is also used of persons who are virtually dead, either because they are no longer around and their whereabouts are not known, or because they are sick and not fully aware of what is going on around them; and (ii) 'quantity', 'set of' with regard to animals, plants, and meteorological items like rain or wind, e.g., **Utxun heno** 'Utxunu, now dead' or 'the late Utxunu'; **royon heno** 'my dead mother'; **torono heno** 'a flock of birds'; **atxowowo heno** 'the big wind'; **waywɨ heno** 'set of arrows.'

komo 'COLLECTIVE', restricted to modifying nouns with human referents when a group of people is involved, e.g., **rowtɨ komo** 'my brothers'; **anar komo** 'other people'. It is also used sometimes with reference to animals and items regarded as an integral part of the culture or environment of the people; **honyko komo** 'peccary' (i.e., in general, contrasted with **honyko heno** 'herd of peccary', which refers to a more specific group); **wewe komo** 'trees of the forest'; **harye komo** 'sweet potatoes'. The particle **komo** is the nearest thing to a plural number, but it is not identical with such a category, since it is not always used when more than one person is being referred to, but only when some sort of focus is being placed on the group. There is another form with the same range of meaning that is used for certain nouns marked for possession: the suffix **-yamo** (see Appendix C.2).

tho 'DEVALUED' marks the items that it modifies as having undergone some change of state or relationship usually involving loss of value, e.g., **ehnɨ tho ymo** (river-DEVALUED-AUGMENTATIVE) 'the big river that has now dried up'; **uro tho** (I-DEVALUED) 'poor me', which may mean either that the speaker has actually suffered some loss or sickness or that he is referring to himself in a self-deprecating way. The morpheme **tho** is distinct from other modifying particles in that it can be used only in noun phrases, that is, it is only postposed to nouns and pronouns. There are two homophonous forms, both suffixes: (i) **-tho** (allomorph of **-thɨrɨ**) 'POSSESSED ITEM, SIMPLE PAST' (see Appendix C.2); and (ii) **-tho** (allomorph of **-toho**) 'THING, TIME OR PLACE ASSOCIATED WITH THE ACTION' (see Appendix F.2).

txko 'DIMINUTIVE', relating to the qualities of being small and/or good, e.g., **roknɨ txko** (my pet-DIMIN) 'my precious pet'; **kana txko** (fish-DIMIN) 'the small fish'.

ymo 'AUGMENTATIVE', relating to the qualities of being big and/or bad, e.g., **toto ymo** (person-AUG) 'the big man'; **okoye ymo** (snake-AUG) 'the dangerous snake'; **kamara ymo** (jaguar-AUG) 'the big, bad jaguar'.

Of these five particles only **txko** and **ymo** are mutually exclusive, and there are frequently sequences of two or three of them in the same phrase: **romsɨ tho txko** (my daughter-DEVALUED-DIMIN) 'my poor (sick) daughter'; **kamarayana ymo heno komo** (jaguar clan-AUG-dead-COLL) 'the much-feared people of the jaguar clan, now dead'.

There are two other particles which, in some of their usages, function like modifying particles, but which elsewhere occur in verb and adverb phrases, where they modify the verb or adverb rather than any noun in the context, and function as discourse particles (see Appendix J). One is **ro** 'EXCLUSIVE', 'HABITUAL', signalling that the item referred to is the only one involved, or is habitually involved, in whatever is predicated of it:

(1) a. **wewe wamano,   uro ro**
     tree I-felled-it, I   EXCL
     'I felled the tree all by myself.'

   b. **wayamakasɨ kahnye   ro**
     comb   one-who-makes HABIT
     'one who makes combs'

The other is **rye** 'SAMENESS', 'TOGETHERNESS', signalling that the referent, usually marked with the collective form, is involved in some mutual relationship or mutual action; it sometimes includes the idea of reciprocal action:

(2) **nosonytxetxkonɨ,   nyamoro rye**
    they-were-hearing-each-other, they   SAME/TOGETHER
    'They were discussing it together.'

APPENDIX J
DISCOURSE PARTICLES

Discourse particles are listed and illustrated here in three groups:

(i) The single, monomorphemic particles.

(ii) Sequences which include **ha** 'INTENSIFIER'. These sequences sometimes have the same meaning as the single particle without **ha** and sometimes have a distinctive meaning. (The particle **ha** is treated in 13.4.2. It is not listed separately in this Appendix, although I now consider it a discourse particle, but it occurs in many cited forms throughout the book.)

(iii) Other sequences of discourse particles that have a meaning distinct from the combined meanings of the separate forms. (There are other sequences, not listed here, where the individual particles retain their meanings.)

In some of the examples one or more modifying or verification particles occur, as well as the discourse particle that is in focus. Many of the examples are from Derbyshire (1965), and references that follow the citations are to this work (page and sentence numbers).

(i) Single particles.

hak(a) 'at this point of time', 'right now', 'right then', 'yet' (for its use with imperative forms see 6.3 and Appendix B.3.1):

(1) a. **toto me   nehxakoni amnyehra haka, kurumu**
       human DENOMLZR it-was   long-ago then king-vulture
       'At that time long ago in the past, the vulture was a man.' (32.106)

   b. **ehxera   ti nehxakoni haka**
       not-being HSY it-was   then
       'There was nothing at that time.' (60.27)

c. **notkukmetxkoni̵, i̵yari̵hnawo, omokhi̵ra haka**
they-were-practicing in-their-absence not-coming yet

ehtokony haka, kurumyana komo
when-their-being yet buzzard-people COLL
'They were practicing in their absence, when the buzzard people were still not yet coming.' (33.132)

htxero 'FIRST IN SEQUENCE':

(2) a. **omoro htxero i̵toko**
you first go
'You go first.' (119.29)

b. **woknano htxero i̵kwarmosi̵ .... haxetmomo**
drink first I-make-it type-of-manioc-drink

i̵kwarmosi̵ htxero
I-make-it first
'Let me make a drink first .... Let me first make the manioc drink.' (128.95-96)

kahpa 'PERIOD (of time that contrasts with some other period)':

(3) a. **i̵ro ma amani̵ri̵ moni̵ wehxakon kahpa**
that CHANGE felling-of-(tree) that I-was PERIOD
'During that time I was felling trees for the first time in my life.' (169.36)

b. **i̵tehe kahpa** (this is a common form of farewell)
I-go PERIOD
'I'm going for now.'

kati̵ 'ALTERNATIVE (in interrogatives)' (this is fully discussed and illustrated in 6.2).

ma 'PERMANENT CHANGE OF STATE, signalling a departure from established norms':

(4) a. **i̵ro ma roti̵mryenkani̵ri̵ i̵ro ma**
that CHANGE my-leaving-boyhood that CHANGE

amani̵ri̵ moni̵ wehxakoni̵, i̵ro
felling-of-(tree) that I-was there
'What was happening to me there was a new experience of leaving behind my boyhood and felling trees for the first time.' (169.21-23)

b. **i̵tos hakahpa ma kay hati̵**
I-go PERIOD CHANGE he-said-it HSY
'"I must go away for a permanent change of location and existence," he said.' (Said by the moon-man, who was leaving earth for the sky at the creation of the moon.) (24.32)

Discourse Particles

The sequence of the third person nondeictic inanimate pronoun **ɨro** and **ma**, as in (4a), produces an idiom with the meaning 'for the first time'.

mak(e) 'ADVERSATIVE', 'CONTRARY TO EXPECTATION':

(5) a. **ohxehra   wehxako;   ɨtek   mak   ha**
       not-good   I-was   I-went ADVERS INTENSFR
       'I didn't feel good, but I went.'

   b. **ɨtono   tho   uro .... ɨto   make**
       there-NOMLZN DEVLD I   there ADVERS

      kohseryehnohye   ha
      I-was-made-afraid   INTENSFR
      'I was a native of that place, but it was there
      I was made afraid.' (143.70-72)

mat(ɨ) 'referring to something just said, by either the same speaker or the addressee':

(6) a. **ahatakak ha   ɨkehe   matɨ,   kekon   hatɨ**
       come-out INTENSFR I-say-it just-said he-said-it HSY
       '"Come out!, is what I just said," he said.' (69.248)

   b. **oske matɨ   texnye   ha**
       thus just-said let-us-INCL-be   INTENSFR
       'Let us do what you say.' (171.18)

nyhe 'MORE, with reference to comparison, time, or activity', 'REQUEST'. The comparative function is discussed and illustrated in 9.1. The time function is seen in a commonly used time expression, **amnye nyhe** 'later on, more in the future', the head word **amnye** being the basic time word meaning 'future'. Other examples of **nyhe** are:

(7) a. **tawasnye mak   naha   ha ....   kohsayano**
       light   ADVERS it-is   INTENSFR .. at-night-NOMLZN

      nyhe mak   kɨwro   tehxan   hamɨ,
      MORE ADVERS   we-INCL   we-INCL-are DEDUCT

      othoko   hamɨ
      occupied-with-each-other   DEDUCT
      'But it is light (all the time) .... It is clear that
      people only have sex later, at night.' (17.30-31)

   b. **uro nyhe   hak ehtxemako**
       I   REQUEST IMP give-medicine-to
       'Please treat me with medicine.'

rha 'SEQUENTIAL', 'in turn':

(8) a. **ɨtoko rha Woxka y**
    go   SEQ Woxka VOC
    'Go again, Woxka.' (61.31)

   b. **anaro rha yowan   yaha   tekonɨ**
      other SEQ inside-of through he-was-going
      'He was going through the insides of different
      ones in turn.' (86.36)

rma 'SAME REFERENT', 'CONTINUITY' (see 8.3 for a reflexive function):

(9) a. **nenyhoryetxownɨ   xarha nyamoro rma**
       they-repaired-it again they   SAME-REF
       'The same people repaired it again.'

   b. **1968 wawo rma wehxakonɨ**
      1968 in   CONT I-was
      'It was still 1968.'

ro 'HABITUAL', 'COMPLETELY', 'TIME(S)', 'EXCLUSIVE'. This particle often functions like a modifying particle (see Appendix I, where the 'HABITUAL' and 'EXCLUSIVE' meanings are in focus). Where it follows a negative word, **ro** has a temporal meaning of 'while, during', which combines with the negative to result in 'before':

(10) a. **wekarymax   hakahpa, rowayehpɨra ro**
        I-promise-her PERIOD   my-not-dying while
        'Let me promise (my daughter in marriage) at
        this time, before I die.' (171.14)

Other examples of **ro** are:

   b. **marar rakatawo ro   nehxakonɨ**
      field middle-of COMPL he-was
      'He was right in the middle of the field.' (37.19)

   c. **neryetɨkryahxakonɨ   ... txomo na tho**
      he-was-piercing-the-end-of-it ... ground to DEVLD

      ro, xaro   tho   ro
      COMPL to-here DEVLD COMPL
      'He was piercing the tail of each arrow all the way
      down to the ground.' (24.42)

   d. **asako ro   wamaye**
      two   TIMES I-felled-it
      'I felled two (trees)' or 'I felled a tree on two
      occasions.' (169.38)

rye 'SAMENESS', 'TOGETHERNESS', 'MUTUALLY RELATED' (for a reciprocal function see 8.4; for the basic meaning, where it functions

Discourse Particles   251

very often more like a modifying particle, see Appendix I). Other
examples are:

(11) a. **ɨsna   rye narymetxkonɨ**
        to-there SAME they-were-shooting-them
        'They were directing their arrows all to the
         same place.' (129.124)

   b. **dɨ   kahrany   haxa, ɨhoko**
      action-of-stopping not-doing-it CONTR occupied-with-it

      rye haxa, dom
      SAME CONTR action-of-eating
      'In contrast to us, they never stopped; they were
       occupied with eating all the time.' (19.93)

ryhe 'EMPHATIC PROMINENCE', 'MILD CONTRAST':

(12) a. **xenyhenɨ   ryhe mokyamo**
        one-not-to-be-seen EMPH those
        'Those are (creatures) we should never look at.'
        (104.13)

   b. **nenamtxownɨ   hatɨ. nenyhoryeye ryhe tɨ. ohxe**
      he-buried-them HSY he-kept-them CONTR HSY good

      ryhe tɨ neryeye,   ewtɨnhɨrɨ   ryhe
      EMPH HSY he-fixed-them his-brother-PAST EMPH
      'He buried them. (At first), however, he kept them.
       He took care of them--the brother of the dead
       man.' (201.23-25)

xa 'CONTRAST'. The contrast is often with another item in the
linguistic context, but it can also be of a more general, universal kind:

(13) a. **ohetxenhɨr   xe   xa   wehxaha**
        your-wife-PAST desirous-of CONTR I-am
        'I want the one who has been your wife (not
         this other woman).' (69.256)

   b. **noro tho   xa   mokro   raheno**
      he   DEVLD CONTR that-one he-seduced-me
      'He (in contrast with all others) is the one
       who seduced me.' (23.23)

xak(o) (the subject of some) MISFORTUNE, DISADVANTAGE, or IN-
FERIOR STATUS', the cause of which is normally indicated in the
linguistic context:

(14) a. **kurum   me   xah tɨ totxownɨ ha**
king-vulture DENOMLZR MISF HSY they-went INTENSFR
'They went in the form of vultures.' (They had
been men.) (32.100)

b. **yakenohnɨ   xak kɨwyamo tahtxoko**
many-NOMLZN-NEG MISF we-INCL we-were
'We have become few in number' (in the context of
talking about deaths in the tribe.) (174.32)

(The phonological conditioning that produces the form **xah** in (14a) is discussed in Appendix A.4.1).

(ii) Sequences involving **ha** 'INTENSIFIER' and certain of the discourse particles just described can be divided into two kinds: (a) those that have the same meaning as the single particle without **ha**; and (b) those that have a distinctive meaning.

(a) Sequences with the same meaning: **hakahpa** (same as **kahpa**), **hama** (same as **ma**), **haxa** (same as **xa**):

(15) a. **otkukmak   hakahpa kekon   hatɨ ɨyɨm   peno**
try-yourself-out PERIOD he-said-it HSY his-father dead
'"Try practicing (as a shaman-healer) for a while,"
said his dead father.' (182.29)

b. **tenahtxe   hama onɨ wyaro rma   xako**
let-us-INCL-eat-it CHANGE this like SAME-REF MISF
'Let us eat it in a completely new way, just like it is
in this (uncooked) state.' (Said when the vulture people
ate dead, decaying flesh for the first time) (32.96)

c. **uro haxa ɨtohtxexe**
I   CONTR I-go-first
'No, I (not you) will go first.' (119.31)

The sequence **hakahpa** sometimes seems to combine the meaning of the separate particles **hak(a)** (in its imperative function) and **kahpa**, as in the following:

d. **wehtan   hakahpa**
I-seek-it-MOT.IMP IMP-PERIOD
'I must go look for it at this time.' (95.24)

(b) Sequences that have a meaning distinct from the single particle with which **ha** occurs: **harha** 'RETURN TO FORMER STATE OR LOCATION', or 'CHANGE OF STATE (i.e., become)'; **haryhe** 'FRUSTRATIVE', 'CONTRARY TO FACT'; **haxaha** 'LAST IN SEQUENCE', 'finally':

(16) a. **komokno harha,   Kasawa hona harha**
I-came back-again Kasawa to   back-again
'I have come back again, back to Kasawa.'

Discourse Particles

    b. **oseryehpɨra   harha wehxakonɨ**
       not-being-afraid become I-was
       'I was no longer afraid' or 'I became not afraid.'
       (168.16)

    c. **nekayɨmyatxkon   haryhe tɨ**
       they-were-climbing FRUST HSY
       'They were trying to climb (but didn't succeed).'
       (13.14)

    d. **ɨhokhura   ehtoko,   enamrɨ   tho**
       without-child if-his-being burying-of-him DEVLD

       haryhe
       FRUST
       'If he had had no children, he would have been buried.'
       (As it was he was cremated.) (176.48)

    e. **kwatxe   yetxownɨ   haxaha**
       river-turtle they-fixed-it finally
       'Finally (after trying one or two other things),
       they used the turtle.' (47.86)

For the special contrary-to-fact conditional construction involving **haryhe**, as in (16d), see 4.9; **haryhe** is also used with a meaning similar to the single particle **ryhe**, i.e., 'PROMINENT, DISTINCTIVE'.

    (iii) Other sequences of discourse particles with a meaning distinct from the combined meanings of the separate particles:

hakarha 'each in turn', similar to the meaning of **rha**, but its use is more restricted in that it always follows a noun phrase and it always signals that there is repetition of an action by a different person:

(17) **uro hakarha wamaxe. Mawarye hakarha namekonɨ**
     I in-turn I-fell-it Mawarye in-turn he-was-felling-it
     '"Let me now take my turn at felling (trees)." Mawarye
     in turn was felling trees.' (52.240-41)

marma 'only':

(18) **nor heno wya marma nekarymaye, ɨyon   heno wya marma**
     her dead to only he-told-it his-mother dead to only
     'He told it only to her, to his (another's) mother, now
     dead.' (171.12)

rmahaxa 'very much':

(19) **ohxe rmahaxa   nahko woto**
     good very-much it-was meat
     'The meat was very good.'

rmarha 'likewise', 'in the same way as (something else)':

(20) ɨme   rmarha   nomokyatxkonɨ,   karyhe
      III-DENOMLZR likewise they-were-coming strong/fast

      rmarha .... ahohsɨra   rmarha   nehxakonɨ
      likewise .... not-catching-him likewise he-was
      'They were coming (back) in the same way (as they had
      gone), just as strong and fast .... And he still didn't
      catch him' (just as he hadn't caught him when they
      were going). (119.40-42)

The possessed form of the 'DENOMINALIZER' relator (ɨ-me) followed by rmarha, as in (20), means 'in the same way'.

romak 'without exception', 'never (when following a negative)':

(21) ɨkokmampɨra   esnɨrɨ   romak hatɨ
      not-getting-dark its-being never HSY
      'It never got dark (i.e., the sun never set).' (16.9)

roro 'PERMANENT':

(22) tawasnye roro nehxakonɨ, ɨkokmanpɨra
      light   PERM it-was   not-getting-dark
      'It was light all the time, never getting dark.' (16.8)

xarha 'ADDITIVE', 'and', 'REPETITION of action':

(23) a. ɨto   tɨ nehxakonɨ asama xarha
         there HSY it-was   trail ADD
         'There was another trail there.' (45.41)

     b. wamay   xarha. asako ro   wamaye
         I-felled-it ADD   two   TIMES I-felled-it
         'I felled a second (tree). I felled two' or 'I felled
         (trees) again. I felled them on two occasions.'
         (169.37-38)

xaxa 'SUPERLATIVELY', 'UNIQUELY':

(24) noro tho   xaxa   xe   wehxaha
      her DEVLD SUPERL desirous-of I-am
      'She, more than any other, is the one I want.' (69.255)

APPENDIX K
VERIFICATION PARTICLES

For the general properties of verification and other particles see 1.5; for the verification particle movement process see 7.7; for the syntactic significance of verification particles see 12.2.3; for their relation to the particle **ha** 'INTENSIFIER' see 13.4.2.

The set of verification particles consists of the following:

tɨ   'HEARSAY', i.e., specifically signalling that the speaker was not an eyewitness of events he describes.

mɨ   'DEDUCTION', i.e., the speaker has made a deduction from facts which he may or may not spell out.

na   'UNCERTAINTY', i.e., the speaker is uncertain. This is also used in rhetorical questions (see 12.2.2).

mpɨnɨ   'CERTAINTY', 'PREDICTION' or 'WARNING'; with imperatives it has the sense of 'see to it that you do this'.

we   'OPINION', 'RECOLLECTION', 'COUNTERAFFIRMATION'.

mpe   'POSITIVE DOUBT', 'SCEPTICISM'.

∅   zero marking signals the absence of any of the above, but it specifically marks 'EYEWITNESS' in contrast to 'HEARSAY'.

There are three other particles which may also belong to this set; they occur occasionally in connected discourse, always in phrase final position, but rarely, if ever, in ordinary conversation, and their meanings are obscure: **-hta**, **-mpa** (cooccurs with imperatives), and **-wa** (cooccurs with the 'NONPAST UNCERT' suffixes).

Some degree of uncertainty is marked in four of the particles: **tɨ**, **mɨ**, **na**, and **mpe**, as evidenced by the fact that whenever these forms occur with a verb in the 'NONPAST', it is the 'NONPAST UNCERT' suffixes that occur: **nomokyan hatɨ** 'he is coming (they say)' (never ***nomokyaha hatɨ**), **nomokyan hamɨ** 'he is evidently coming' (on hearing the sound of an outboard motor) (never ***nomokyaha hamɨ**); **nomokyan hana** 'maybe he'll come' (never ***nomokyaha hana**), **nomokyatxow hampe** 'they are coming!--I don't believe it' (never ***nomokyatxhe hampe**). The other particles occur with the other nonpast forms of the verb: **nomokyaha hampɨnɨ** 'he's coming--be warned', **nomokyaha hawe** 'but (in spite of what you say) I think he will come'. So far as I know, the 'NONPAST UNCERT' forms never occur with these last two particles. Where the zero member of the set occurs, the resulting form can be either 'NONPAST' or 'NONPAST UNCERT': **nomokyaha** 'he is coming' or 'he will come' or 'he can come'; **nomokyano** 'will he come?' or 'is he coming?'

REFERENCES

The following abbreviations are used:

BLS   Proceedings of the Annual Meetings of the Berkeley Linguistic Society.

CLS   Papers from the Regional Meetings of the Chicago Linguistic Society.

IJAL International Journal of American Linguistics.

Abbott, M. 1976. Estrutura oracional da língua Makúxi. Série Lingüística 5.231-66. Brasília: Summer Institute of Linguistics.

Abreu, C. de. 1895. Os Bacaerys. Revista Brazileira 3.209-28. Rio de Janeiro.

Anderson, J. 1972. The ghost of times past. Foundations of Language 9.481-91.

Andersson, A.-B. and O. Dahl. 1974. Against the penthouse principle. Linguistic Inquiry 5.451-53.

Armellada, R.P.C. de. 1943-44. Gramática y diccionario de la lengua Pemon (Arekuna, Taurepan, Kamarakoto) (Familia Caribe). Caracas: C. A. Artes Gráficas.

Bach, E. 1975. Order in base structure. In C. N. Li, ed. (1975).

Ballard, L. 1974. Telling it like it was, Part 1:4. The 'hearsay particle' of Philippine languages. Notes on Translation 51.28.

Basso, E. B. 1977. Introduction: The status of Carib ethnology. In E. B. Basso, ed. (1977).

Basso, E. B. (ed.). 1977. Carib-speaking Indians: Culture, society and language. Tucson: The University of Arizona Press.

Berman, A. 1974. On the VSO hypothesis. Linguistic Inquiry 5.1-38.

Bresnan, J. 1976. Evidence for a theory of unbounded transformations. Linguistic Analysis 2.353-93.

Brockway, D. 1981. Semantic constraints on relevance. In H. Parret, M. Sbisà and J. Verschueren (eds.), Possibilities and limitations of pragmatics. Amsterdam: John Benjamins.

Burgess, E. 1976. Focus and topic in Xavante. Ms. Brasília: Summer Institute of Linguistics.

Callow, K. 1974. Discourse considerations in translating the Word of God. Grand Rapids: Zondervan.

Cauty, A. 1974. Reflexiones sobre 'Las formas flexionales' del idioma Panare. Antropológica 37.41-50.

Chafe, W. L. 1970. Meaning and the structure of language. Chicago: University of Chicago Press.

———. 1976. Givenness, contrastiveness, definiteness, subjects, topics, and point of view. In C. N. Li, ed. (1976).

Chapin, P. G. 1978. Easter Island: A characteristic VSO language. In W. P. Lehmann, ed. (1978).

Chomsky, N. 1957. Syntactic structures. The Hague: Mouton.

———. 1965. Aspects of the theory of syntax. Cambridge, MA.: MIT Press.

———. 1977. On WH-movement. In A. Akmajian, P. Culicover, and T. Wasow, eds., Formal syntax. New York: Academic Press.

Comrie. B. 1978. Ergativity. In W. P. Lehmann, ed. (1978).

Culicover, P. and K. Wexler. 1974. The invariance principle and universals of grammar. Social Sciences Working Paper No. 55. Irvine, CA.: University of California.

Dahl, Ö. 1979. Typology of sentence negation. Linguistics 17.79-106.

Derbyshire, D. C. 1961. Hishkaryana (Carib) syntax structure. IJAL 27.125-42, 226-36.

———. 1965. Textos Hixkaryâna. Museu Paraense Emílio Goeldi, Publicações Avulsas No. 3. Belém.

———. 1977a. First report on an OVS language. Presented to the Spring Meeting of the Linguistics Association of Great Britain.

———. 1977b. Word order universals and the existence of OVS languages. Linguistic Inquiry 8.590-99.

———. 1977c. Discourse redundancy in Hixkaryana. IJAL 43.176-88.

———.1978. Another kind of 'hearsay particle'--Hixkaryana, Brazil. Notes on Translation 70.8-13.

———. 1979. Hixkaryana. Lingua Descriptive Studies 1. Amsterdam: North-Holland.

References

Derbyshire, D. C. and G. K. Pullum. 1978. Object-initial languages. Presented to the Summer Meeting of the Linguistic Society of America.

———. 1979. A select bibliography of Guiana Carib languages. IJAL 45.271-76.

———. 1981. Object-initial languages. IJAL 47.192-214.

Dik, S. C. 1978. Functional Grammar. Amsterdam: North-Holland.

Dixon, R. M. W. 1977. Where have all the adjectives gone? Studies in Language I:1.19-80.

Durbin, M. 1977. The Carib language family. In E. B. Basso, ed. (1977).

Edwards, W. (ed.). 1977. An introduction to the Akawaio and Arekuna peoples of Guyana. University of Guyana, Georgetown: Amerindian Languages Project.

Emeneau, M. 1964. India as a linguistic area. In D. Hymes, ed., Language in culture and society. New York: Harper and Row.

Epée, R. 1976. A counterexample to the Q replacement and COMP substitution universals. Linguistic Inquiry 7.677-86.

Faltz, L. M. 1978. On indirect objects in universal syntax. CLS 14.76-87.

Firbas, J. 1966. On defining the theme in functional sentence analysis. Travaux Linguistiques de Prague 1.267-80.

———. 1971. On the concept of communicative dynamism in the theory of functional sentence perspective. Sborník prací filosofiské fakulty A19.135-44. Brno.

Fock, N. 1963. Waiwai. Religion and society of an Amazonian tribe. Nationalmuseets Skrifter, Etnografisk Roekke, Copenhagen.

Foley, W. A. 1976. Comparative syntax in Austronesian. Berkeley: University of California dissertation.

Frantz, D. 1979. Grammatical relations in universal grammar. Supplement to Work Papers Vol. 23 of the Summer Institute of Linguistics, University of North Dakota session.

———. 1981. Grammatical relations in universal grammar. Bloomington: Indiana University Linguistics Club.

Frikel, P. 1958. Classificação linguístico-etnológica das tribos indígenas do Pará Setentrional e zonas adjacentes. Revista de Antropologia 6. São Paulo.

Green, G. M. 1976. Main clause phenomena in subordinate clauses. Language 52.382-97.

Greenberg, J. H. 1966. Some universals of grammar with particular reference to the order of meaningful elements. In J. H. Greenberg, ed., Universals of Language. Second edition. Cambridge, MA.: MIT Press.

Grimes, J. 1975. The thread of discourse. The Hague: Mouton.

Gudschinsky, S. 1973. Sistemas contrastivos de marcadores de pessoa em duas línguas Carib: Apalaí e Hixkaryana. Série Lingüística 1. Brasília: Summer Institute of Linguistics.

Guerios, R. F. M. 1947. Pequeno vocabulário Uiaboy (Indios do Nhamundá). Arquivos do Museu Paranaense Vol. VI. Curitiba.

Gundel, J. K. 1974. The role of topic and comment in linguistic theory. Austin: University of Texas dissertation.

———. 1977. Stress, pronominalization and the given-new distinction. Ms. Ohio State University.

Guppy, N. 1958. Wai-Wai. London: John Murray.

Haiman, J. 1978. Conditionals are topics. Language 54.564-89.

Halliday, M. A. K. 1967. Notes on transitivity and theme in English, Part 2. Journal of Linguistics 3.199-244.

Halliday, M. A. K. and R. Hasan. 1976. Cohesion in English. London: Longman.

Hawkins, R. E. 1962. Waiwai translation. The Bible Translator 13. 164-71.

Hawkins, W. N. and R. E. Hawkins. 1953. Verb inflection in Waiwai (Carib). IJAL 19.201-11.

Hess, H. 1968. The syntactic structure of Mezquital Otomi. The Hague: Mouton.

Hockett, C. F. 1948. Potawatomi. IJAL 14.1-10, 63-73, 139-49, 213-25.

Hodsdon, C. A. 1976. Análise de cláusulas semânticas na língua Makúsi. Série Lingüística 5.267-300. Brasília: Summer Institute of Linguistics.

Hoff, B. J. 1968. The Carib language. The Hague: Martinus Nijhoff.

———. 1978. The relative order of the Carib finite verb and its nominal dependents. In F. Jansen (ed.), Studies on fronting. Lisse: The Peter de Ridder Press.

Hyman, L. M. 1975. On the change from SOV to SVO: Evidence from Niger-Congo. In C. N. Li, ed. (1975).

Jackendoff, R. 1977. X syntax: A study of phrase structure. Linguistic Inquiry Monograph 2. Cambridge, MA.: MIT Press.

References

Kakumasu, J. Y. 1976. Gramática gerativa preliminar da língua Urubú. Série Lingüística 5.171-97. Brasília: Summer Institute of Linguistics.

Kantor, R. N. 1977. The management and comprehension of discourse connection by pronouns in English. Ohio State University dissertation.

Keenan, E. L. 1976. Remarkable subjects in Malagasy. In C. N. Li, ed. (1976).

———. 1978. The syntax of subject-final languages. In W. P. Lehmann, ed. (1978).

Koch-Grünberg, T. 1908. Die Hianákoto-Umáua. Anthropos 3.83-124, 297-335, 952-82.

———. 1924. Vom Roraima zum Orinoco. Vol. 2. Stuttgart: Strecher und Schröder.

———. 1928. Vom Roraima zum Orinoco. Vol. 4: Sprachen. Stuttgart: Strecher und Schröder.

Koehn, S. 1974. Processes and roles in Apalaí clause structure. Ms. Brasília: Summer Institute of Linguistics.

Koster, J. 1978. Conditions, empty nodes, and markedness. Linguistic Inquiry 9.551-93.

Kuno, S. 1978. Japanese: A characteristic OV language. In W. P. Lehmann, ed. (1978).

Lehmann, W. P. 1973. A structural principle of language and its implications. Language 49.47-66.

———. 1978. The great underlying ground-plans. In W. P. Lehmann, ed. (1978).

Lehmann, W. P. (ed.) 1978. Syntactic typology. Sussex: The Harvester Press.

Levinsohn, S. H. 1975. Functional sentence perspective in Inga. Journal of Linguistics 11.13-37.

Li, C. N. (ed.) 1975. Word order and word order change. Austin: University of Texas Press.

———. 1976. Subject and topic. New York: Academic Press.

Li, C. N. and S. A. Thompson. 1976. Subject and topic: A new typology of language. In C. N. Li, ed. (1976).

Longacre, R. E. 1976a. 'Mystery' particles and affixes. CLS 12. 468-75.

Longacre, R. E. (ed.) 1976b. Discourse grammar: Studies in indigenous languages of Colombia, Panama, and Ecuador, part I.

———. 1977. Discourse grammar: Studies in indigenous languages of Colombia, Panama, and Ecuador, parts II and III. Dallas: Summer Institute of Linguistics and University of Texas at Arlington.

Loukotka, C. 1968. Classification of South American Indian languages, ed. by J. Wilbert. Los Angeles: University of California, Latin American Center.

Lowe, I. 1969. An algebraic theory of English pronominal reference. Semiotica 1, No. 2.397-421.

———. 1972. On the relation of formal to sememic matrices with illustrations from Nambiquara. Foundations of Language 8.360-90.

Lyons, J. 1977. Semantics 2. Cambridge University Press.

McCawley, J. 1970. English as a VSO language. Language 46.286-99.

McLeod, R. and V. Mitchell. 1977. Aspectos da língua Xavánte. Brasília: Summer Institute of Linguistics.

Perlmutter, D. 1978. Impersonal passives and the unaccusative hypothesis. BLS 4.157-89.

Perlmutter, D. and P. M. Postal. 1977. Toward a universal characterization of passivization. BLS 3.394-417.

Pickering, W. N. 1973a. Command in Apurinã. Ms. University of Toronto.

———. 1973b. Gapping and constituent order in Apurinã. Spirit duplicated. University of Toronto.

———. 1977. A framework for discourse analysis. University of Toronto dissertation.

Postal, P. M. 1966. A note on "understood transitively." IJAL 32.90-93.

Pullum, G. K. 1977. Word order universals and grammatical relations. In P. Cole and J. Sadock, eds., Syntax and semantics 8: Grammatical relations. New York: Academic Press.

———. 1978. Language and genocide. Survival International Review 3.2.16-17.

———. 1980. Syntactic relations and linguistic universals. Transactions of the Philological Society, 1-39.

Rhodes, R. 1977. Semantics in a relational grammar. CLS 13.503-14.

Rivière, P. G. 1977. Some problems in the comparative study of Carib societies. In E. B. Basso, ed. (1977).

Ross, J. R. 1967. Constraints on variables in syntax. Cambridge, MA.: MIT dissertation.

———. 1973. The penthouse principle and the order of constituents. In C. Corum, T. C. Smith-Stark, and A. Weiser, eds., You take the high node and I'll take the low node. Chicago Linguistic Society, University of Chicago.

Speiser, E. A. 1941. Introduction to Hurrian (The Annual of the American Schools of Oriental Research 20), American Schools of Oriental Research, New Haven.

Sperber, D. and D. Wilson. Forthcoming. Relevance. Oxford: Blackwell's and Cambridge, MA: Harvard University Press.

Steinen, K. von den. 1892. Die Bakaïri-Sprache. Leipzig: K. F. Koehler's Antiquarium.

Vennemann, T. 1973. Explanation in syntax. In J. P. Kimball, ed., Syntax and semantics 2. New York: Seminar Press.

———. 1975. An explanation of drift. In C. N. Li, ed. (1975).

Vincent, N. 1977. Some issues in the theory of word order. Presented to the Autumn Meeting of the Linguistics Association of Great Britain.

Voegelin, C. F. and F. M. Voegelin. 1977. Classification and index of the world's languages. New York: Elsevier.

Wheatley, J. 1973. Pronouns and nominal elements in Bacairi discourse. Linguistics 104.105-15.

Williams, J. 1932. Grammar notes and vocabulary of the language of the Makuchi Indians of Guiana. Anthropos Internationale Sammlung linguistischer Monographien 8. St. Gabriel-Mödling near Vienna.

Yde, J. 1965. Material culture of the Waiwai. Nationalmuseets Skrifter, Etnografisk Roekke, Copenhagen.

Zwicky, A. M. 1977. Hierarchies of person. CLS 13.714-33.

www.ingramcontent.com/pod-product-compliance
Lightning Source LLC
Chambersburg PA
CBHW070241230426
43664CB00014B/2378